Cobr & Pyramids

Adventures of a Teaching Couple in Pakistan, Bangladesh and Egypt

To Hermann & Traute —
thank you for all your organic &
delicious produce!

Jane Cundiff

New Haven Press ~ Floyd, Virginia

We hope you enjoy the stories —
Jane Cundiff
& Ken Cundiff

Published by New Haven Press
Floyd, Virginia

Cover and All Images
by Ken & Jane Cundiff

Copyright © 2015 Jane Cundiff
ISBN - 13: 978 0996181501
ISBN – 10: 0996181504

Library of Congress Control Number - 2015904141

Dedication

I am eternally grateful to my loving husband, Ken, my lifelong partner in adventure and wonder. This book is ours, not only in action but also in the two-year process of writing and publishing.

Acknowledgements

To my readers; especially those who are in the stories - I apologize for my writing skills and publishing errors and hope you enjoy the stories despite them. I hope my notes and photos from those many years ago accurately and positively portray our times together.

Thanks to our families for encouraging us to ask questions and pursue our highest goals in life. To the Cundiffs – Will, Claudia, Sybil and Mitch. To the Owen's – Earl, Ann, Cindy, Christie, David, Mary Lisa, Paul, Grandma and Aunt Fay. Especially to Mom (Ann Owen) who shared so many of our adventures and kept all of my letters.

Thanks to all my friends who encouraged me and helped me to edit this book – Ann Owen (Mom), Sybil Phillips, Paul Owen, Vicky Nelson, Paula Marr, Nanette Johnson, Virginia Klara, Fred First, Randall Wells. Special thanks to my friend Diane Davis who helped edit chapters from beginning to end, spending many hours on the phone.

For the substance of the stories I am forever grateful to all of the people around the world who have filled my life with glimpses into their own. To my students, teachers, friends and family and even the strangers from whom I have learned so many lessons. In the end, it is the people who matter most.

Table of Contents

Pakistan

Maps

Bangladesh

Egypt

Maps

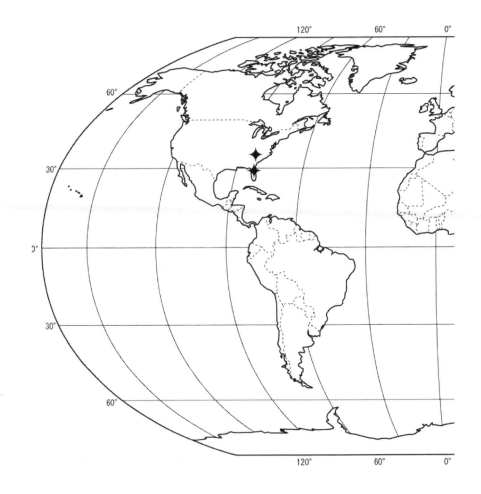

Teaching Around The World

Oak Hall School - Gainesville, Florida, 1983 – 1987
Lahore American School – Lahore, Pakistan, 1987 – 1989
American International School of Dhaka - Bangladesh, 1989 - 1990
Cairo American College – Cairo, Egypt, 1991 – 1995
American Embassy School - New Delhi, India, 1996 – 1998
Roanoke Valley Governor's School - Roanoke, Virginia
1998 – 2000

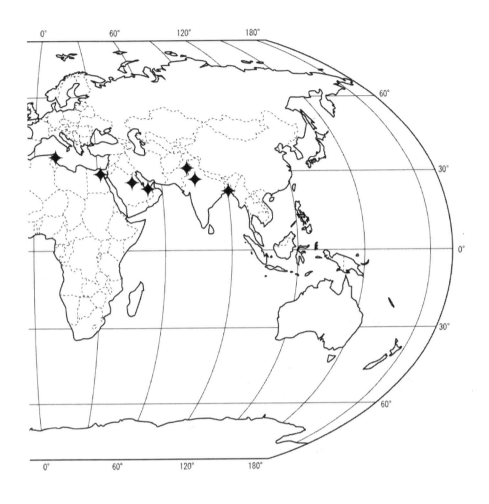

American Cooperative School of Tunis- Tunis, Tunisia,
2001 - 2003
American International School of Riyadh – Riyadh, Saudi Arabia
2004 - 2006
Dubai American Academy - Dubai, United Arab Emirates,
2007 - 2008
Radford University and Virginia Western Community College
2008 - Present

Pakistan

Teach Overseas?

"Not all those who wander are lost."
— J.R.R. Tolkien,

I am struggling with reality, dreaming of turbans, vaguely aware of a remote buzz. It is two o'clock in the morning, four nervous unsure weeks after the international hiring conference. The phone rings and rings again, rousing us from a deep groggy sleep. Trying to sound coherent and knowing that I'm not, I answer the call from Gene Vincent, the superintendent of Lahore American School in Pakistan. "Yes! No! I mean I don't know. Ken is sleeping. I mean Ken is awake but can't talk. I guess we'll say yes and just go with it!" Gene is pretty bad at remembering about the time difference. Or maybe he is very good at it and just wanted to catch us by surprise. Lahore is not a preferred destination for many folks and it can be difficult to hire two good science teachers.

So that was it. We couldn't believe we'd done it. We were actually going to quit our ideal local teaching jobs, leave our safe little Florida nest and go venturing into the vast unknown. Pakistan! A wild, foreign place on the other side of the world we knew very little about. There was not much sleep happening that night.

I don't really know what made us do this. We were happy after all, Ken and I, still in love after sixteen years of marriage. We had 80 idyllic rolling acres in the country outside of Gainesville, Florida, which was once listed #1 place to live in America by *Money* magazine. We had close supportive families, friends, dog, goats and a garden. We had good jobs teaching science at Oak Hall School, a quality private college-prep school. We had kept close connections to the University of Florida where we had earned our degrees and worked in research for a few years. We had it made. Recently I read about a gene that makes one adventurous. That must be it, an incurable disease. We just have it in us.

Ken and I spent time in the Peace Corps in Colombia, South America in the 1970's but our term was cut short by serious illness in our families at home. The hunger to travel and work with others was

1

still with us. About the time our hearts were stirring for serious adventure again, our good friend and major professor, Dr. Mary Budd Rowe from the University of Florida, was there to help fan the flames. Not only had she lived and taught in Germany for eight years but she also knew lots of other people who were involved in international education in wild and wonderful places. Knowing our creative and diverse science teaching backgrounds, Dr. Rowe gave us great recommendations and pointed us in the right directions.

Paging through notices for teachers needed from Amsterdam to Zimbabwe, we were hooked the moment we walked into the International Schools office at the University. "Oh, look at this, Nairobi! We could go on safari and stalk lions," Ken points out an ad to me. "What about Japan or Singapore? I love Asian foods and culture," I reply, showing off another notice. "Well in Singapore you can get arrested for not flushing a toilet where on safari there are none." Ken responds chuckling, trying to tempt me into adventure with his raised eyebrows. They had us. We found it hard to believe we could actually live and travel in a foreign country and even get paid for it. I knew this teaching business had more to offer than some people let on. It seemed like a perfect fit for Ken and I, both learning junkies, energetic and adventurous. Having chosen not to have children would make it even easier.

"The opening ceremony starts in the ballroom in ten minutes. Are you psyched?" asks Ken as I check the mirror for final touches and he leans down for a quick kiss. "Can't wait! Let's go get a seat right up front," I respond as he opens the hotel room door for me. In February 1987 we arrived at our first hiring conference. The International Schools Services in Princeton, NJ, the largest organization that brings overseas administrators together with prospective teachers, held their hiring fair at the Omni Hotel in Washington D.C. Teaching opportunities ranged from tiny village elementary schools to dense metropolitan K-12 schools of over 2,000 students. Most of the international schools tout strong academic programs and small classes. Usually two-year contracts, salary packages range from barely survivable to big bucks. They expect to hire highly qualified, certified teachers with classroom experience, enthusiasm and flexibility. We hope we fit the bill.

2

High excitement permeates the conference. Hundreds of applicants and administrators come from all over the world to court each other. The air is charged with emotions as the latest job offers are posted or removed and prospects change. Gym rooms, breakfast tables and even elevators become good places to meet and chat about possible positions in exotic places. There are jitters during interviews, fears of not getting a job, competition with other well-qualified teachers, doubt of the unknown and anticipation of adventure. The well-traveled and experienced wear special nametags so newbies can ask them questions. "Where in the world have you taught?" "Do you know if Malaysia or Bangladesh are good places to live?" "What is it like to teach science in Viet Nam?" Just rubbing elbows with all these international folks stokes anticipation.

"Let's check out the openings in India and Nepal first," I suggest. "Thinking of teaching in an ashram?" Ken teases. Over 100 school administrators are stationed at their tables in the ballrooms of the hotel for the ISS conference. Each table carries a sign advertising the name of the school and the jobs available as lines form to sign up for interviews. The queues for European schools are long. For some, it is the dream of a lifetime to live in Madrid, Rome or Munich. But for us that doesn't sound like as much fun as Katmandu, New Delhi, Kuala Lumpur or Pakistan. Finding a school we want with two high school science positions open is not that easy and we get discouraged when we don't see physics and biology written on the posters for Nepal or India. But Malaysia, Pakistan, Uruguay and several others have good matches so we march into seven different interviews with our song and dance and condensed resumes. Then we fly home to wait on pins and needles while the schools sort out whom they want to hire.

Four long, anxious weeks passed before that call came from Pakistan. Two more calls from other schools came right after that but we made an agreement with Gene in Lahore, and we were happy with our decision.

3

There will be so much to learn with unfamiliar languages, unique job skills, different foods, new friends, and untrodden ways of looking at the world. Arriving in a totally different part of the world for the very first time with a one-way ticket and no tour group is like being born again. Like a couple of children, we will be ignorant, helpless, wide-eyed and lousy at communicating. Our new life will require humility and flexibility. We will be starting from scratch in a place that will be our home and our job for the next two years - or who knows how long. We knew from the moment of that first phone call from Pakistan that we'd need to prepare for the rollercoaster ride of our life.

New teachers in Lahore

During the months of preparation many well-meaning friends responded to our plans with "How nice! We hope to travel when we retire." In our mid-thirties, retirement is incomprehensible to us. Besides, it would be much more difficult to throw on a backpack and take off hiking into the Himalayas or through the busy streets of Bangkok at the age of 65. There is a real difference between living in a place or just visiting, between adventure and tourism. This will be our life, not just a vacation. We are ready now.

We decided to keep our house. My sister Mary Lisa needed a place to stay while pursuing a nursing degree in Gainesville. Living overseas is tough and it will be wonderful to return and relax in our very own comfortable place in the summers. Some teachers sell their households and enjoy visiting, renting or travelling in summer. Only a few actually take up residence in their newly adopted country.

"Danger?" I respond to the questions. "We are scientists, remember. Statistics show you are far more likely to die from heart disease than terrorism. If we fear something it should be cigarettes and sausage biscuits." We are leaving the good ole USA to live on the other side of the earth. "How exotic!" "Sounds very exciting!" "Isn't that dangerous?" "What in the hell would you want to do that for??" We drew very mixed feelings from friends and relatives. We love them but it is our life and our necks after all. We intend to send lots of letters and pictures and, yes, there are telephones over there.

The excitement of anticipation can be almost as much fun as the journey itself. We poured over any literature we could dig up on Pakistan. (There was no Internet available in 1987). We mangled Urdu words from a tiny language primer and dug up friends of friends of friends that once traveled to the country. We made sure we had our passports and visas, hiking boots and cameras, treasured classroom reference books and bags of chocolate chips. We got ready.

"Do you think we can take our TV?" I ask Ken as I wander around the house making a list. "It will probably be easier to buy one there; besides, don't ship anything we can't stuff with socks. And we should probably leave the goats," he teases as he packs some tools in a box.

We discuss what to bring and leave behind, what to sell, store, ship, trash or give away. Some teachers don't bring much to their new posts, planning to buy things when they arrive. Others bring everything and just pay extra shipping costs in hopes of feeling more at home when they move in. There is always a chance of losing part of a shipment. Not common, but it happens, especially in countries where things tend to 'disappear.' We bring as much as we can within the shipping allotment. It is often difficult to find everything one needs in a new country but being without is a good lesson in how to be creative and improvise.

Schools vary greatly in their facilities, student populations and the financial packages offered to teachers. Housing, shipping, vehicles, insurance, retirement and lots of other things may be included in "hardship" posts. Teachers may have to pay local income tax. Schools with a good benefit package usually have high academic standards and compete for the best teachers. Equipment and facilities vary and teachers need to be adaptable and inventive. Most of the staff and some of the faculty are locally hired and have their own, culturally unique, way of doing things. Patience and flexibility are definitely prerequisites.

Somewhere, deep down in our souls - or in those wandering genes or empty hiking boots - we feel the need to GO. We ache to get off our comfy couch and see the world. We long to experience aspects of life around the earth - its nature, religion, culture and humanity. We hope to leave expectations behind and learn so much more about who we are as individuals and how we fit into the big picture. And, of course, we plan to pass on these most valuable lessons to the young, future leaders of this planet.

We pack our bags for Pakistan.

"Travel brings power and love back into your life."
 - Rumi

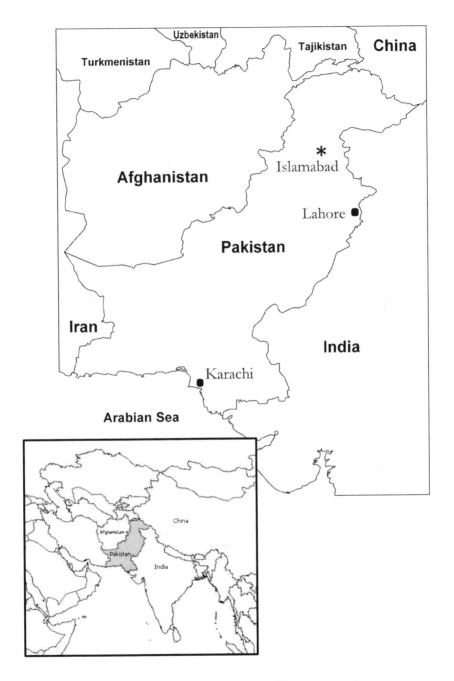

Pakistan and surrounding countries

As-salaam Alaikum
Arriving in Pakistan, August, 1987

"The purpose of life is to live it, to taste experience to the utmost, to reach out eagerly and without fear for newer and richer experience."
— Eleanor Roosevelt

"Can you see anything out there yet?" Straining to get closer, Ken leans his tall comforting body across me to ask. My nose has been glued to the plane window ever since takeoff. Vast expanses of tawny shades of parched desert stretch to the horizon under brightness of an unrelenting summer sun. It is mountainous, grand and serene but quite desolate. Starkly void of visible life, mile after never ending mile, it seems a very barren planet from 30,000 feet in the air. Flying from Europe, across Turkey, Iran and Afghanistan we head to our new life in excited anticipation.

"All I can see is your big head in the way, my Dearest," Ken continues as I squish to the side to give him some space. "Look! Over there! Just to the right of that tallest mountain," Ken says while tapping on the glass. "It looks like a village!" We can barely pick out the adobe buildings and the dusty trees of a small compound that blend right into the brown desert mountains below. Cheek to cheek, we focus on a few other isolated villages in the vast expanse. No highways, no shopping malls or factories. Not much out here on the fringes of life. This is really going to be different from our home in sub-tropical wet, green, modern Florida. Linking arms, Ken and I are so glad that we are in this together. Craning our necks and twisting our bodies to view our new home, we chat nonstop about all the exciting possibilities ahead.

"Insha'Allah we will be landing at Karachi International Airport in twenty minutes." Announces the pilot in Arabic and English. After months of sorting, planning, packing, communicating with school personnel, getting passports and visas, hard goodbyes and anxious anticipation, we are here at last, circling in the air above our future.

Some of the women passengers are digging into their bags to pull out veils to cover themselves before landing. I roll down the long sleeves of my loose pink cotton blouse and check to make sure that my baggy cargo pants properly cover my provocative ankles.

Suddenly realizing we really are on the other side of the planet, in a Muslim country with a culture unlike any we have ever experienced and a one-way ticket, we cling tightly to the plush arms of our seats, our last connection to our known world. "What are we doing here?" "Are we crazy?" "Whose idea was this, anyway?" we banter back and forth, joking nervously. As the plane touches into a smooth landing and rolls to a stop, we breathe deeply and hope everything will be OK.

Hot, dry, hazy air, blistering overhead sun and strange new spicy odors of a summer day in Pakistan overwhelm our senses as we step out the plane door and breathe in this new place. Two handsome young Pakistani military guards stand in pressed blue uniforms below the metal boarding stairs with automatic rifles resting across their arms. They watch nonchalantly as passengers pour out the exit door and down the steps onto the hot black tarmac.

Almost everyone here really does wear traditional clothes. Somehow I thought that all of those movies, videos and articles about Pakistan were filled with actors in costumes. The long loose shirts and billowing long pants, known as shalwar-kamis are standard dress for both men and women. Men are in white, grey or subdued pastels and women mostly in bright flowery or embroidered patterns. Some of the people wear western clothes and a few women are covered totally from head to toe in full black burkas, looking rather like Catholic nuns with face veils. Westerners are not really common here but, thanks to three hundred years of British occupation, English is widely spoken. Urdu is the common Pakistani language but not the only one. We hear the sounds and phrases but don't understand more than a few words.

"Look at that cute little girl, behind you." "Did you see that old man over there?" "Stop staring or someone may take offense." "That machine gun over there looks way too serious." Our heads twirl as we whisper back and forth and take it all in while trying to adjust and pretend we know what we're doing.

Moving forward on the baking hot black asphalt, we slowly file into customs. A stout middle-aged woman, heavily panting in the heat and sun and fanning her face with a folded paper, squats down on her haunches as her flowing garments billow beneath her. Some of these people are only recently descended from nomads who lived without chairs and they still seem to be fairly comfortable in a squat that makes my ankles hurt just to watch. I think that I might try to work on it. It could be quite handy when I'm chair-less.

Finally, standing nervously before a tall customs desk that I can barely see over, an officer frowns in concentration as he slowly pours over our passports and visas. Anxiously hoping everything is in order, we aren't sure what to think when he asks an unexpected question. "Why are you here?"

"To teach at the American School in Lahore" we answer, thinking the paperwork should show that.

"Ahhhhh Muderriss!" he exclaims as a smile spreads across his face. He ceremoniously stamps our papers and finally hands them back with a big welcome. 'Muderriss' means teachers in Urdu and teachers are highly respected in this culture. Our tension lessens a little as we take our passports and head to the main terminal to layover for our final flight to Lahore.

A pretty, dark-skinned little girl wearing a frilly white western dress runs her small hand over the top of a dusty, dirty counter. As she licks her fingers to clean them her mother, fully covered in restrictive black garments, tries to grab her. As a couple hours pass, Ken and I sit in awe just watching and experiencing all that is going on around us. A wrinkled old man with a long white beard and a small round cotton hat, kneels and prostrates on a mat facing the west wall toward Mecca. It is the midday time for one of their five daily prayers and a few other men gather to join him.

"Is that veiled woman staring at me or just turned this way?" I ask Ken. Sitting in the vinyl seats cracked by years of waiting, we are trying some delicious Chai tea spiced with cardamom, purchased from a small bustling teashop in the airport. The milky rich, sweet, flavorful hot brew is common and much loved in East Asia and we look forward to drinking more of it. From a tiny bank exchange window in the corner of the crowded noisy terminal we purchase some rupees and closely study

10

the different colors and sizes of the unusual bills and coins so that we can use them correctly.

Preparing to board the last leg of our flight to Lahore, we visit the restrooms. "Did you have one of those squat type Asian toilets in the men's room?" I ask Ken. "I was really glad I didn't have to use one just yet. They had a few western type ones in the ladies room. That squatting thing does not look easy." He agreed, smiled at me and started to grab my hand to go, but pulled away, remembering the rules of this Muslim country.

After gluing our noses once again to the window as we fly from Karachi to our final destination, we finally stepped off the plane and into our new life.

Lahore is a very old city, a cultural center with legendary beginnings. Some believe it was founded by the son of the Hindu God, Rama, thousands of years ago. Ptolemy, the second-century Egyptian astronomer mentions it in his writings. Once part of the Indian subcontinent, which consisted of Pakistan, India and Bangladesh, Lahore is now a densely populated city of about six million people in the independent Muslim country of Pakistan. We disembark from the plane to join hundreds in the arrival terminal.

"Mim Saab need help?" "Please, I help you!" "No, let me!" As throngs of humanity pulse through the busy Lahore airport, we are bombarded with men who want to help carry our large extra suitcases from the baggage claim carousel. I worry it might be the last we see of them as we finally choose a porter. The men wear grey-blue uniforms and a little official porter badge that says to tip them 10 rupees (about 30 cents). We hire one named Mohammed and the rest of them leave us alone to look for other customers.

"Hey!" "Ken and Jane!" "Over here!" Shouts and waves from the side and two familiar, smiling faces in the throngs of people at the arrival terminal are a sight for anxious eyes. "Hey! You made it!" Gene Vincent, the superintendent of Lahore American School, and his wife Terry are waiting patiently to pick us up. Lots of hand shaking and chatter, but no hugging allowed. "As-salaam alaikum. Welcome to Pakistan!" each in turn gives us the traditional Muslim greeting meaning "Peace be with you" as they help us with our bags.

Gene and Terry are the ones who hired us in Washington, DC during the recruiting fair in February. Our contact with them over the last few months has helped to prepare us. As we hear our names and their welcoming words and smiles, we feel so much more comfortable, knowing they will guide and look out for us.

Leaving the airport, we drive through tree-lined boulevards where adults stroll, children play, and water buffalo yoked to lawn equipment rest from their chores. Ancient Moghul forts, historically unique Mosques and whimsical fountains adorn this cultural "City of many gardens." The traffic pattern is unusual. You drive on the left side - unless you really don't want to, and if you have a large vehicle you can do whatever you please. There are as many motorcycles as there are cars and the donkey or buffalo carts with their turbaned drivers seem not to care about either. Horns blare constantly as most drivers use them non-stop just to let everyone know they are coming. The cacophony tends to leave us newly initiated a bit wide-eyed and white knuckled, clutching the seat of the swerving fast moving school van, as if that will save us from sure demise.

The locals don't seem to even notice. "Look over there at that family. That's crazy," Ken says as he points to a small motorcycle with a man driving, a woman riding side-saddle and two children, sitting on their laps clinging tightly to their parents' waists. Motorcycles careen wildly though the traffic, passing on right or left, sidewalk or not, missing and hitting the potholes, and no helmets. Kids on bicycles or just walking in groups weave on and off the roads because, either sidewalks don't exist, or they are so filled with rubble to be useless.

"As-salaam alaikum. Welcome Saab and Mim Saab." Our new housekeeper, William, dressed in a white starched shalwar-kamis, bows and humbly greets us at the door of our new home. We had heard that workers are easily affordable and a necessity here to run the household and negotiate the local markets and that we "rich" should help provide jobs. We weren't sure we would like having someone around the house so much. But after William greets us in almost perfect English with fresh homemade bread and iced tea, carries in our bags and asks what we would like him to make for dinner, well, we think we might be able to handle it.

Gene and Terry leave us with William for the evening, promising that a driver will come to get us in the morning to bring us to school for our first day of orientation. The house came complete with a moving-in kit to use until we got our shipment, so our bed was made with clean sheets and the table was set. There was even food in the refrigerator. After a small but delicious meal of local curried beans, rice and veggies, we hit the sack quickly, overwhelmed, jet-lagged, and totally elated!

Ken, Jane and William at Lahore home

Most American schools overseas are quite helpful with assistance to their new teachers, especially when coming to difficult places. We had been sent preliminary information on what to bring and not to bring and even tips on how to act. We are helped to get customs paperwork done, and shown around town to find the little things we need to settle into our furnished house.

For the first couple months Gene comes often to visit in the evenings. With a hard to get six-pack of beer tucked under one arm and his cute little three-year-old Nicole, latched on to his fingers, they sit with us on the back porch to chat, see what we need and how we are adjusting. Good administrators like Gene and Terry act more like parents than bosses and the other teachers soon become like family. Their physical and emotional support was fundamental to our years in Pakistan.

First Letter Home
September, 1987

"Allah ho Akbar". The call from the mosque to praise God comes drifting through the early morning stillness of dawn. In the streets, there is only an occasional clomping from the hooves of the buffalo or pony cart. A few turbaned men, in long white robes or shalwar-kamis are sweeping outside their shops or quietly headed toward some early morning destination. The sweet smell of gardenias and jasmine floats from the well-manicured gardens and mixes with the not-so-nice manure and diesel odors of the street. Another morning has dawned in a very old country, as we awaken on the other side of the world.

Only three weeks have passed, yet it seems like months of new adventures here in Lahore.

The computer made it to Pakistan with lots of worry but no damage. In order to collect our freight we have to spend about five hours at 100 degrees in airport customs offices. Sitting on crowded wooden benches, water bottle in hand, sweat on face, we soak up the foreign images around us. Men in long white garments wearing turbans are squatting comfortably in clusters, chatting in words not yet understandable to us. I think I'm hot until I look into the eyes of a woman sitting next to me. Covered head to toe in long black robes she has just a slit for her eyes open to the air and they drip with perspiration. While gathering about a dozen different signatures and stamps from customs offices, we have tea with several friendly officials. As self-conscious foreigners we shake hands with everyone, saying lots of please and thank you or "shukran", very happy that all our airfreight has actually arrived intact, only three weeks later than expected.

We are still hoping that our sea freight, which seems to be coming by donkey from Karachi via Antarctica, will be arriving soon but it could be another month. You can usually double or even triple the amount of time American shipping companies tell you it will take. Meantime, we learn more about making-do in our new culture.

We are living in an old large home, surrounded with wide, shady porches, that has been converted into a duplex. Mrs. Latif, our landlady and neighbor, is an elderly Pakistani woman who speaks little English and lives alone. We rarely see or hear from her as the school takes full responsibility for our residence. Both the house and the yards are divided with tall, thick walls for privacy. We had requested a yard and we have a nice one that came with a gardener.

In the Middle East culture, the traditional home consists of a solid walled-in compound, with small rooms forming the perimeter facing inward to a courtyard. The tall walls are for seclusion, especially for women of strict beliefs who are not supposed to be seen by any men outside their extended family. The central open area is used for daily living, including cooking and sleeping in the warm dry nights of summer. It is usually filled with children, animals, women and the elderly. Electricity may not be available and fresh water must often be carried from a community well. Usually several generations share the home. Most of the people live this way, but the wealthy have more modern life styles and fancy, large, western-style homes, surrounded by gardens and tall walls topped with broken glass. Covered with flowering pink and purple Bougainvillea, the barriers serve to keep out the noise and dust of the city or desert, as well as maintain family privacy. Although this concealment can be quite nice it prevents us from getting to know our neighbors as we would like.

Once a palatial family home, Lahore American School lies within a 4.5-acre compound in a pleasant, older area of the city. There are only 340 students K-12. My largest class has 15 students. Our science labs are spacious but old and leaky. Getting some dry ice or other science materials I am used to will be unlikely. But I am excited about having a lab assistant. Dubash teaches a couple of classes, prepares materials for our science experiments and even helps me clean up after my biology and chemistry labs.

"What kind of computer lessons are you going to teach the younger kids?" It is just two days before school starts when our superintendent, Gene Vincent, with a cigar in his mouth, is chatting with Ken. Thinking Gene is referring to kids about 14, Ken answers, "Probably a shotgun approach with word processing, a little programming, spreadsheets, etcetera." Gene removes his cigar, lets out a puff, smiles

15

and says, "No, I mean the little ones. Aren't you teaching a computer wheel?"

Ken had not heard yet. He had been assigned children from grades one through six to come to him once a week for a computer lesson. He is a high school physics teacher. Ken was ashen. He had never taught little kids. What should he do with them? So he scours his programs and comes up with the simplest one he can find - a spelling game.

Entrance to Lahore American School

On the first day of school twenty first-graders come in and sit two to a chair they are so tiny. Ken welcomes them and introduces himself as Mr. C. He boots up all the computer programs for them and stands in the center of the room expectantly waiting for them to read the instructions and get started. The kids stare at the computer screens, fidget in their shared seats and look around squirming. Finally one cute little boy with round glasses raises his hand. Ken slides to his knees beside him to help out. "Mr. C", he says in a timid voice, "We can't read." Ken had not considered that. As a high school physics teacher he thought kids were just born reading. "Those little guys are really cute but boy are they a handful of energy. Thank goodness for those wonderful elementary teachers who can manage them and teach them to read."

"For me, it's easier to teach Einstein's Theory of Relativity," Ken shares. In small schools we sometimes learn to wear unexpected hats.

A daily routine is finally starting to emerge out of our chaos. Sometime around 4 AM we stir between sleep and wakefulness as we hear the early morning call to prayer from the loudspeakers on the neighborhood mosque. It comes at the time "when dawn brings enough light to tell a black thread from a white one". Many devout Muslims rise at this time to observe the first of the required five prayers per day. We roll over and try to get much needed sleep.

At 5:45 AM our alarm rings. The sun is already up shining through the dusty haze. We do some yoga and calisthenics in our study or out in the backyard as our breakfast is being prepared for us by William. At 6:45, as requested, we sit down to a fresh fruit salad, some scrambled eggs, freshly baked whole wheat bread and fresh squeezed orange juice. After we finish we give William 65 rupees (about $3) to do the daily grocery shopping. He carries the lunches he has made for us out to the car provided and serviced by the school, and opens the front gate for us to drive away. Tough life.

It is already hot and humid. Monsoon season is late or not coming and it may get over 100 degrees Fahrenheit today. We prefer to say 38-Celsius because it doesn't sound so bad. The streets are fairly quiet this early, with mostly bicycles and a few pony carts so we make it to campus alive.

"Happy Birthday Dear Tamir, Hassan and Natasha....." School starts at 7:45. Once or twice a week the whole school meets together for some announcements about birthday wishes, new library books, or sports and such. Most of the students and faculty dress in the shalwar-khamis, a few in blue jeans or other western dress.

Learning new and different names is a challenge. Shandar and Shehzad, Tahira and Ilham, Mizna and Fatima. There are over thirty nations represented at this school but most of the students are from Lahore. There are seven class periods and lunch. We teach five with two for planning and time to share our picnic, packed by William.

Kids are kids like everywhere. They want to learn but also want to play. Most International schools are much like quality private, college-prep schools in the U.S, but with more variety in the faces and more flexibility in the attitudes. They may or may not have many American students. They are established for students who want to get a good education to go to top colleges anywhere in the world and can afford the high tuition. Standards are especially high and people around the globe recognize the quality of the International educators who strive to foster the imagination and problem solving abilities required in our fast-changing world.

Lahore American School has a lot of local Pakistani teachers and staff who have graciously brought us into their lives, inviting us to their family celebrations and helping us in any way they can. Shahnaz Ali, our high school principal, is an amazing woman with great talent and a thoughtful leader. (She eventually went on to be the Federal Minister of Education for all of Pakistan.) Tahira, our proficient high school computer teacher, was educated in Canada. Although it is not law, it is rare to find working women in this country as seclusion and poor education are the norm. Some Pakistanis are highly educated at universities in London or America and enjoy working within the compound of our school. It is a pleasure and an honor to get to know them.

"Are you ready? Is your insurance up to date? Have you told your Mom you love her?" asks Ken as he takes the steering wheel on the right side of the van to drive through the street on the 'wrong' side of the road. The school has generously provided a vehicle for us. We chose a Toyota van as it is bigger and feels safer in the traffic mayhem. While shifting gears with his left hand and steering from the right side of the car, Ken keeps his grip on the wheel and close to the horn. "Watch out for the bicycle! That kid is going to run right in front of you! Geez, you almost hit that water buffalo," I encourage Ken on the drive home from work. I am glad he is driving and not me, as I prefer to hold tight to the seat, clench my teeth, hold my breath, and even sometimes shut my eyes. It seems that the bicycles, motorcycles, cars, ox carts, camels and pedestrians have the philosophy that if they get hit, it must just be the will of Allah. Nobody looks behind them as they swerve from lane to lane or stomp on the brakes. Red lights seem to be optional and the biggest vehicles with the loudest horns have the right of way. Mrs. Rana, one of the local teachers told us that she never heard of anyone getting a speeding ticket.

In Lahore, traffic is mostly cars, as big trucks are not allowed in the city from 5AM to 12PM.

The drive through the streets is full of variety and excitement. There is no falling asleep at the wheel. Some of the roads in our section of town are quieter, wide and one way, with well-manicured lawns, tall trees, flowers and sometimes a camel or water buffalo working or grazing in the median.

Original Toro mower

"Salaam alaikum." Pulling into our driveway, we say hello with the traditional greeting to the mali, our gardener. He has been cutting our lawn with hand clippers and carefully weeding around the rose bushes and potted plants that line the porches. "Walaikum, salaam," he answers with a shy crinkled smile. A small, wiry man with a loosely wound turban, bare feet and hard-working weathered hands, he only speaks Urdu, and right now all we can say is hello and thank you.

The house has been swept, mopped and dusted, the laundry washed, ironed and put away, and flowers from the garden fill vases throughout the house. Fresh groceries were purchased and dinner will be ready shortly. William has been working all day and smiles broadly to welcome us at the door after a long day at school.

We are pleased with our new home. There are two large bedrooms, two full baths, a living and dining room, all freshly painted. The high ceilings all have fans. Rows of French windows in the living room open up to view our wide veranda and spacious yard. We have mango, citrus and shade trees as well as rows of rose bushes, bougainvillea, and gardenias. A small area is being prepared by the gardener for some vegetables and there is even enough room for a tight badminton or croquet game. We requested a place with a nice yard and not everyone has one. We are a bit too close to the busy street but a six foot wall covered in vines helps keep out some of the noise and dust. A small two-room servant's quarters behind a row of bushes houses William and his family. The back porch is nicely shaded by a large tree and is a pleasant place to sit as the evening brings gentle relief from the heat of the busy day.

We try to have low expectations of a new home, preferring to be pleased rather than disappointed. We thought we might have to live in very meager conditions, maybe even dirt floors. Someone did say it was the third world. But it is not too bad after all. Things are not so finished and elegant. Paint splashes on windows, no baseboards, and peeling walls. Electric wiring and lighting are very sloppy and sometimes downright scary.

"Oh my God, what is that?" I screech, jumping up from grading papers on the couch to the sound and smell of sparks coming out of the wall behind me. "Ken, come here –quick!" Sparks continue to fly as Ken runs to find the fuse box, cut off the electric, and call the school electrician who comes over right away. Ken immediately befriends the electrician, hovering over the work and asking all kinds of questions, as he is wont to do. Chaos can be an opportunity to make new friends.

Our electricity is out frequently in a process called "load shedding." Lahore does not have enough energy to distribute to everyone at once so they cut off sections of the city at different times of the day. Even though the newspaper announces the times, it doesn't make being without electric easy. A hot day with no air conditioning, no fan and no refrigerator can be trying. The school and most businesses have back-up generators to run fans but we do not.

Our water faucets often stopped flowing late at night. It was months before we found out that our landlady was cutting our water off after ten o'clock at night to save money. The school finally intervened. Our queen-size bed, with just a thin pad on a solid wood frame, was hard as a rock until the school finally brought us an extra pad that helped us softie foreigners get some sleep.

A load of lumber arrived on a donkey cart for an addition to the house on the landlady's side. A telephone repairman just climbed up the utility pole using only a rope. A turbaned man on a motorcycle, carrying large copper and tin jugs strapped to the back, delivers our fresh milk twice a week.

Our mobile Milkman

Every day is different. Our servants make life easier. William speaks English well and we are getting to know his family better. He is a wealth of information about our new life and how to do things around town.

"Do you want to go explore a bit?" asks Ken after we finish grading papers and the evening is cooling down. "Maybe we can practice some of our Urdu on unsuspecting merchants." As dinner is being prepared, we take a walk over to Liberty Market, one of the newest shopping areas in town, only a block away. Over a hundred small shops are squeezed in an area about 3-4 square blocks. We have not investigated many of them yet. I think you can get everything from gold jewelry to donkey manure there.

Across from the market is a delightful park, filled with all kinds of new and interesting trees, flowers, birds and people. In the early mornings we jog on the wide winding paths, probably close to 3/4 of a mile for one loop. The large fountain in the front is turned on and lit up at night. Lahore has many beautiful parks and is often called the city of fountains. It is nicer than we expected, but definitely dusty, busy and noisy.

At 7:00 P.M. we sit down at the table to a home-cooked meal. The teachers who lived here before were, like us, vegetarians and William learned to make all kinds of delicious foods, from veggie curries to spinach lasagna. Because we can get many "American" food items from the commissary and all kinds of new things locally, almost anything goes. Although William speaks English quite well and interprets Urdu for us, he cannot read. I will have to teach him any new recipes that I would like. I was afraid that I might really miss cooking our own food but so far this has not been a problem.

"Can you come over Thursday for dinner?" asks Kris. "Brad and I are having Lulu, Nighat, Eve, the Werbers and the Reykdals over for some curry." About two or three times a week we are invited to dinner or evening parties. Since everyone has servants, there is a lot more time for entertaining and spending time with friends. The parties are especially interesting because of the international gathering of people and we are making good friends already. There are six new American teaching couples who are getting especially close as we all have a lot to learn and discover in our new home, job and country. The Pakistani teachers and school staff are quite graciously inviting us into their lives, showing us around town and answering our zillions of questions.

"How do I look?" I ask Ken as I parade around in my new yellow flowered shalwar-kamis, just completed by my tailor. "Like a genie in a magic lantern. Can you make my wishes come true?" answers Ken as he grabs a hug. The material is a very light, thin cotton and the outfit is much cooler and more feminine than the long pants that I brought from home.

Hand-made is the norm here. A tailor came to our house with his sewing machine to reupholster our living room chairs and a couch for less than $200, including the material. He sat cross-legged on the back porch to do his work. With his careful stitching he can even sew men's suits. Some people here get all their clothes hand-tailored.

Tailor on our porch

The shalwar-kamis is comfortable and I have four outfits already. The long blouse and billowy pants are worn by all the women. I like the thin cotton and bright summer colors. I don't like the dupata, a long scarf, wrapped loosely all around the body at the shoulders, drooping down to hide the outline of the breasts. It is quite dainty and soft looking and most women wear it, but I just haven't mastered the ability to keep it from falling off.

"Will you take 200 rupees?" "No, Mam, I will need 400." "Maybe I can pay 250." "I must have at least 350," "OK, then 300." I am learning the fine art of bargaining with the 'wallas', or door-to-door salesmen. We have had our own personal art show with antique Persian carpets filling our living room. Their prices are usually reasonable and sometimes it is nice to avoid driving around searching in this massively complex city. It is also reason to call over other new teachers to have a little home shopping party. We have already purchased oil paintings, wicker furniture, jewelry, brass pots and a small, very old, worn, red Persian prayer rug full of wonderful vibrations that I call our "flying carpet."

We have not done a lot of sightseeing yet.   The weather is way too hot and only early morning is reasonable.   Nighat Agha, one of the friendly local teachers, took us downtown to the Badshahi Mosque built in the 1600's. One of the largest in the world, it is still in constant use. Lulu Chaudry, the school's administrative secretary, guided us around the Old Fort of Lahore with foundations over a thousand years old and surrounded by beautiful gardens. The inlaid marble work was stunning, even 600 years after it was done.   Most of the jewels have long since been removed but the magnificence still remains. We plan on returning to these monuments of culture to spend more time on cooler days.

We have heard from Mitch. Ken's brother went into the Navy the same time we were leaving for Pakistan. He is headed for Guam to be trained for service on the nuclear aircraft carrier, the USS Eisenhower. My brother, David and his wife, Dawn just opened a new business; *Shanley Flooring* in Boynton Beach, Florida. Seems like change runs in families.

We hear that in March there will be an education conference in Thailand.   NESA (Near East South Asia Council of Overseas Schools) sponsors amazing training institutes for over 100 international schools in this area. It will be held in Bangkok, and we get to go. AND the school will pay 75% of the trip! It is a four-day conference followed by our spring break, so we can spend another five days traveling all around Thailand. We are thrilled to say the least. This is what I call professional development!

Each day is a new adventure. We wanted to experience a really different culture and we surely have our wish.

Gods and Basketball
Oct 1987, LAS basketball team travels to India

"You are looking for God. That is the problem. The God in you is the one who is looking"   - Rumi

At just five feet tall, this game has never been one of my specialties. My only background was high school gym class too many years ago. But I shouted across the basketball courts, like I knew what I was doing.   Our enthusiastic athletic director, Cheryl Rutten had convinced me that I could help coach the girl's team. So I read a book on the sport that I found in the school library and agreed to try my best. Cheryl's husband John had already talked Ken into helping coach the boys.

"Come on, Short Stuff. You can do it! Just a little more oomph." Ken encourages me as we try some baskets. At six-foot-one-inch tall, Ken is much better at it than I, and even knows most of the rules. So we are enjoying some after-school hours on the courts getting exercise and spending fun time with our students.

"Shandar!   Stop dribbling and pass that ball to Katja!"   "Take that shot, Fatima! You can do it!" "Good play, Adrienne!" I am getting better at coaching. We have been practicing basketball after school for about six weeks and the kids really do thrive on the extra direction and cheering. Dressed in our baggy cotton shorts and T-shirts acceptable in our walled-in school compound, three afternoons per week in the sweltering heat on hot asphalt, we practice moves and play some games.

Team sports are considered an integral part of an American curriculum. Learning how to work and play together is just as important as other school subjects, maybe more important. This is especially good for our teenage girls who live pretty sheltered lives outside of school. For me, playing is almost more fun than teaching science.

"Are you ready to go up against India or Nepal?" "YES!" is the resounding reply.   Local schools in Pakistan do not play the same competitive sports. So five American schools in the region have play-off

25

tournaments over long weekends. Only the teams and coaches participate and Ken and I are needed to coach and chaperone at the games in New Delhi, India at the end of October.

India and Pakistan seem to have an unofficial mutual harassment agreement, trying to top each other in hoops needed to jump through in order to get across the border. Getting travel visas for all of our international students is even more complex than playing basketball in a land of soccer. Finally, paperwork in hand, we become a travelling team.

"Welcome to the American Embassy School of New Delhi!" announces the pretty Indian woman with a red dot on her forehead. The dot or 'bindi' represents divine insight in the Hindu religion. Dressed in a flowing blue sari with white trim, she hands each of us some papers as we pile out of the bus that picked us up at the airport. "Your sponsor families will be here shortly to take you home. Please enjoy snacking on some samosas while you are waiting, and read over the schedule."

Nine teams have come from four countries - Bangladesh, Nepal, India and Pakistan. Over fifty nationalities are represented and all here to compete, cooperate and have fun. Visiting students and coaches are staying in the private homes of our hosts from the New Delhi school. We pick up our nametags and head to assigned areas of the gymnasium to locate our host family.

LAS basketball team at New Delhi school

It can drive some non-coaching teachers crazy to loose these students from several days of school just to compete in a sport. The kids love it and playing and staying with such a wide variety of international people is an amazing experience for all of us. Ken and I stay with a teaching couple living on campus and get some insight into a country and a school in which we eventually accept a job.

Even though much of our time is spent with the players during the games, Ken and I get to sneak out on a few fast and furious excursions of our own. India is a place we might like to live someday so we take every spare moment we can get between basketball games to explore its fascinating diversity. We are especially interested in all the different religions represented, as religion is so important to understanding culture and worldviews.

The Sufi Order is an esoteric group of Muslims, a small minority group in present day India. Most Muslims, including Sufis, left the country during the Partition of India in 1947, fleeing to Pakistan and Bangladesh (then East Pakistan). We had been involved with the Sufi Order of the West while living in Gainesville, Florida, had met some Sufis in Pakistan, and were interested in finding a Sufi center in India.

For many years we have been contributing money to the 'Hope Project', a program to feed and educate the poorest of India. We really want to visit this place to see how it works. It is a fairly small organization run by the Sufi Order International near the tombs of renowned Sufi Saints in New Delhi. Bastis (shanty towns) tend to build up around these sacred places where the poor live and hope to receive donations from those who come to worship. Knowing that the project is somewhere in this city of about 10 million, we hope to find and visit it.

The Hindi phone book is no help, even when we have a translator try to look up 'Hope Project' for us. The taxi drivers who sit at the school entrance have never heard of the place. Our host suggested we see the cultural advisor at the school who is quite helpful. She knows the location of several Sufi shrines and tells us where to look and what to ask for.

"Can you take us to the tomb of Nizamuddin Auliya?" Ken inquires as we jump in an old yellow cab with torn back seats that lists a bit to one side.

"Yes, Saab, as you like", the taxi driver assures us, bobbing his head with a smile, in the typical Indian fashion that I find endearing. Success! At least we feel we are on our way.

In the quiet early morning streets we venture out into the city passing just a few buffalo carts on the way to the tomb of the great Sufi Saint - Hazrat Shaikh Nizamuddin Auliya. As one of the Chisti Order who lived in the late 1200s, Nizamuddin believed in drawing close to God through service to humanity. He is well loved by Sufi followers as well as most Muslims of India.

The taxi driver drops us in front of an imposing twelve-foot high stone wall blackened and mossy with age, spreading for hundreds of feet in both directions. Stepping through the wide-open iron gate the intensely sweet fragrance of overflowing flower baskets and burning incense fills the sales stands surrounding the entrance. A towering, ancient Moghul tomb stands as the centerpiece ringed with gardens and surrounded by a park. Along the garden paths, the snake charmers are already squatting on the ground, toying with their cobras and playing their flutes to attract a few rupees.

Snake charmer with his cobra and python

28

"Hi! Nice day isn't it? "There are no information or business offices in the park so we ask questions about the Hope Project to anyone who smiles at us. Ken and I keep strolling around smiling and asking until we make some friends.   Here in New Delhi on Fulbright scholarships, two Americans out for a morning walk with their baby in a stroller want to help but know even less than we do. Finally, persistence pays off. An elderly Indian gentleman wearing an oversize dark blue winter jacket and a smile tucked between a thick white mustache and his fuzzy white beard knows of the program we are in search of. He leads us out the back gate of the park into the crowded city and away through a confusing maze of narrow alleys.

Hazrat Inyat Khan Sufi Center

Recognizing the large winged heart symbol of the Sufis above the entrance, we finally stand before the sanctuary containing the tomb of Pir Hazrat Inyat Khan. A great spiritual teacher of our time, he was founder of the Sufi Order of the West and his followers run the Hope Project. We have studied many religions, finding wisdom everywhere but have been most impressed by the teachings of this amazing man. The book "The Message in Our Time" tells of his life in service to humanity. We are over-excited to be at his tomb, right here in India and ask our gentle guide if we can take a picture.

While removing our shoes in the entry alcove, Ken grabs my arm, pulls me close to whisper, and points over to a group of people in the courtyard. "Jane, look over there, isn't that Shahabbudin? What's he doing here?" We are shocked to recognize a spiritual teacher and a few others in the group we had met at various retreats in Florida. "Oh my! What are you doing here?" we all seem to ask at once. "We are travelling together on a tour of the spiritual places of India and have just arrived in

29

New Delhi." Shahabbudin answers. We renew friendships and Ken and I explain how we just happen to be in India too, teaching Pakistani students and coaching basketball. Coincidence or cosmic connections? Who knows?

After arranging to meet again later in the evening, the tour group heads off. We climb the stairs alone to sit and meditate in the quiet cool space around the marble tomb of this saint.

"La, ilaha, illallah," (There is no God but God) I chant the common Arabic words of praise to myself quietly, wishing all religions could see that a true God must be greater than all religions put together.

Like frozen white lace the intricately carved walls and ceiling are open to nature and allow a light breeze to flow across the cool marble room. Birds sing and fly about like protective free spirits in the giant tree just outside that spreads its wide arms over the tomb. Our minds and hearts lift ever higher, carried with their wings; our chants join their songs.

Hazrat Inyat Khan preached a unity and respect for all religions in the search for a personal path to God and service to humanity. Sufism is considered a mystical school of Islam that is focused on a search for Truth rather than blind obedience to a text. As scientists we like this philosophy, as science is also a search for truth. Fundamentalist Muslims often look down on the more global, less strict Sufis.

Tomb of Hazrat Inyat Khan

Just outside the entrance to the center, a yogi, draped in an old white cloth with long black-knotted hair, staff in hand, stands quietly like a sentinel. Women and children in tattered clothing sit under a tree and sift through a pile of garbage to find anything that can be salvaged or recycled. A baby, wearing only a string around his waist to keep away evil spirits, crawls over the top of a gravestone, which also serves as the corner to his family's home built of trash.

In the Basti over 500 people live in shacks built of old scraps. Everything from sticks to plastic bags and rags are leaned against or attached to the monuments in this ancient graveyard. About the size of two large city blocks, it is called the Nizamuddin Basti. The poor gather here to live off garbage picking and the charity they beg from pilgrims who come from around the world. But their best salvation comes with the Hope Project.

A young, polite Indian nurse shows us around the community. Material poverty is not considered "bad" in this culture and is sometimes a chosen method of reaching God. But these people have not chosen to be poor, especially the children. Yet they smile and do not seem too worried as their culture teaches that God sets their lot in life and if they live it well they will be rewarded in their next incarnation.

Our guide walks us to a classroom explaining, "The Hope Project distributes milk and food to over 200 children, sick and destitute each day. We run an infirmary, family planning and health programs, provide blankets, clothes and other essential supplies, and teach pre-school through adult vocational classes." Smiling shyly, a group of young women look up from their sewing lessons on their old donated machines as we enter one of the classrooms. We tour other rooms where some study health care, child rearing and family planning. Men are learning mechanics and carpentry. Most of the equipment is old but useable.

Amid the poverty there is hope as the dark-eyed, brightly dressed women smile timidly and the naked children laugh and play happily. This is the only life most have ever known but they are working hard to improve it with the help of this organization. Their own deep belief of karma and the prejudiced caste system will work to keep them in their place so it is a challenge against both ignorance and culture. Graduates from this project have gone on to open their own small businesses and become respected members of their community.

After attending the afternoon basketball games to coach and cheer on the kids, we return to the tomb of Nizamuddin Auliya for evening services. We gather with our Florida friends to participate in the age-old Sufi tradition of Qawwali, a devotional and boisterous chanting lead by musicians.

Surrounded by piles of flowers and the heavy sweet smell of burning incense, we are welcomed whole-heartedly at the vaulted entrance. Each of the pilgrims in our group is wreathed with a garland of tiny orange marigolds by a smiling heavy-set old man. We leave our shoes in his care to enter sacred spaces. Our bare feet feel the cold dampness of the stone worn smooth as we step carefully around the beggars wrapped in rags who line the dark passage. We respectfully make our way to the inner sanctuary.

"Ya, Illah-ha, il-Allah!" Chanting and music echo around the tomb. Men in turbans and robes, tattered clothes or designer blue jeans, women in saris or pants with a scarf over their heads, all touching shoulders, sitting cross-legged on the matted floor around the tomb. One red-turbaned musician taps a small goat skin drum called the tabla, another pumps a harmonium (a small keyboard with a bellows). In blue jeans and T-shirt a young man strums a twelve-stringed sitar. Another in a shalwar-kamis claps a set of small bronze cymbals in each hand. Loud and joyous chants echo across the dark damp tomb walls, warmed by the glow of candlelight and the sweet harmony of the devotees. We join in, adding our own voices and sway in unison with this diverse group joined together as one. The air is close, warm and muggy so a lean old man in a loincloth swings a large palm leaf over our heads to cool us as we sit crowded together on tattered oriental rugs. Absorbing the spiritual feelings emanating from the voices as well as the very walls, permeated with centuries of prayers, we chant. An experience so totally foreign to my eyes and mind is yet so familiar to my heart and soul.

Nations, religions, schools, sports teams and many other social groups use song as a way to connect their congregations in a harmony that binds them together. Perhaps if we taught children the songs, chants and anthems of people around the world, we could stress understanding and community instead of borders and conflicts. With today's technology children of different countries could actually sing together over the Internet. Imagine a world joined in song.

"Om Sri Ram, jai Ram, jai, jai Ram!" chant the Hindus. The next day across town we remove our shoes again, to climb the wide staircase to the Temple of Hannuman, the Hindu Monkey God. The large sanctuary is filled with statues of many prominent Hindu Gods each adorned with wreaths of flowers, flickering candles, burning incense and offerings of sweets. There is so much variety, color and shapes in

the Hindu religion. Female and male, monkey and elephant, lion and mouse, Gods with many arms holding symbolic talismans, are all represented. Gold and red dominate as colors of divinity, royalty and strength. It is a religion that seems to see God in a wide variety of forms, human and animal, yet intricately linked across time through their different incarnations.

Hindu Altar

As we enter the temple we pause to watch quietly from the side so that we might learn how to behave and not offend anyone. Barefoot Hindu men and women chant softly as they move through the corridors, bowing in supplication to each of the enshrined Gods, stopping to pray at their favorites, ringing bells in corridors. As Ken and I walk over to a statue of Shiva, one of the bald priests robed in orange, smiles, waves and corrects us to turn and walk in the opposite direction. Ringing a large bell, another priest motions for us to come over and receive a handful of sweets that had been given as an offering to one of the Gods. I accept it with a smile as I bow, quietly moving backwards and away, not knowing what I am supposed to do with it. Do I eat it? Do I offer it to a God? Offer it to another? Around the corner I quickly wrap it in a tissue and stick it in my purse.

Sitting quietly at the entrance of the temple in the twilight, on an old table next to a policeman, we watch as others come and go, often cleansing their hands and face with water poured from a copper kettle by an old man.

"Can I help you? Would you like to know of our Gods?" An orange-robed priest with a blaze of red painted on his forehead symbolizing divine insight approaches us shyly.

"Yes, please, we would like that," Ken answers as I nod and we both join our hands in a slight bow before him. We stand up to follow him to his small, private meditation room packed with statues, flowers and candles where he proceeds to explain in broken English the life and times of each of his beloved Gods.

"Vishnu is a supreme God with at least ten incarnations, including Rama and Krishna. Durga is a supreme Goddess and protector who re-incarnates as Lakshmi in her mild form and Kali in her wrathful form." We get lost in the lecture as the sweet gentle man before us recites a litany of names and stories in a reverent monotone. Each of the Hindu gods represent a face of the encompassing One God. It is sort of like each of our beings are just pieces of way more than we will ever know.

Throughout our travels we have found most religious places are not only a cultural experience but also a quiet haven from the busy streets. If approached with reverence and respect for customs (removing shoes, wearing a veil) most of the "priests" are very friendly and quite willing to talk about their religion and holy places. Religion is a major portion of the foundation of a culture. We must understand what people believe to figure out how they think and why they act. This study often gives insights into my own cultural behaviors, as seen from the eyes of a very different perspective. The Hindus are particularly accepting of other Gods and cultures. They have so many of their own who have reincarnated that they figure any new one could be a new face of Shiva or Durga or Kali.

On our last day of basketball we make one last pilgrimage during a long break between games. The Lotus Baha'i temple outside of the city of New Delhi is one of only seven "mother" Houses of Worship around the world. There is one for each continent. A huge building in the shape of

Bahia Temple in New Delhi

34

an opening lotus flower, the seven petals partially divide the church into sections with seven pools of water spreading out from around the base. The temple can be seen from a great distance and is surrounded in beautiful open gardens. The lotus, a symbol of purity, is a majestic flower rising from the pools of water, symbol of spirituality.

Founded in the nineteenth century, the Baha'i religion is fairly new. Followers believe that it is time for all people of the world to recognize basic truths and join together in a global spiritual unity. They are very practical and stress education for all and a common world language. Some of our good friends at school are Baha'i and involved with helping refugees from Iran who had to leave the country because they were persecuted for their non-Muslim beliefs. Surely, 'God' would have to be infinitely inclusive, far more than any one religion could ever claim to understand.

After lifting our thoughts in early morning meditation inside the lotus temple we enjoy a nice walk through the spacious flower gardens before the noisy tuk-tuk ride back to the school and the final basketball play-offs.

The basketball tournament was fun. We lost. But what do we expect from a group of kids who never heard of the game before they came to our school. They played their hearts out and I think they did pretty well. The Delhi school had quite an advantage with more students and more Americans who grew up with the sport.

Camel rides at American Embassy School - Delhi

All the basketball teams and coaches were treated to a celebratory Indian mela on our last night. Painted elephant and camel rides, belly dancers, music, and tables filled with delicious curried foods. Decked out in vibrant shades of red and shiny gold, musicians fingered their string instruments as lithe young dancers moved among the guests. There was even a performer in an orange and blue cardboard horse costume to greet each arrival, and monkeys with little hats and vests to come and grab our food.

"Think you have enough stuff? I saw an elephant down the street you could buy to carry your bags back home." Ken teases as I hand some of my bulging packages over to him. Having spent most of our time temple hunting and coaching basketball, we have about two hours before our plane leaves to explore the shops. New Delhi is definitely a shopper's playroom. That is, if your preference is for the exotic. I bought a sandalwood Shiva, five thin cotton outfits, a blue tablecloth with hand-done white embroidery, a small fan made of peacock feathers, and some hand-painted silk art. I spent only about $70.00. But you must have some stamina for the persistent beggars and sidewalk merchants. It is hard to ignore the starving skinny hands in your face and the more you give, the more seem to show up. Most stores are the size of a large closet and specialize in only a few items. Prices are low because salaries average about $300 a year. I try to beware of 'antiques' as thousands of tourists buy them yet there are always more available.

After our exciting, exhausting, whirlwind tour of basketball and the temples of Delhi, we were more than happy to board the flight back "home" to Pakistan.

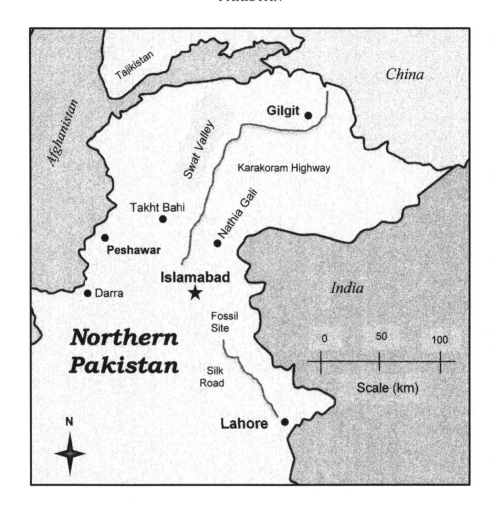

Into the Countryside
Nov 1987 to Nathia Gali

"Stop, say-ay, what's that sou-ound? Everybody look what's going -rou-ound". American music blares from our Pakistani boom box as we jostle around in the back of the Japanese Toyota van, leaving the city of Lahore on our first road-trip to the countryside.

R'Delle (school counselor), Tim & Paula (literature & history teachers), Kris and Brad (library and administrative faculty), Ken and I, are spread out in the 15 passenger van, having decided to take a long weekend and turn it into an adventure in the foothills of the Himalayas. As our driver listens to the World Cup cricket match over the van radio in Urdu, we snack on cheese, bread and fruit from boxes of familiar food that will supplement our local diet for the next 3 days. After all, we wouldn't want to starve if we can't find Cheetos.

Horns bellow as we speed around buffalo and donkey carts, squeezing between vibrantly painted trucks and busses, barely missing bicycles and motorcycles, bouncing through potholes with the dusty wind blowing through the open windows of the van. We are glad Ayub, our required, experienced driver from the school is at the wheel so that we can absorb the sights and sounds of the countryside while trying to ignore the maniacal traffic.

Water Buffalo traffic jam!

The five-hour trip to Islamabad is well worth it. Even though most people take the thirty-five minute, thirty-dollar flight, we want to experience more of Pakistan. We have been in the country for just three months now, which seems like thirty in terms of life experiences. Every day has brought a menagerie of problems and wonders. The intense heat of summer is gone and we are finally getting out more to explore.

"Slow down, Ayub, I want to get a picture" Kris calls from the back of the van. Each village and scene along the way has its own peculiar character. One small camel caravan with turbaned, dark skinned riders is a vision of the Wise Men of the Bible. An old weathered man cups water over the wide back of his rugged black buffalo as they both stand knee deep in a muddy pond. Barefoot little children in tattered clothes playing in the dirt jump up to wave a greeting. "Slow down, Ayub, I want to get another picture."

"Why is that bus pulled over?" Brad asks our driver-become- tour-guide. "Prayer time." Ayub states matter-of-factly. Everywhere, loud speakers on the minarets of mosques chant the required five daily prayers for the faithful. A large inter-city bus has stopped on the desert roadside to allow passengers to disembark, spread their small worn prayer rugs to face Mecca and prostrate humbly before Allah in the hot afternoon sun. The melodic "Allah-ho-Akbar" calls faintly from a nearby village. The devotion of the people is built into their daily habits and social expectations.

Bedford lorrie

We ride along the Grand Trunk Road, one of Asia's oldest and longest. The nation's capital Islamabad and Lahore are both located on the Indus Plain in the Punjab region, the fertile "Land of Five Rivers" that flow down from the Himalayas. Signs of once flourishing civilizations dot the countryside.

"Ayub, please stop just ahead, I think I see it.' Paula requests. An ancient Buddhist Stupa, believed to contain some of the actual remains of Buddha stands high and alone just off the road. Built about 300 B.C., the huge mound can be seen from several miles away. A stupa is a kind of hemispherical structure usually containing ashes of revered Buddhist monks. There is historical documentation that suggests that this pile of old bricks and stones, grown over with tough desert vegetation, was once a beautiful monument, neglected in recent times. Buddhist monks occasionally come as pilgrims to circumambulate the shrine of their Lord, gaining grace as they meditate. These old stones seem vibrant with their presence, even though we are the only visitors today.

After spending the night in the home of generous teachers working at the International School of Islamabad, we rise early to make the two hour drive into the mountains. Climbing up the valley on the newly paved highway, the clean cool country air is a welcome relief of the dusty pollution of the cities. Even though it is November the 4th (Ken's birthday) the temperatures in Lahore are still reaching the 90's during the day. Because of the Himalayan barrier, it does not frost in Lahore even though the city is at the same latitude as southern Georgia.

Buddhist stupa

Natia Gali is a small resort hill station at the base of the mountains used to retreat from the heat of summer, known for its scenic beauty and hiking trails. At an altitude of around 8,000 ft., they have had one snow already. But I guess Allah is with us and the weather is clear, sunny, dry and cool, perfect for exploring.

"Ayub, would you mind checking into the rest-house for us?" asks Tim as we all pile out of the van, anxious to get hiking on the mountain trails. "Yeah, and go ahead and unpack and shine my shoes," Ken teases.

Sparse cedar-green pine trees give way to scrubby wild grasses and brush as we hike upwards into the clear deep blue sky. The view is more breathtaking around each emerging corner. A quick glimpse of a monkey and the squawk of a flamboyant partridge erupt from a stunted tree off the edge of the trail. Colorful shalwar-kamis flowing, thin shawls covering their hair, smiling eyes curious and shy, the local women carry unimaginably high stacks of branches on their heads down the paths to sell as firewood. They giggle and wave to us when they discover that most of us are women, all dressed up in those funny boots and clothes like men wear.

We climb the steep worn paths to 9,700 feet, the highest point within about 50 miles. The brilliant afternoon sun sparkles on snow-topped Nanga Parbat, the ninth tallest peak in the world. At 26,660 feet tall it is clearly seen, yet 100 miles distant from us. Small, simple huts of stone and mud, carved into the mountainsides dot the landscape in distant clusters below us. Clumps of forest give way to the barren peaks, too high for trees, crowned with glaciers sparkling in the brilliant sun.

Lying in the grass at the top of the treeless ridge, resting lazily in the sun, I am consumed with the astonishing beauty of this earth. At the top of the mountains minor problems disappear and my own tiny significance merges into the incredibly expansive world before me.

Natia Gali in the Himalayan foothills

Our first view of the awe-inspiring majestic Himalayan Mountains is not a disappointment.

The chill in the rustic old cabin perched on the ridge of a small mountain brings a shiver to my worn-out bones. But the warmth from the glowing fireplace and the lively chatter of our friends are plenty to relax our hike-weary bodies as we settle in for the night. I can't help but stare out the window at the full moon shining on the alluring white peaks of the Himalayan Mountains.

Have Mom Will Travel
Winter break 1987

From the beginning Mom was just as excited about going overseas as we were. Although we did have a few people come to visit over the years, she was the only person of all our friends and family with enough flexibility and sense of adventure to take off work and re-arrange her life anytime we invited her. She started planning her visits even before we arrived in Pakistan. Game for anything, she looked forward to unique adventures, trying unusual and perhaps difficult experiences and meeting culturally different people. At a spry and healthy 58, Ann Owen was eager to join Ken and I in Lahore for our first big travel vacation over Christmas break.

It would be easy to have her stay in our home with William to help and a separate bedroom and bath for privacy. We began preparations in September just as soon as we settled in. Mom would buy a round trip ticket from Miami to Lahore and we would make arrangements here for the rest of our travel. Since we had been adventuring locally on most weekends, we thought we would go to India over Christmas. We knew Mom was an easy companion and happy to do everything we did. Even though she is his mother-in-law, Ken is always quite the gentleman and protector of both of us, helping with anything we need. I like to mold and organize the plans and so the three of us make a pretty good team.

Letter - September, 1987
Dear Mom,

Be sure to call around to get a good price on your flight, as there are wide variations. We have had trouble with our phone, especially long distance, so if you need to talk with us, know that you may have to try again. The weather here in December should be something like South Florida and you will need a few warm clothes a light jacket, good walking shoes and maybe a sweater if it gets cool. Think conservative and baggy to cover legs and arms. And, of course, bring a party outfit for it will indeed be Christmas and even the Muslim Pakistanis like to celebrate at our

American School. You can always buy more clothes here or have them made by a tailor if you need to. Bring four or five rolls of 200 ASA film for us, and some for yourself.

Some travel tips – store money and passport in a waist pouch attached to your body at all times. Stash other valuables in your backpack that you use as a "purse" and keep it on your back. Use your soft suitcase as your carry-on so it is lighter and will squish into more spaces. As soon as you get to the Lahore airport, exchange some dollars for rupees, as rates and dependability are better at airport banks.

OK – now for the requests from us.

Can you buy and bring us a telescope? Ken would really like to have one both personally and for our students and there are none to be found here. A four-inch Bausch and Lomb Schmidt-Cassegrain is compact and you can make sure it is packed well in checked bags. If customs interrogates you tell them it is for your camera to take pictures of mountains and wildlife, but ignore it completely unless you are questioned. They get touchy about possible spies.

After a week here in Lahore we are planning to fly with you to India as the train has too many border problems. We would really like to visit the Taj Mahal and will figure out how to do that when we get to New Delhi and ask the teachers who have been living there a while. Other than that one flight, we will not make reservations, as we want to remain flexible.

Mom arrived without a hitch and settled into our home. Age garners respect in this part of the world and she enjoyed the extra friendliness and consideration of everyone from the local shopkeepers to the students and staff at school. As Ken and I prepared our classes for semester exams, all three of us stayed busy with invitations to dinners and parties as we prepared for our holiday travels.

The Wedding Greens

"She is stunning in her shimmering green gown and golden jewels, but she sure looks tense and a bit frightened," remarks Mom, as we sit on rented wooden chairs inside the spacious red, blue and yellow festive shamiana tent. We have been invited to the wedding of Iffat, one

43

of our young, Pakistani elementary teachers and we are watching the proceedings and chatting about the marriage arrangements.

"The bride came to see me a few days ago and she was terrified," confides our school counselor, R'Delle, sitting next to Mom. "She has barely met her husband-to-be and would soon be expected to be his loving wife. I can't even imagine such a thing."

Pakistani wedding day

After years of arrangements the full wedding ceremonies are two weeks long and we have been cordially invited to the culminating public celebration.

First, there is a selection of a spouse. For several years, sometimes from childhood, a fitting mate is sought. It is the parents and other relatives who search out possible partners. Choices are based on the religion, culture, personality, education and financial background of the individuals. Traditionally, couples are not allowed to meet before marriage. For strict "purdah" a woman is cloistered from the time she reaches puberty and never shows her face to a man outside her immediate family.

Vows to sanctify a marriage are pronounced to their own parents before the couple even meets. The relatives of the bride follow a different set of rituals than those of the groom. Divorce is rare as the union is held together by extended families and strong traditions.

Tonight in public celebration of the final night of vows, the couple is brought together and unveiled, to finalize their commitment before Allah and the united families and friends.

From head to toe a veil of woven lace and gold thread covers the beautiful bride in her richly embroidered green satin gown. Green, symbol of hope and fertility and thought to be the favorite color of Fatima the daughter of the Prophet Mohammed is the typical color for wedding dresses. Layers of heavy gold jewelry lie against her bodice, surround her face to highlight her shy smile and bring wealth to the union.

The Handsome groom wears a gold trimmed finely tailored white brocade sherwani. A garland of red and white roses symbolizing energy and purity adorns the outfit that is similar to a shalwar-kamis but more elegant and form-fitting. About ten years older than his bride he appears more sure of himself. There is often quite an age difference in a marriage here as men are expected to have established careers and a home before taking a spouse and raising a family.

"That delicious aroma is making me hungry. I hope you can't hear my stomach growling. Maybe they'll serve some of that grilled chicken tikka doused with garlic, ginger and red chili" Ken sighs as the sweet spicy odors fill the air. About a hundred people are gathered under a ceremonial shamiana, a circus-sized, brightly colorful, closed-in tent. Dark red Persian carpets overlap to cover the ground and a few polished brass coal burners keep off the evening chill. Hundreds of tiny white lights shine a soft festive glow. No alcohol is served but there is plenty of good food and festivity. Wafts of roasting meat, cinnamon, turmeric and ginger drift in from the back yard where a sumptuous feast is being prepared over small wood fires in brass pots the size of bathtubs.

The bride and groom sit enthroned on a small carpeted stage in front as the rest of us sit in rows of chairs in the audience, socializing and waiting our turn to go up to congratulate them. The couple sits shoulder to shoulder avoiding each other's gaze as they are not supposed to look at each other until this final ceremony is complete.

Finally it is our turn to go to meet the wedding pair. "The two of you look like such a fine couple. May you have a wonderful life together."

Mom speaks gentle words of encouragement as the bride clings tightly to her hand in nervousness and quietly confides in perfect English, "Tomorrow morning we leave early for my husband's home about a hundred miles away where he has a good, successful accounting business." The bride will now be more a part of her spouse's family than her own and hopes to teach at a local girl's school, if her new husband permits it.

Wedding feast prepared in the backyard

They say that ninety percent of marriages in Pakistan these days are still arranged by parents. Dating and even mixed socials are not acceptable for un-married women. As women are getting better educated many are trying to modernize these traditions.

India, Golden Triangle Trip
December 1987

India seems more open and relaxed than Pakistan and I think Ken, Mom and I released a sigh of relief as we arrived at the Delhi airport. Women in colorful flowing saris showing a bit of midriff are friendly, not so shy and more active in public. Rainbows of color appear in the dress, the turbans and even on painted animals thronging the streets. Diversity of customs and beliefs is common in the ancient Hindu religion of many faces of God. Hindus seem to have fewer restrictions and more tolerance than Muslims. You can tell the difference in their dress alone.

We taxied to the Lodhi hotel near the Nizzamudin Basti Sufi center we visited in October during the basketball tournament. The hotel's vegetarian restaurant was well known for sumptuous food and recommended by some New Delhi teachers.

It was Christmas Eve when we entered the shrine of the Sufi saint, Nizamuddin Aulyia ablaze with candlelight surrounded by marigolds and gardenias and filled with pilgrims paying homage. After time spent inside showing Mom around and sitting in meditation for a while we stepped out into the dark chilly night to be bombarded with poor beggars calling "backshish, backshish" holding their open hands up to our faces. We just kept walking, trying our best to ignore their pleas for money hoping they would go away. Finally one spoke out in English, "but Saab, Memsaab, it is Christmas!" We stopped in our tracks, looking at each other and deep into their pleading eyes. "Yes, you are right, it is Christmas," we answered, as we finally stop to fully acknowledge them.

What good is it just to meditate and speak of God when these people right in front of us are in such need? So we sighed, laughed and emptied our pockets of all our change and small bills. Shaking their hands we wished everyone a Merry Christmas. Hindu, Muslim and Christians alike, it is a time for sharing. This pleasant memory of giving to those in need stays with me more than other events of that day.

The Golden Triangle

Following suggestions from teachers at the New Delhi school we taxied down into the depths of the city to hire a car with a driver rather than try to take trains or planes around India. We would have a lot more flexibility to stop and see whatever interested us and by splitting the cost with Mom, it would even be quite affordable.

Climbing into our hired Ambassador car with a driver named Om, I knew we would have it made. The Hindu incantation 'Om' is considered the highest spiritual mantra harmonizing us with God and the universe. This shyly confident man seemed like he could be trusted to take the wheel.

The Golden Triangle Trip is a favorite tourist loop in northern India from the nation's capital of Delhi to the Taj Mahal in Agra to the "Pink City" of Jaipur. Each leg should be about a 4-hour drive but it could be 8 or more if traffic is slow and we stop to sightsee.

Busy narrow roads filled with animal-pulled carts, trucks, bicycles and sacred wandering cows are all dodging each other in a menagerie of close encounters and honking horns. Traffic was backed-up where we had to maneuver around a deadly accident. There was a corpse, tightly shrouded in white cotton still lying next to the smashed car. Om is a very careful driver but we still cling to the edge of our seats as we wind through the traffic praying to all the gods for a safe trip and no cotton shrouds.

Iron Pillar of Delhi

A twenty-three foot tall, seven ton steel pillar erected in the fourth century to the Hindu God Vishnu still stands strong with no rust at a ruin not far from Delhi. Steel is made of iron, carbon and a few traces of other metals that must be smelted at high temperatures. It usually rusts rapidly unless a modern method to turn it into stainless steel is used. Apparently some other unknown process was used in ancient times making this pillar something of a mystery to metallurgists.

"Come on, you can do it!" Mom and I call encouragement to Ken. It is said that if you can wrap your arms around this ancient, mysterious edifice backwards, locking your fingers, your wish will come true. So we try our luck. No one in the crowd can manage it until Ken steps up to the sleek cool metal. As he forces his fingertips to grab, the crowd breaks out into smiles and cheers. Being over six feet tall with long arms has some unusual advantages. He smiles and winks at me hoping his wish will come true.

Jane and Ann in Om's taxi stop for a sacred cow

"Saab, just ahead is another Hindu religious temple. Would you like to visit?" At first we were a bit skeptical about riding around India with a stranger at the wheel, but as Om starts to point out and stop at interesting sights along the way we begin to appreciate his enthusiasm and knowledge of the land and its history. The birthplace of Krishna; a place that makes jewel-inlaid marble; and a temple to Hanuman the Monkey God are all along our way on the first day drive from Delhi to Agra. Our heads are still spinning a bit from the busy day as Om pulla up to drop us at the towering entry gates of one of the Wonders of the World.

What an amazing tribute to love, a manifestation of life's most powerful emotion. Built by Mughal emperor Shah Jahan in memory of his third wife, Mumtaz Mahal. The Taj Mahal is widely recognized as 'the jewel of Muslim art in India' and one of the universally admired masterpieces of the world's heritage. Construction began around 1632 and was completed around 1653, employing thousands of the world's best artisans and craftsmen. The polished delicately carved pearlescent marble changes hues from dawn to dusk as the light shifts from pink to golden to white to blue-grey and back.

It is difficult to fully experience the whole of it in the bits and pieces that our senses allow. It is touristy of course, with lots of things for sale, pushy hawkers and noisy crowds. But it is not too hard to step away to the side, take a deep breath and just stare at the magnificence of this wonder in our world still so majestic hundreds of years after construction.

Taj Mahal in all its glory

We arrived in the late afternoon to stand in line for a tour of the inside of the resplendent mausoleum. The grandiose central dome towers more than a hundred feet above our heads and the Islamic architecture that was made to "display the Creator's glory" does just that. Typical of Muslim tradition, geometric and floral murals adorn the polished marble walls. Blue lapis flower petals with jade green leaves are highlighted with luminescent mother-of-pearl and stemmed in coral. Semi-precious stones embedded in intricate designs show the fine artistry of the time. No photograph can do it justice. The Taj Mahal.

We returned just after dawn the next morning to enjoy the wonder in the quiet stillness before the crowds moved in. Fog envelopes the mausoleum as if it were rising from the clouds with the 130 feet tall minarets at four corners of the massive dome that touches the sky.

Majestic, serene and luminous, it stands in all its glory as a tribute to sublime creativity in the name of love.

The Pink City

Driving is relatively easier the second leg of the trip as the Agra to Jaipur road is less populated than Delhi to Agra. Cues of camels and elephants calmly tromping along carrying freight are much more fun to travel with than noisy trucks. The narrow, worn blacktop hummed with the feet of all kinds of animals and people coursing through their day. My brother David once remarked that he was jealous of the low-tech self-guided transport of the elephants who can find their way home as their drivers sleep on their swaying backs.

Elephant caravan

"What is that big white building standing on that hilltop to the left?" I ask Om. An especially long staircase winds up the stark mountainside to a white temple perched at the top.

"It is the Chulgiri Jain temple. The Jains follow a path of nonviolence and do not believe in killing any living thing." Om answers. "It is one of the oldest religions in the world."

"Are we allowed to visit them?" Mom asks.

"Yes, of course. I will stay right here and wait for you," he answers while pulling off the road into a small dirt parking area.

Ken, Mom and I jump out of the car to spend the next hour climbing a stairway to heaven right along with other devoted pilgrims. Three small, dark, totally naked men coming down the stairs smile at us as we climb up past them trying not to look pop-eyed. The Jain religion is a path not only of non-violence but also of renunciation and these guys had definitely renounced. Wearing only big grins they motion for us to take a photo if we like, but we are too embarrassed. I wish we had. Mom and me with three naked Jains.

The majestic white marble and alabaster temple springs from the top of a steep hill overlooking the entire valley not far from Jaipur. Mahavira is the latest incarnation of their prophet who stands naked as a tall stone statue in the center of the temple. Peacock feather fans are sold at a kiosk so that you can brush away bugs from your path as you do not want to hurt any creature. The Jains claim to have counted over eight-million species on the earth over 2,000 years ago; which isn't too far from today's estimate. Probably the originators of vegetarianism, they say that other animals have souls and consciousness and should be treated with respect. There is modern research that supports some of their claims as even mice can show signs of altruism and all social animals communicate complex issues with each other.

In a world where biodiversity is being annihilated at a record pace because of our disregard for nature, perhaps we could learn from the Jains. In their renunciation of material goods and their love of a non-violent life they must be the best environmentalists on earth.

"Here taste some of this. It'll be sure to wake up your mouth." I offer a snack to Ken that I just purchased from an old woman wearing a brown woolen shawl crouching over a hibachi-like stove in a village market. "You first. I want to make sure I don't die. Who will carry your bags?" he responds. Fast food in India is spicy dried lentils filling cones of rolled newspaper, fresh fruit and fried samosas stuffed with herbs, potatoes and peas. Our travelling lunches are an experience in the foods we can find in open roadside stands; generously flavored with those infinitely variable spices we call "curry". Although the foods are delicious and mostly healthy we try to be sure they are clean and freshly made as food-borne disease is a major problem for weak-bellied travelers in this part of the world.

Palace of the Winds. The Pink City of Jaipur has lots of sights but the namesake, locally called the Hawa Mahal is an ornate and elaborate five-story palace made of pink sandstone on the main road to Agra. Decorated with hundreds of arched windows covered by intricately carved latticework, it was built in the seventeen hundreds as a harem for the women of the royal household. Observing a life of strict purdah they could see out to watch the daily activities below them but could not be seen behind the lattice. Many spent their entire life in these shadows of the palace, never leaving the premises.

Looking out through the tiny holes from within is not all that easy and the rooms are fairly dark inside. Where western outsiders may proclaim enslavement, insiders may have strived to reach an honored piety expected in the cultural upbringing of their time. Every lifestyle seems to have facades of tradition to aspire to or hide behind.

From Delhi we had been able to book a fine room in the Moghul Sheraton Hotel near the Taj Mahal for our night in Agra but we could not get a reservation in advance for a night in Jaipur. We wanted to stay at the Rambagh Palace but it was full. So we asked Om to find a place for us as he knew the area.

Darkness and exhaustion had settled in before we finally found a vacancy after a few tiring stops in nicer places. Travelling without reservations in high season is not easy and we have to settle for a not so first class place. With only one room available, they set up a cot for Mom to sleep beside our sagging double bed.

After our busy day of touring we decide to have a simple dinner at the hotel. It takes about two long hours for them to serve the chicken vegetable soup we ordered. The soup is filled with neck bones and tastes off, but our hunger overides other senses.

So very tired, Mom still remembers falling off to sleep watching and ignoring a mouse scurry across the room to squeeze under the door.

We have running water but it is plenty cold and our morning cleanup is a bit shocking in the unheated room.

"I'm not feeling too hot." Mom says as she emerges from the bathroom. "Must have been last night's dinner as I've already needed the toilet a few times this morning." I reply uncomfortably. By late morning we are all feeling nauseous from food poisoning and poor Ken is horribly sick through the entire ride of six hours of winding traffic back to Delhi. Soda crackers and ginger-ale doesn't seem to help much. Next time we visit this area we will secure reservations in a better hotel and be more careful about ignoring our food sense.

"Oh, my God, I can't find it!" blurts Mom, looking quite ashen.

"What is it, Mom?" I ask, worried

"I can't find my passport." As we are just arriving back into the outskirts of Delhi, Mom is organizing her purse and terrified by her conclusion. Losing a passport in another country can mean weeks of problems before getting a new one issued. After a stressful discussion we decided it must be at the mouse hotel we stayed at last night in Jaipur at the main desk where they hold your passports until you leave and the bill is paid.

We really did not want to drive all the way back to Jaipur to that awful hotel, probably having to spend another night there.

"Don't worry, madam, I will travel to get it for you." An angel in disguise, Om calls the hotel and arranges to spend the entire next day diving all the way down and back to pick up the passport and deliver it to our hotel personally, requesting only gas money in return.

We were so very, very thankful. Traveling is quite energy intensive and doing a bad trip over is definitely not on our list of fun things to do. Many years later when we were living in India, Mom came to visit and was quite excited to hire Om Prakesh, who had started his own tour company, to drive her all around the city sites for a couple of weeks while we were teaching. They became friends, he invited her to visit his family in Nepal, and they even exchanged a few letters after she went home to Florida. Now, at the age of 85, Mom still remembers his helpfulness.

Finally returning to the Lodhi Hotel where we had left some of our luggage, we are happy to relax and take a day off before our flight back to Lahore. After a morning sitting on the sunny deck Mom and I leave Ken to recover in the room from the mouse hotel food poisoning as we head out to shop the streets where export clothes are sold for enticingly cheap prices. The Indian cottons are some of the softest and coolest garments in the world and are great bargains. Western fashions locally made for export are heaped in piles, some of them with a torn hem or other small flaw, with good brand names, sold for just one or two dollars apiece.

"Backshish!" "Coolie!" "Mim-saab, I be your coolie!" About a dozen ragged children surrounded us in a cacophony of want. Some had their hands out for money, others begged to help us shop and carry our purchases in their baskets and be our 'coolies'. We were up to our necks with pleading hands. So we each chose a girl with a basket, as it is better to hire than to just give money. They were beautiful girls with their dark skin, huge brown eyes and bright smiles. Taking their jobs seriously they chased off all the rest of the children and anyone else who might bother us. That alone was worth their meager salary.

Blue cotton shorts, a pink flowered gauze blouse trimmed with lace and a red jacket. For the next hour we dug through the piles collecting some cotton clothes that we hoped would fit.

Ann with her basket helpers in the market

"What is your name?" the little girls ask. "How old are you?" They are trying out their best English. We chat with our helpers who have just enough English to tell us their names are Orang and Moolie, they are nine and ten years old and they are not in school because they have to work. Well, OK, the work part we just surmised. They show us some tricks to be able to balance and carry baskets on our heads. We laugh, take pictures and enjoy being with them. Mom buys a pretty pink sweater for each of the girls and we both give them some extra money so they can buy books for school. Most likely they will re-sell the clothes, take the money home to their families and come back to work.

After returning to Lahore, Mom packed her bags to head home and back to her job at the social security office in Florida. But not before we discuss exciting plans to meet in Thailand during our summer vacation. Seems obvious. I must have inherited that incurable adventure gene from my Mom.

Teaching Ali - Then and Now

"I'm hoping this is the Mrs. Jane Cundiff who taught at Lahore American School in Pakistan in the late '80s. My name is Ali Riaz. I used to be your student in biology and medical biology. I was talking to some of my old LAS friends and your name came up. Did a little googling and got this email address (scary, but also very useful!). I hope this is the same Mrs. Cundiff I knew."

There is nothing more fulfilling for a teacher than to be remembered by our students. I received this query in November 2012 in my email at a Virginia college where I presently teach. I couldn't believe it. Even though it was twenty-five years and seven countries ago, a distant memory from a different land came bubbling up.

I remember Ali Riaz quite well. Tall, lean and handsome with a head of thick black curly hair he was vivacious, inquisitive and always in the middle of the fun. Exceptionally bright, bouncing up and down in the back of the class enthusiastically, always asking the difficult question and doing well on exams.

Today Ali is a transplant surgeon at one of the best hospitals in the United States and travels around training and giving lectures. He searched me out to thank me for inspiring him to go into medicine. I am so very proud of him and his accomplishments and so honored that he remembers me.

As teachers we tend to forget how much of an impact we have on the lives of our students. So impressionable, they are like sponges soaking up what they feel and learn. There is always so much going on in their lives and in a classroom. Those young faces are each individuals who have their own paths in life. They will all learn something but you may never know exactly what.

With a few pictures, conversations and excavated bits of thought, the memories of these kids came flooding back. Especially of those I taught in more than one class. My Pakistani kids: Kasim, quietly trying to get the highest grades, Shandar and Shagoo chatting secretly in the corner, Majid a gentleman, Ambreen loving critters in biology, Shezad full of questions, Mohsin and Zully brilliant and independent, Umar, Habib and Faisal cooking up trouble. The new American kids, Noelle, Tory and Ty, a bit shy and sometimes feeling left out. Alex, Arno and Katja, the Germans who have been here a little longer have learned to fit in better. In fact, I am surprised at how well I remember them.

All the old pictures in my photo albums and getting re-connected brought them right back to me. After Ali's suggestion to get on Facebook, my life expanded once again to include so many of the people I have known and loved around the world.

Lahore earth science laboratory

We had been at Lahore American School only a few days. School had not yet begun and we were frantically trying to prepare our classes while getting acquainted with our new home and country.

"The chemistry book for the students is antiquated, boring and too simple, can I order another?" I report to Gene, our superintendent as he sits pensively at his office desk.

"I don't know. The last chemistry teacher said these kids weren't very bright" he replies. "Are you sure another book would help?" I just roll my eyes and answer, "They might learn more with good textbooks and active lab experiences." I persist until Gene gives in to my determination.

My Lahore students were far from slow. In fact some of them were exceptionally bright and just needed some direction and high expectations.

Mohsin was a senior in my Advanced Placement College Biology course my first year there. Very smart and rebellious, I remember he would shout out a question while taking a test that would give away the answer to the rest of the class. Cute. I had to make more rules. Twenty years later Mohsin's novel is on the New York Times bestseller list and has won many awards for his unique perspective and voice of someone torn between two cultures. He wrote *The Reluctant Fundamentalist,* a powerful novel that portrays some of the wrenching personal experiences experienced by a citizen of two different worlds. I highly recommend it.

Katja is an artist in Germany, Omar is a prominent businessman in Dubai, Shezad is an accountant director in Kenya and Tory is a civil engineer in Oregon. Fatima, a thoughtful, studious girl, is teaching and tutoring with a degree in economics. Shugoo, a social organizer and leader in the classroom, is now in Pakistan politics trying to make real democratic changes against difficult odds.

"Free thinking has gotten more difficult here in Pakistan as there are strong groups who try to stifle it," confides Khurram as we Skype between Lahore and Virginia in 2014. "It is easier to exchange ideas on the internet than to talk with my neighbors who might cause a problem." Khurram is working in Lahore with social media, in concert with a Harvard program, to bring a better education to low income children. He posts interesting international topics on Facebook as he gathers materials. We had a wonderful conversation over Skype, each of us in our own comfy chairs on opposite sides of the earth, having a long discussion in which we solved most of the world's problems. He runs a Facebook site called "Indo-Pak Heart-to-Heart" in hopes of getting people of these two countries communicating better.

Twenty-five years after high school these students are leading successful, meaningful lives. They work all over the world in a wide variety of professional occupations, emissaries of their countries and of their international education.

Never sell them short.

Lahore classroom

Lahore American School was small. Ken and I were able to teach most of the high school science classes and so we had some students for two or even three full year courses. We got to know them even better on extended field trips and after-school activities. We remember them. We loved them. We had trouble with them. They were kids like anywhere else, pushing boundaries. The boys were a bit more assertive in this male dominated society and the girls a bit more shy. Most were physically more mature than my American students, sporting mustaches and well-developed bodies at younger ages. All had pretty good manners. I enjoyed each of their individual personalities as I tried to keep them concentrating on their subjects instead of everything else that popped up.

Our international schools in general have many bright, capable students. They are children of diplomats, international business executives and the local elite. Many speak two or three languages fluently. Their parents, usually world-traveled college graduates themselves, pay top dollar for a good education that will allow their kids to enter the best universities in the world. Students work hard to make high grades and many go on to be major players on the world stage. Their international education and global views make them amazing assets for almost any occupation. If only all our world leaders and all of our children could have such a background.

"Mrs. Cundiff, you should get on Facebook. I know a bunch of your students would like to get in touch with you," encouraged Ali. "Oh, I'm not so sure about that. Seems like opening Pandora's Box," I replied reluctantly. "Besides, I already spend too much time on the computer."

I have to thank Ali for getting me into writing this book. I gave in to his suggestion and am having a wonderful time connecting with the kids that I knew and taught and loved who are now amazing adults living and working all over the world.

Chemistry students experimenting with hot air balloons

Ali and I have had a few really good phone conversations. He is a Pakistani surgeon with a degree from Swarthmore, living in Pennsylvania, with an Argentinian doctor as his wife. He still travels around the world frequently and has been back to Lahore and LAS recently.

He says he vividly remembers the medical biology class that I taught him. I laughed and told him that I had totally made up that class by myself. The school needed another science elective and many of my students wanted to be doctors. Medical training in Pakistan at the time was pretty limited and I decided to help in any way I could. I ordered more copies of the *Family Medical Guide* that I had brought with me and designed a curriculum around health, human physiology and basic medical treatments.

Ali especially remembered our trip to a local teaching hospital. Medical students there were studying anatomy using old, dried out human cadavers. Unclaimed bodies had to sit for a few months before they were allowed to use them for dissection. Very few people donate their bodies to science as they think it is against their religion. Ali remembers the black mummified face of the body on the table. Looking at his own face in the mirror that evening he "saw a cadaver in the making." It affected his life and choice of medicine as a career to prolong the lives of others.

You never know what will impress your students. Now, as Ali transplants livers and kidneys he is saving many lives, giving his patients more chances to fulfill their dreams and to push away that corpse in the mirror.

"Pakistan is in trouble and the people there are too immune to violence." Ali reports as we chat on the phone. "Over 50,000 people have died in terrorist attacks just since 2003 and my friends say it is not so bad. The wealth and power is concentrated in just a few families and there is much corruption. Over the years most of the good, quiet people have learned to put up with serious problems instead of trying to stop them."

"The scariest thing is when I meet with old friends. I still sometimes see the irrational child I knew in them." Says Ali, who is now forty years old. "Their emotions, their basic desires, are now in adult bodies who are quite influential."

It is no wonder that behavior becomes irrational when even the best of us can still carry childish prejudice, beliefs and fervors which could go on to contribute to some international conflict. Pakistan is now a nuclear power, a Muslim country struggling to remain stable with conflicts around and within the nation.

Global environmental and political problems must be addressed at the cause behind the cause. Controlling the emotional child within each of us begins with a good education. We can learn respect and compassion for every being on this planet. But it must be carefully taught.

Most of my international students, including Ali, are different from their compatriots. This is why his education was so important. He was brought up with children and teachers of other nationalities with an excellent background, learning how to respect other ideas and use an analytical point of view. He learned to ask questions instead of rejecting them, searching for evidence instead of just memorizing. Ali has become a global citizen born and raised in a Muslim world, but with an essential difference.

Imagine a world in which resources were shifted from military to a global education for all. Imagine children learning to understand, appreciate and celebrate cultural, religious and environmental differences instead of fearing and hating them. In learning to promote compassion over conflict we wouldn't need so much military. We could be connecting with friends instead of blowing up enemies.

"All people are a single nation." - Koran

"Education is the most powerful weapon which you can use to change the world" - Nelson Mandela

Swat Valley Mischief   (see map Page 37)

"Our youth now love luxury. They have bad manners, contempt for authority; they show disrespect for their elders and love chatter in place of exercise; they no longer rise when elders enter the room; they contradict their parents, chatter before company; gobble up their food and tyrannize their teachers." - Socrates

Every year Lahore American School sets aside a "Week Without Walls" to take high school students on extended, experiential field trips. Having chosen not to have children of our own, Ken and I feel justifiably worried when we are asked to be responsible for a large group of teenagers for a week on the road in northern Pakistan. There is way too much freedom for them without walls, without parents, and with the peer pressure of rambunctious young friends. They will be pushing boundaries in dangerous places. There will be two other adults with us, but as the American teachers, we are expected to take full authority and guide the students twenty-four hours a day.

"Has everyone put your luggage in the other van? Do you have your backpacks with water and snacks with you? Is your money secure? Have you used the toilet?" I ask twenty-two excited tenth grade students crowded into the school bus and ready to take off on an adventure.

For our "cultural enrichment" we are headed off for a weeklong expedition to the historical sites in Swat Valley. This area of northern Pakistan is narrow, less than 200 miles across, with Afghanistan to the west, India to the east and both Russia and China to the north. Historically called "the Switzerland of the East", it is a beautiful, mountainous area with a wide, lush green valley that has been inhabited for over ten thousand years. But there is often armed conflict in the area, due to tribal clashes. The Russians are at war with Afghanistan not very far away. Gun manufacturing is an industry here. Sometimes there are earthquakes. Not a really safe place, to say the least. The school has been taking cultural trips to this area for many years and so far, the excursions were successful, so we come again.

LAS students at Takht Bahi ruins

From our small cabins nestled in the mountains we take a trip out to nearby Takht Bahi. These Buddhist monastery ruins contain remnants from the first to seventh century. In America we are used to thinking of a two hundred year old building as ancient. Moving to the Middle East and Asia, where civilizations began, has totally changed my view of antiquity.

The students are not quite so impressed. Most have already visited similar ruins and they are having much more fun trying to escape the historical tour to go running and jumping through the crumbling foundations on the steep hillside. Site caretakers will not discipline these privileged teenagers. That is our job and not an easy one. There are pieces of this ruin for sale and we purchase a small stone Buddha head that was cut from the face of the shrine during some decimating religious purge. In my hand is a piece of worship from fifteen hundred years ago. Mind-boggling. I am hoping this relic is a fake and they are not really selling off this ancient shrine.

The students are having a grand time with days of touring and picnicking and nights of slumber parties. Meantime, Ken and I are gritting our teeth and holding our breath as we watch them climb slippery crumbling slopes of ruins, teetering on the edges of mountain ravines, and daring their friends to join them. We keep calling them back with "Be careful!" "Get off that wall!" or "What do you think you are doing?" All this activity, while we are trying to teach about the history and ecology under their feet.

We are enjoying the students in spite of their antics. They are smart, energetic and interested in just about everything. "How did you and Mr. Cundiff meet?" asks Shugoo. "Yes, tell us," pleads Shandar. Like girls everywhere they want to know of romance.

"Were you really in the army, Mr. Cundiff?" asks Habib. "Did you get to drive any big tanks or shoot down helicopters?" Faisal quizzes. The boys have their own sets of questions.

Guy's night out

I get out the first aid kit to patch the blisters on Natasha's heels and put some salve on Majid's cut hand. Ken and I race the kids to the top of a hill and are able to beat most of them. We hike trails through the mountains and visit ruins in the valley. It is fun to get to know these amazing individuals outside of the classroom.

"It's your turn," Ken says to me as he shines the flashlight on his watch. "I've been twice already. I think they are probably asleep now but we still have to make sure the girls are separate from the boys." The nights worried us most. Will the boys escape and get into trouble? Will a girl sneak out and get pregnant? Ken and I get up periodically in the middle of the night to check on them and wish we could somehow handcuff all of them to their beds.

So it was with a huge sigh of relief, we were quite relieved to return to Lahore with everyone in tact, hopefully having learned a lot. I know we did. We might try sneaking out the back next time they ask for week-long field trip leaders.

Girl's night out

"I need to see you in my office before you leave today," a note from Gene Vincent, our boss is brought to our classroom the first day back at school. Ken and I wonder what this urgent message is about as we enter his office immediately after classes are over.

"I heard that some of your field trip students went out in the middle of the night and bought guns from a local village," Gene says as we sit down near his desk.

"GUNS??!!" "No. Couldn't be." "We kept a really close eye on them, even getting up in the middle of the night." "Must be rumor. You know kids." "No. Couldn't be. I just can't believe that."
Gene frowns, frowns again, pauses, then smiles and says, "Let's hope it was rumor". We leave not really knowing, hoping we are right. We could not see all of them for every second of a week full of sleepless nights and slumber parties. Who knows? All inquiries to the students, of course, end with a "no, not me!" We decide to believe them.

Twenty-five years later we get the truth.

In 2014, I phoned my student Ali Riaz, who was on that trip, to ask what he remembered. "Yeah. A bunch of us went into the nearby village and bought some guns and knives. No drugs, though, guess we weren't into that much. The guns were a bunch of junk and one of them went off in somebody's hand. And I remember one of the guys got mad at somebody about a girl and jammed a knife through a chair. I can't believe the school let us go on trips like that. There was always so much trouble to get into. There is no way I would want my kids to do that. We were mostly spoiled rich kids that were always looking to get away with something. I think I'd have to kill kids like that if I had to teach them! I don't see how the teachers can shoulder that kind of responsibility."

Ali was quite forthcoming with his memories and comments. I was glad he waited 25 years to spill the truth. He obviously learned some lessons that we did not plan on teaching, or want his parents to know about.

Students and villagers in Swat Valley

This is why I still shiver and go bug-eyed when anyone talks about extended student field trips. Great adventures for all, but only really fun for me when they are over, successful, without casualties, and with a few good stories to tell.

Our kids do grow up. We have to allow them to test their mettle and spread their wings, even if they might get a little hurt and tell stories about our neglect. Most of them make it with only a few bumps and bruises along the way. But school sponsored trips into dangerous areas might not be the best idea.

Swat Valley field trip students from Lahore American School

Sufis, Celebrations and Weddings
1987-1989 Pakistan

"When all your desires are distilled; you will cast just two votes: to love more and be happy" - Rumi

Six great religions have shaped the major civilizations of our day. The three Western or Abrahamic religions of Judaism, Christianity and Islam, along with the Eastern religions of Hinduism, Buddhism and Taoism. Although these faiths might be at odds in some of their doctrines, if one digs deep enough there seems to be a fundamental core, some moral truths shared by all humanity.

In 1927 Werner Heisenberg presented the "Uncertainty Principal". The measurement of one phenomenon can affect the measurement of another and we cannot know both at once. The pursuit of basic truths in physics can be similar to the pursuit of truth in religion. Physics is looking for the one universal force that encompasses all other forces. Religion is looking for the same thing. Can physics discover the full truth without religion? I think not. Our minds, spirits and emotions are truly part of this universe and we must continue to study all angles to understand anything.

We had learned of Sufism while living in Gainesville, Florida. It is a religion based in Islam, focusing on a search for truth and spirituality, much like mystical groups of Christianity and other faiths. In the Sufi Order of America there is an emphasis on the truth behind all religions and you do not have to be Muslim to be Sufi. After our visit to the Sufis in India during the basketball tournament, we asked around the school in Lahore for any information about local Sufis.

Tahira, our high school computer instructor, just happened to be the niece of Pir Rabbani, a well-known leader and Sufi teacher who draws students from as far away as Malaysia. Pir is a title given only to Sufi masters; so we are honored to meet with him and to be invited to their Friday evening prayers and teachings.

"Come, sit with us," Pir invites with a big wave as we remove our shoes at the front entrance. There is a small blue couch across the middle of the spacious living room, set there to separate the men from the women and children during prayers. Pir is up front with nine other men, all cross-legged on the wide scarlet-red Persian carpet. Not used to this kind of division, I sit right in the middle, near the couch, close to Ken and the men so that I can join in the Zikr (group chanting). Most of the seven women are tending children behind me and just a few are quietly joining in. The powerful voices of the men ring out loud and clear from a lifetime of practice. Soon

Pir Rabbani

we are all swaying with the rhythm of "La, Illaha, Il Allah" (there is nothing but God).

Chanting is different than singing. Singing focuses on the meaning in the words. Chanting is meant to free us from words, to go beyond our body and join consciousness with something more vast. I find chanting especially powerful when I'm with a group who puts all their heart and soul into it. We are, after all, made up of a bunch of freely interchanging energy and atoms, all connected to each other, to nature and to our universe. Feeling that connection by vibrating to the same rhythm brings me a larger sense of global harmony as I tune into the chant, "La, Illaha, Il Allah" (there is nothing but God).

After the ceremony Pir asks us if we would be interested in going to a big yearly celebration of the famous Sufi saint Moinuddin Chishti. Because Chisti's tomb is in India and it is difficult to cross the border, the ceremonies and festivities are to be held at the tomb of a more local Sufi saint in Pakistan. Jumping at the chance, we offer to transport as many as can fit into our school van – about seventeen. Although our teacher friend, Tahira cannot join us, the crew includes her brother, Monsoor, and her daughter, Bushra who are great translators and guides for us throughout the trip.

After a four-hour drive we pile out to go to the homes of those who have offered to put us up for the night. The men head off in a different direction from the women. "Whoa! I think we're going to have to switch gears," Ken says to me. We have all our stuff in one suitcase so we have to do a very quick division. He got the brushes, I got the toothpaste. Luckily, we grab the right clothes.

*Jane tries
the Islamic path*

So I get to spend the night in a very old adobe home in an ancient village called Pakpattan with eight women and two girls from different provinces and from all different walks of life. They welcome me with open arms to stay with them for this special spiritual event. We gather in a circle, sitting cross-legged on a straw mat in the living room to share dinner. A simple evening meal of the traditional curried dalh-bhat (lentils and rice) with pickled carrots and cauliflower are all set in large platters in the middle of the mat to share. Simple, tasty and sufficient, with sharing as the most important ingredient.

"Do you have enough to eat? Can I get you some more? Would you like some tea?" My gracious host offers. Not being very fluent in their language, I smile and nod a lot and occasionally ask my friend Bushra, for translation. They are all very friendly and curious to know what had brought me to them. One of the women, who is wearing a full burka, gladly allows me to try it on. It is a strange feeling looking out from behind that face screen knowing that no one can recognize me. Like being a ghost. I can see how someone could become attached to this feeling of being invisible. You can just do your business, moving unseen through crowds, without anyone knowing who or even what you are. I might recommend it for celebrities or for really bad hair days.

As dusk draws closer we head off to evening prayers, joining with the men of our group as they file out from their rooms across the

72

alley, led by Pir Rabanni. Hundreds of others join the throngs of pilgrims heading to the mosque shrine of the saint Hazrat Baba Farid for prayers, chanting and celebrations of the birthday of the great Sufi saint Moinuddin Chishti.

Our shoes wait on the edge of a pile at the entrance as our bare feet move across the cold, worn, marble floors. Crowded shoulder-to-shoulder, we take our places in the open mosque, in tight lines for evening prayers. Ken is just in front of me with the men, and I am surrounded by women, all standing together in the back. In unison, like one living body, we bow and prostrate five times to Allah for the evening prayer. After a sermon by the local mullah some leave while others begin to gather in concentric large circles for the evening qawwali and the celebration of a Sufi saint.

Celebration of Moinuddin Chishti, Sufi saint

For hours we chant in tune with the vibrant music played on the tabla drums and harmonium. As the night grows dark, hundreds of tiny twinkling lights sparkle around us as our bodies sway in rhythm and our prayers and spirits rise together in harmony into the deep expanse of the starry sky above.

It must have been close to midnight when, tired but relaxed, I crawl into my sleeping bag atop a straw mat next to Bushra for a little quiet conversation amongst the other women preparing for sleep. I want to know a bit more about her and at eighteen years old she is excited to tell me about her recent engagement to be married.

They say that more than 90% of marriages in Pakistan are still arranged by parents. Bushra was born and spent her early years in Canada when her parents were in college there. Having graduated from Lahore American School she was quite westernized and global in her ideas and attitudes.

"Who will you marry?" I ask.

"My parents picked five different men from which to choose," answered Bushra, drawing closer to whisper her story, so she would not wake the others.

I was surprised to learn that her engagement was indeed, arranged. Well, mostly arranged. All of her suitors were quite a bit older, between 28 and 38, as it is customary for the men to be well established before taking a bride. One was a lawyer in London who sounded quite attractive but she had barely met him and she would have to move away. Her choice ended up being a military man, a distant cousin of the family whom she had known from childhood. He was 35, had a good stable occupation, and most importantly, she liked him and she would be living close to home.

We all take chances when we get married. What is love anyway? Shouldn't we be able to grow to love anyone? Chemists say that some of our strong attractions could be due to body chemistry. They have shown

Bushra's wedding day

that women seem to prefer the smell of men that have an immune system complimentary to their own. Religions say that we should love everyone. Long-term relationships must be based on far more than body chemistry or rules. Arranged marriages are practical and many work just fine, as long as both individuals wish it so. I relate love to passion, commitment and a never-ending desire to understand and share life's changes. It is all way too complex to analyze and diversity in relationships, like diversity in people, is probably the best thing anyway.

74

Several months later we are honored to receive an invitation to Bushra's wedding. Her shyness on her wedding day is bedecked in a stunningly beautiful green and gold gown, the traditional colors of a bride on this last day of ceremonies before she begins her new life with her new husband. The young reserve of a naïve girl, not yet twenty, contrasts with the exuberance of the groom's age and eagerness after many years of planning and waiting for this day. I hope they live happily ever after.

We were able to spend more time with Pir Rabbani over the two years we spent in Pakistan. He was eager to know how we came to be interested in Sufism and was excited to write and communicate with Pir Vilayat, our teacher in America. We learned more from him about the stricter Muslim traditions. He learned some of our modern, global views about spirituality and religion. We read his books and he read ours. We all grew in knowledge and acceptance.

Perhaps if we all could spend some time really experiencing the deep beliefs of other people, it would be much easier to see them as friends, all wanting the same basic things in life. All searching for Love, Happiness, and Community.

Sufi Dervish

Basant - Flying High in Spring
1988 Pakistan

Red, green, white, yellow, multicolored and multi shaped, thousands of them, looks like millions were flitting about the clear blue skies of springtime in Lahore. Kites. Today is Basant. They say it is a celebration that dates far back into Hindu tradition to celebrate the coming of spring in February. These days it is non-denominational and it seems as if everyone gets involved in this happy energetic festival, the most popular holiday in Lahore.

"I am dressed in yellow, the custom for the day!'" I announce to Ken as I dance around in my new, flowery shalwar-kamis. "Do you have a yellow shirt to wear?" We have been invited to spend this holiday on the rooftops of the old city with a large extended family of one of the teachers and are getting ready for a fun party.

After carefully maneuvering the van down the narrow streets thronged with people and animals, we arrive at an old mansion where around sixty or more of the 'wealthy and important of Lahore' are already chatting, flying kites and meeting friends. Many of the Pakistani teachers at the school are wives or daughters of dignitaries. All are well educated, generous, friendly and sociable, often asking us to be their guests. The spacious time-worn, once-beautiful home consists of a large open courtyard surrounded by several stories of oddly shaped rooms and tiny winding staircases; like a rambling story-tale palace. But the real action is out on the wide-open, and dangerous rooftops.

Almost everyone participates, even if just to watch or picnic. Flying kites is a sport here and the competition is intense. The goal is not just to fly but also to try to cut down or pull other kites out of the sky. Small and maneuverable, many of the strings are even coated with crushed glass fragments to make for sharp attacks. Those who love the game have a stack of kites made especially for them, knowing they will lose many. Mostly it is family fun and everyone all over the city, probably millions of people join in to celebrate spring.

Reaching the roof I hold my breath watching a young boy standing on the edge of a precipice. He yanks on the tough string of his small fragile kite to hoist it into the breezy blue skies above, happily ignoring the three story drop from the edge of the roof where he stands. A small girl perches on a crumbling wall with her feet dangling far above the busy street below to watch her brother run around with his kite.

Each year more than a dozen people are mortally wounded because of Basant. They get hurt from falling off rooftops or getting badly cut when the glass-coated strings wrap around them as they ride through the streets on bicycles or motorcycles. Safety is not a priority. Either Allah is with them or not and many don't seem to worry about it much.

Our hosts have brought a stack of kites for us and we each choose one to fly. "I'll take the bright yellow one, to match my outfit" I say as I pick one out. I try to launch my lofty toy into the air by pulling and jerking it like the others are doing but without their success. "OK, this is the third time I have crashed this thing and have not even gotten close to flying it." Disappointed in my failure, but still eager to participate in the fun I pass it over to Ken. "Here, you try." Ken gets a better grip on it, joining in the play and with persistence he pulls it into the sky on his fourth attempt. He laughs and jokes and dodges the blue and red kites handled by our friends Brad and Dubash. I sit back and enjoy watching the activity, cheering on the players while chatting with Freeha and Ayesha about the latest happenings at school.

Wearing bright red and blue costumes with silver bells around their feet and a kettle drum hanging from a long strap, they treat us to some exuberant music. A young lady dances in the traditional joyous style of jumping, kicking and adroitly beckoning the crowds on the roof to join her.

While drums beat and the group sings, a 'picnic lunch' is served in the courtyard. More like a royal feast, three long tables are covered with platters of meat curries, grilled chicken, yogurt raita, salads, pickled vegetables, sweet puddings and fresh fruit. Waiters are decked out in white uniforms, sashed in red with white top-hats of starched cloth and red plumes that stick straight up.

The sky darkens into evening and kites slowly disappear as we share stories and finish our lovely meal. Suddenly there is a loud cracking right beside us that jolts us to our feet. Someone is lighting a fireworks display less than ten feet away. Startled, we quickly grab our chairs and move a good distance back to watch and enjoy the celebrations lasting late into the night.

Basant entertainers

"Hey, what do you guys think of going down to the old city? I hear the celebrations there go all night long." Still wide-awake at the end of our Basant party, Tim and Paula suggest Ken and I join them to explore the festivities in the heart of Lahore in the middle of the night before we head home.

"I'm not sure, it's getting really late" I reply.

"Oh, come on, it's good to go out of your comfort zone now and then," Tim responds, "You can do it."

Ken takes the challenge, nods at me, and shrugs with a smile.

"Alright then, I guess we can sleep tomorrow," I capitulate as I reach into our bag of city maps to help plot the course.

With Tim driving the school van and edging us on to stay awake, we wind our way through the sleepy alleys at 2 A.M. way past our bedtime. We heard that the kites would still be flying even in these wee hours of the night, so we keep looking for signs of life.

The Walled Old City is the heart of Lahore. Some of the ruins date back four thousand years. Not far from the Ravi River, one of the largest rivers in northern Pakistan, the area has seen many civilizations come and go. Most of the crumbling walls have been torn down and replaced with gardens and streets but some of the ancient gates still remain. Towering arched stone tunnels, just wide enough for a donkey cart or one vehicle, still stand as entry gates taking you through the thick old city walls and a step back in time.

The intricately carved stone and woodwork adorning the old and decaying homes packed tightly together near the inner city attests to what once must have been a beautiful and wealthy area. Just below the shuttered windows, open gutters cut into the base of buildings as they carry runoff and even some sewage from leaky pipes down the narrow streets. Bundles of dirty ragged blankets hug the edges of the cobblestone here and there covering the homeless. Tiny shops display fresh food on tables just above the open sewers. It is no wonder that the average life span here is in the low 50's.

As we draw closer to the center of Lahore and pass through one of the ancient, arched stone gates, signs of festivities begin to erupt. "Kites!" Paula points out the front window. "Over there! Head to the right!" Tim responds, weaving closer to the spotlights and fireworks lighting up the rooftops of the old city in jubilant festivity.

For two o'clock in the morning, it is pretty unbelievable. Food stalls and kite shops are open for business and people bustle through the streets eating samosas and sweets, flying all sorts of kites and having fun. Curious smiles from the dark men wearing their traditional simple garb, are wondering what our

Baking bread in a tandoori oven

white faces in a fancy large van are doing here in the narrow passages of this ancient center of life at these wee hours.

"Salaam Alaikum! Chai?" One of the men invites us to come and have tea. Others beckon us to fly kites with them. One is excited to offer us freshly made flat bread, hot and right out of his tandoori oven that sits molded into the floor. Bowing with thanks we accept and savore these gifts of life freely offered. We make small talk with our limited Arabic, asking about their families and enjoying their hospitality.

There may be a lot of discouraging things in this part of the world, but there are not too many places where one can go into the poorest areas of a dense inner city and feel safe and welcomed in the middle of the night. Alcohol is illegal and crime severely punished and that has its advantages. But mostly it is about a culture and tradition of being friendly and generous to strangers. We have found this graciousness common in Pakistan and, really, in most countries around the world. We have learned that meeting people with smiles, handshakes and humility we usually receive the same in return.

The kite flying fervor of Basant lasts for about a week. We ask our servant William to purchase a stack so we can fly them with his family in our backyard. Darting here and there, up and down, catching in the trees, laughing like crazy, we try our best to fly these small "maneuverable" kites with no tails. William is a pro and even wraps around and brings a neighbor's kite right down into our yard. Even his little daughters whip their kites high into the brisk spring air. Although we do not master the skill of cleverly flying the brightly colored toys we get pretty good at crashing them and delighting in the family fun.

Mountains, Goats and Mujahedeen
Pakistan, June 1988

"It's impossible," said pride.
"It's risky," said experience.
"It's pointless," said reason.
"Give it a try," whispered the heart. - Unknown

"Can we really do this?" "This is a dangerous area for more than one reason. What if we fall or get lost or killed by bandits?" "Do we have the equipment and the ability to hike the tallest mountains in the world?" Ken and I ask each other and anybody else who might know something.

"What about drinking water and food and our poor language skills?" "Will people on the trail be friendly or hostile?" "What will we do if we run into trouble?"

The *Lonely Planet Guide for Pakistan* and *A Traveller's Guide to Pakistan* by Hilary Adamson and Isobel Shaw were our main sources of information at the time and they offered little to answer our questions. Our local friends knew even less as none of them had ever ventured into the area.

We were young, energetic, smart and naive enough to feel fully confident that we could make the journey.

The Gilgit-Baltistan area of Northern Pakistan is in the rugged Karakoram mountain range of the Himalayas where four mountain ranges meet. With the remnants of a primeval ice age, it contains the greatest concentration of lofty mountains in the world. Getting only a little rain each year and having very few good roads, simple lives have been scoured out from the sparse, tough landscape. Villages are small, isolated and quite independent.

Unknown to us, there were many conflicts brewing in the area at the time. Close to the border with Russia and China, along with the stirrings of Islamic fundamentalism, as well as local tribal disagreements, there was much to argue over. Many men were armed and dangerous and funds were being used for things other than maintaining roads, trails or guesthouses.

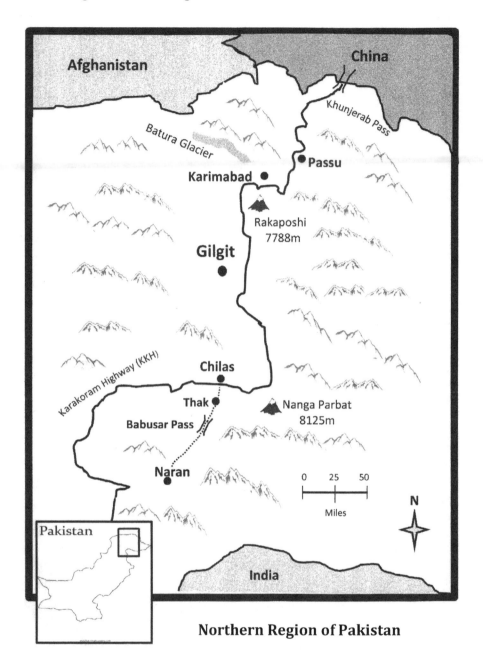

Northern Region of Pakistan

But we did not know these things. No Internet. We couldn't read Urdu or Arabic newspapers or understand their newscasts and this remote area was not really talked about in Lahore. The guidebook just says that the first trail we want to follow through Babusar Pass, "is a 5 to 6 day moderate trek through the mountains," and gives minimal directions to find it. We will search out more hikes after completing the first.

Excited about hiking and camping at the top of the world at the end of a long, intense school year of teaching in a different country, we make our plans and pack our gear.

5 A.M. June 3, Day One

"OK! Over here everyone. It's time for our final check. Does everybody have your passports, credit cards and some cash?" asks Ken. "Let's see them." He wants to make absolutely sure we have these essentials we can't travel without.

"Our maps, compass and guidebooks are behind the driver's seat," Tim assures.

"What about filled water bottles, iodine pills to sterilize river water, food bags and handi-wipes?" I want to know. Most of our gear had been loaded in the van the night before and marked off of our long list. Only our last minute essentials and our weary bodies are left to carry on board.

"Did anybody sleep last night?" asks Paula, as she climbs into the back seat next to the food boxes. "I think I was way too excited."

"I'm sure glad we have a driver so I can get some sleep on the road," answers Tim as he curls up his long body in the middle seat of the van snuggling into his pillow against the window.

"I'll ride shotgun and help navigate for a while," proclaims Ken as he jumps into the front seat with our driver.

Our high-energy, adventurous friends, Tim and Paula, had arrived in Pakistan the same time as we had. We had spent a lot of time with them already, jaunting and exploring all around Lahore, and had excitedly prepared for this major trip for months. Paula's sister Jean, who flew in from America to join us as soon as her college let out, was primed to rough it right along with us.

Two days after LAS high school graduation, very ready for summer vacation, the five of us load up. With tons of traveling, hiking, camping, and driving gear, enough food for an army, and our sleepy bodies we pile into the Toyota seventeen-passenger van with our best school driver, Ayub, at the wheel.

Tim Marr, English, literature and history teacher, Stanford graduate, tall, thin, blonde, 27, married just last June to Paula, is an old hand at backpacking – having traveled through New Zealand, Europe and the U.S. with the carefree attitude of "whatever man", making friends everywhere.

Jeep and passengers before glacier ride

Paula Marr, social studies, English and history teacher, Stanford graduate, petite, long blonde braided ponytail, 28, energetic, always asking questions, seeking to understand both intellectually and emotionally, forever the wonderful optimist. Both she and Tim have been studying Urdu (the local language) more diligently than Ken and I, which will be a valuable asset to our trip.

Jean Phillips, Paula's sister, is a psychology student at the University of Alabama. At 22 she not quite as experienced as the rest of us, but is ready to carry her own load and more when needed. For a pretty southern sorority girl, she is relatively tough.

Ayub, our talented and patient driver, doesn't speak much English but is trying to learn and is a fair translator. Since the school owns the van they require that we have a driver to take us around the countryside. Getting paid less than $10 per day, which covers his food and room on the road as well as salary, he is happy to make the extra money as he travels to places that his family has not yet been able to visit.

After lots of research in the *Lonely Planet*, other guidebooks, the school library and info from teachers and locals, our plan to backpack through some of the rugged mountain trails of the Karakoram Range took shape. The itinerary includes two or three hikes with recuperation between treks at small hotels or guesthouses where Ayub will meet us with our van full of supplies. Each trip will be three to five days of backpacking and camping through the steep, rocky, magnificent Himalayan Mountains.

Most of the first day is spent weaving through cars, trucks and ox carts, pointing out new sights along the Grand Trunk Road to Islamabad, the capital city of Pakistan. There is an International school there and we have arranged to spend a night with the same teachers who generously hosted us on our trip to Nathia Gali last fall. The 'new' city of Islamabad has been built from scratch near the crowded old city of Rawalpindi and the wide, open boulevards and modern buildings are quite a contrast to Lahore. It even feels a little barren but is not likely to stay this way with the fast growing population.

"Welcome! Come on in and make yourself at home. We have two spare bedrooms and dinner will be ready shortly," Sylvia invites. Other American teachers seem to become immediate friends and we settle in as if we have always known them. The Stites had lived in Lahore before coming to Islamabad and still had mutual friends at our school that had introduced us.

Sylvia and Tom have much to tell us as they are still recovering from the huge explosion of a military arms depot not far away, just outside Islamabad. They were at school when they felt the blast. The athletic coach was filming his team and caught the sound and the image of a huge mushroom cloud covering the sky. "Holy shit!" were his exact words as he dropped the still running camera to yell at the students to run to the theater, the planned emergency shelter. A missile rammed into the ground right behind them as they fled. As all the students

85

huddled in the theater another missile tore right through the wall to land on stage and start a fire. Sheer terror. No place to go.

The missiles were not armed but they were deadly projectiles. Hundreds of them had exploded out of the arms depot and across the city. Thousands of people were killed. With great luck, there were no serious injuries on the International School campus. Right now there is an American marine crew out in the street, very carefully removing one of the missiles that tore into the ground fairly close to the Stite's house. The American embassy has taken responsibility to dis-arm and remove these missiles that could still explode, from any areas near their citizens. Ken is out there chatting with the supervisor. I wish he would back away and come up to the house.

The depot contained millions of dollars of ammunition, mostly provided by the U.S., given to Pakistan to fight the Russians on the northern border. There is speculation that the explosion was a purposeful cover-up of a huge Black Market. A recent investigation could not locate some $30,000 stinger-missiles. Some of the politicians had been getting unexpectedly rich recently.

June 4, Day 2

After spending the night in Islamabad we forge ahead north into the mountains to the town of Naran - our first 'base camp.' As cities fall away and the mountains get steeper we leave the main road to follow a minor gravel road, once part of the ancient Silk route followed by Marco Polo. Nomad herders with their goats, sheep, donkeys, and camels are also moving along this road making for tricky, slow driving. They are taking their herds and their families to greener pastures for summer.

The hot summer temperatures of Lahore do not reach the mountains. Shivering, I pull my thick blue stocking cap tightly over my head when just yesterday we were sweltering. There is still ice and snow here and some of the glaciers have not yet melted back from their winter fullness. We each have a set of long underwear, gloves, woolen socks and layers of clothes to keep warm. Right now the glacier across the road bothers us even more than the cold. Although there are tracks over it, crossing the slippery ice will be dangerous.

"OK, what do we do now? Walk?" asks Paula.

"I cannot drive across this ice in the van, and it is too far to walk to Naran," proclaims Ayub. "It isn't safe. But I can find someone with a jeep to take you the rest of the way. There are some shops here beside the road and they might be able to help."

As Tim heads out with Ayub to find a four-wheel drive to hire, the rest of us unload all of our gear and food from the van and tightly organize our backpacks with what we will need for our first hike. It isn't long before they return in a jeep with two men driving. "Thank you so much, Ayub. We think we'll be fine from here. We will hike from Naran through the mountains at Babusar Pass and you can wait for us in Chilas on the other side. We should arrive in about five days, Inshallah (God willing)." Tim and Ken explain the plan to Ayub, hoping he fully understands. Ayub is not happy about leaving us. "Are you sure, Sahib? He asks them. "The area is rough, it is a long journey and I can drive you to Chilas." He is worried about losing all these teachers he is in charge of, but we assure him everything will be OK and urge him to enjoy a few days' vacation without us.

Chunks of ice kick out from under the jeep tires and skid over the edge of the glacier into the freezing, roaring river over one hundred feet below. I am sure the American Automobile Association would not approve this road. We insist on watching another vehicle pass over, slipping this way and that, before trying it. Slowly and carefully our jeep driver starts across.

"Whoa! I swear we almost went over the edge. We are slipping way too much," cries Jean. "Shit!" "Go slower!" I shout to the driver while clinging to the seat of the sliding, bouncing vehicle. Wide eyed and white knuckled, shouting encouragements and threats, we perch on the edge of the seats, hands on doors, ready to bail. Sliding sideways, inching forward, bouncing, slipping near the icy edge, we FINALLY cross about 300 feet of terror. "We made it!" we shout in relief. We have to cross 2 more glacial arms during the two-hour drive to Naran. It does not get any easier.

The little town of Naran is a tourist spot for the area; boasting stunning mountain scenery, deep clear lakes and abundant wildlife in the

Jeep crew takes a breath on the glacier

surrounding pine forests. Being a bit early for summer tourist season, the paths are not yet clear of ice and the main hotels and restaurants are still closed. We finally find a small guesthouse with about six small rooms to welcome us in and feed us dinner. Dirt floors, mud and wood walls, chipped cloudy drinking glasses, bare light bulbs, hot, spicy lentils and rice sit before us. We chat with the local men in the cool evening, accumulating news of Babusar Pass and the route we wish to hike through the mountains. With very little Urdu on our side and very little English from them we are translation challenged. Some say there is too much snow and ice, others say it is possible, but what do we want to do that for? At least we think this is what they are saying. We have eyes and ears out for a guide. Friends at the Islamabad school have recommended a man called Bashir, but no one seems to know who he is.

June 5, Day Three

"Oh, my God, this water is cold!" Freezing water rushing down my back forces shivering yelps and jump-starts the day. Our guesthouse provides "showers" - a bucket of frigid ice water drawn right from the glacial melt river behind the building. The water swirls silvery as it glitters with mica, a mineral worn from the mountains as glaciers move across them. The icy slush is not for the timid bather. I should have brought more baby wipes. There is no electricity or heat here either, but hey, with few choices and only $10 for all six of us for one night, it is easier than camping.

To get into the spirit of things and scout out more information, we decide to hike for a few hours up to a recommended tourist picnic spot on Bashkiri Lake. They didn't tell us the trail was still mostly covered in ice. "Be careful! Here, do you want to take my staff?" Ken offers protectively as we proceed across our first glacier by foot, slowly and carefully. "Do you see that dead horse? Are you sure we want to do this?" I grab Ken's hand and point to the animal lying at the bottom of a deep ravine that cascades over the side just inches from our path. "Just take it slow. There will be more ice in the higher mountains and we need to get used to it," he encourages.

Tightening our boots, taking tiny steps and holding our breath we inch slowly along. Not to faze the locals, however. "I can't believe it. They must be crazy," I murmur as a local family of four passes us slipping and sliding along the icy trail in their best Friday leather shoes and billowy clothes. It is their vacation and they came to see the mountains whether the paths are clear or not. There are even two women ahead of us wearing high heels. I can't really know if they have poor planning skills or they just don't own the tough jeans and gripping boots we find an utter necessity. They certainly aren't showing much fear about falling. It could be they have been moving through these steep icy mountains since they were children while I grew up in flat, sandy, warm, Florida.

"OK. If they can do it so can I." I smile at Ken, take a deep breath, straighten up and try to get my balance, move a little faster and not be such a wimp.

Drizzling, freezing rain begins to fall, adding to the slippery ice and even though we have raincoats, our boots and packs are getting soaked. "The rain is getting worse and I don't think we want to go any farther," Ken calls ahead to Tim, Paula and Jean. We agree to return to town.

"As-salaam Alaikum! Come! Join us!" A welcome call comes from a worn grey tent already packed with men and goats. "Aiwa! Shukran!" (Yes! Thank you!) Answers Tim, happy to squeeze in with them as Paula and Jean follow. Ken and I decide to pass on the party and head back to the quiet of the guesthouse.

The tent party turned up some good information. Although Ken and I are glad we missed the crowded, wet, noisy crew, we are also glad that Tim had joined them. Some of the goat-herders knew the man, Bashir, who could guide us through the mountains and they offered to find him for us.

"Saab, you need guide?" Later that evening Bashir shows up at our guesthouse, ready to discuss hiking plans. With a round kindly face, and a small, healthy, strong body wrapped in a brown woolen shawl Bashir speaks only a few words of English. He has just returned from a trip, leading two French men through the mountain pass of Babusar. It had taken a full four days with lots of snow and ice but it is possible. Worn folded letters of recommendation he pulls from his wallet speak highly of his skills as guide, porter and cook. Offering to carry 25 kilos (55lbs) of our gear for only $6 per day, we hire him.

He has his own old backpack with an aluminum outer frame, a worn sleeping bag and his woolen shawl that doubles as a blanket and tent. With plastic jelly loafers for hiking boots, and some chapattis (flat bread) and catsup in his food sack, he is ready to go. I am amazed and love his simple approach to life. It takes us 4 hours that evening to prepare our expensive packs loaded with all the "essentials". Bashir will carry his own things along with our tents and cooking gear while leaving us with about 12-20 kg each of food, clothes, water and stuff like flash lights and toilet paper.

This is the first time Ken and I have done any serious backpacking. We thought the Himalayas would be a good place to really get the feel of it! Sink or swim? Ken checks on me constantly to make sure my load isn't too heavy but I am doing great and loving it. Our tents, mats and cooking equipment are heaviest. Weighing only 45kg myself, I can only carry about 12, Ken and Tim probably have more than 20 and I am so glad that Bashir can hoist so much more than his own needs. We only pack a liter of water each and will use iodine pills to treat stream water along the way.

The Naran valley is part of the Karakoram range in the very north of Pakistan - 30 miles from Afghanistan, 20 miles from China and 40 miles from Russia - five times farther through mountain trails. A sort of intersection of world-class problems. An interesting and yes, dangerous area both politically and physically. We will hike about 100 kilometers over about five days to go over the mountains from Naran to Chilas and over Babusar Pass, at an elevation over 4,000 meters high, close to 14,000 feet.

June 6, Day Four

The sun has not yet topped the mountains. Heavy backpacks full and tightly secured, outfitted in our best hiking outfits, we are excited and ready. Laughing and breathing deeply of the cold fresh morning air we lace up our boots. "OK, Bashir. Lets go!" Striding out of the village, one after the other, we follow our guide up the path and into the Himalayan Mountains.

"Baaah, Baaah", the soft bleating of the goats with little bells tinkling around their necks, part around us like a flowing stream as we pass through them. The caravans are already on the move. It is early summer and time to lead the herds to higher, greener pastures. Extended families and hundreds of animals, mostly goats and sheep are headed up the mountain trails. Women and little girls are decked out in their full native dress - long, heavy, embroidered red and black skirts, thick silver jewelry and woolen shawls to cover their heads and wrap round their bodies in modesty. I think they wear all the clothes and jewelry they own instead of carrying them, looking a lot prettier than I do. Men in shalwar-kamis, and loose turbans typical of the area are wrapped in warm, locally spun, woolen wraps. Little boys sport western style jeans and parkas. Us westerners in our North Face down jackets, stretchy Nike shirts and expensive hiking boots have too many extra clothes in our packs. The herders are using packed donkeys, which follow right along with the goats.

The air is crisp, the sky a deep blue and a small black-capped wag-tail flits just before us, rock to rock, perching and serenading us along the trail. We walk at a leisurely pace to enjoy the scenery, the life and just being here.

Hiking with local shepherds

A wide, shallow bubbling stream tumbles down the mountain over boulders and rushes across the path before us. Bashir tells us that we must ford it, as there is no bridge. It is only about a foot or so deep, but looks over twenty-five feet across. If our heavy leather boots get soaking wet they will not dry. So, with our boots tied to our backpacks we decide to ford the stream barefoot, rolling our pant legs up as high as we can.

"Yikes! This water is freezing my toes off and I can't move them anymore." Bashir has taken my pack, but just walking over the slippery rocks through rushing, icy water and trying not to fall is difficult. "Come on, you can make it!" cries Tim, already on the other side. Ken gets across, drops his pack and comes back to carry me the rest of the way. With our feet frozen in the icy water, stumbling across the slippery rocky stream, we now understand why Bashir wears plastic jelly shoes. He keeps them on, has much better footing, and they are dry in less than an hour.

A knurled old man with a long black beard carries a tiny white baby goat in a sling hung over his bent back giving it safe passage near a steep cliff. A young teen-age boy waves a long stick at us as we attempt to photograph some of the women. The women sometimes smile but more often turn to avoid our glance and pull their shawls lightly across their face. We move along a bit faster, picking our way slowly through the herds, passing them one by one.

"Chai? Chai?" A group of about ten Afghan men are waving us to join them for their afternoon tea break. Chai is their favorite drink. A milky, hot sweet tea spiced with cinnamon and cardamom, it is my favorite too.

They are nomadic Afghan Mujahedeen or freedom fighters who have come into Pakistani pastures with their families and goats for the winter and are now making their way back through the mountains to fight the Russians in summer. Americans have been supplying some of their weapons. Since we are white and look an awful lot like their Russian enemies we

The mujahadeen leader

are quick to introduce ourselves as Americans. Ken offers them some American Marlboro cigarettes, which they heartily and gratefully accept. Although he doesn't smoke, Ken likes to carry small gifts he knows tough mountain men may enjoy.

While cleaning their rifles and handguns, they spread another blanket for Paula, Jean and me to sit separate from the men. They are gentlemen and ignore us, as they have been taught to do. This does make it easier for me to take more candid photos. Their wives and children are lunching at another tent about 50 meters away. A tall, muscular, handsome man with the slow quiet intense bearing of a leader sits in the center of these rugged characters. He has four wives and 11 young children and I can understand why. Had I to make the choice of being wife number five or the wife of another in the group, I may have chosen him too.

After placing a target some distance up the mountain, the men gather to do some practice shooting. The leader takes a couple of shots with his Kalashnikov rifle and then hands a 1903 Springfield bolt-action rifle to Ken. Oh boy! The tough mountain fighters glue their attention to this American in jeans and a yellow T-shirt striking his best prone shooting position. I try to focus the camera in the cloudy, dim light. A great shot. A rousing cheer! And some terrific pictures. They were quite impressed at Ken's expertise and excited to learn that he had been trained in the American army. They wanted to know if Ken had brought any weapons with him and would he fight along with them to defeat the Russians.

Ken's invitation to join the Mujahedeen

With a brown woolen shawl wrapped around her long red, embroidered dress, an older woman makes tea for all of us over a stick fire. Her little grandchild in a blue woolen tunic crawls around on the ground keeping busy by playing with bullet cartridges.

"Jane, can you figure out what these pills are for?" Tim had been conversing a bit with the men, using his own Urdu and Bashir as a translator. One of the men had an injured leg and wanted to know if we could help him understand some medications he had. Since the chemical names are international, I was able to describe what some of the pills were for. We also gave him a few pain pills from our own medical kit. Even though they had previously ignored me, they were quite attentive and respectful when I was giving them medical advice.

It is such a tragedy that war tears apart these simple mountain people. They are a microcosm of the plight of man in conflict. We are carefully taught to fear and hate those who have fought against us in the past and who may strike in the future. Right now these men are fighting Russians right over their border who are not so different than themselves. Although they are proud of their warrior capabilities they all express a desire to live and raise their families in peace. Perhaps one day we will all be taught to cooperate instead of fight.

Feeling bloated after three or four cups of tea we start out again, travel about twenty more minutes and again hear the call: "Chai? Chai?" from another group of Mujahedeen. "Shukran! Shukran!" We wave, bow and thank them, but we have to get hiking before dark.

Our goal for the evening is a small town that Bashir tells us has a guest house. If you can call three huts and ten nomad tents a town, I guess we found it. Throwing back her plaited black hair a young woman in her long red tribal outfit clambers from a tent, dragging her toddling baby by the hand. She follows and waits with us for the owner of the hut

that is the 'guesthouse'. Squatting down on the rickety wooden porch she flings her shawl over her child to nurse, while chatting merrily away in a language we cannot understand. We guess she is just being friendly and welcoming so we smile and nod a lot.

The chowkidar (watchman) finally comes and settles us in for just 50 rupees rent and another 50 backshish (tip) for him. A roof, stonewalls, charpoys (rope cots) and plastic chairs for the night. At least it gave our group some indoor privacy. Tenting can sometimes draw quite a crowd of curious villagers.

June 7, Day 5

"How long do you think it will take to hike to that mountain perch up there? " Jean asks. "It looks like a good spot for a spectacular view." With no trees or other familiar structures to judge size, it is difficult to estimate distance in these high mountains. After an hour of steep rock climbing without getting much closer we give up and return to the main trail to see a spectacular view right around the corner.

Stark, snowy white peaks reach up into the deep blue sky. At these high altitudes you can stare right up into the darkness of space even in the day. Crisp clear cool air with an intense sun comes straight through the thin atmosphere. Raging rivers from melting glaciers cascade over boulders and forge through crevices as they leave the heights, pummeling into the valley.

Now I understand why people climb mountains. It is tough, dangerous and exhausting but the freedom that comes with having everything you need strapped to your back, the adrenalin of the physical achievements and the exhilarating views cannot be beat. It seems as if you can see forever. Little problems dissolve away. The awesome expanses co-mingle with our lifted spirits and it feels so open and free at the top of the world.

After two days hiking, we leave most of the caravans behind. Even the goats cannot go where we will climb. The glaciers have not yet melted back.

Looking over sheer drops of hundreds of feet to the rocks below while slipping along on the ice is not what we had planned for. "The paths are not bad," said a hiking guide. Somewhere it actually says that jeeps can get through them, which is totally impossible now. Maybe the tour guide writers have never been here in early June.

We are not equipped well for ice. We have no spikes or crampons for our boots or even any ice picks or walking sticks. Slowly and deliberately we kick each foothold as we hike (crawl?) along the sloped trail covered by remnants of a slippery glacier with a dangerously downward angle. Bashir leads the way, trying to forge a narrow path in the wet snowy ice, making footsteps we can follow. I find his steps just a bit too long and am getting a bit off balance.

A blood-curdling scream pierces the thin air, freezing me in my tracks. I twist round, trying to keep my footing, to catch a glimpse of Jean as she slides over the edge, off the frozen path and down one of the long, steep inclines. It must be well over a 500-foot icy, sliding fall to a raging glacial river below. None of us are near enough to even try to grab her. We can only stand desperately still and hold our breath, as she screams and we wait, what seems forever, until she stops. We cannot see her.

"JEAN!" screams Paula in wild desperation. "JEAN! JEAN! WHERE ARE YOU, ARE YOU OK??" "JEAN!"

"I'm here!" comes a frightened, rattled answer from somewhere below.

God was with us, or Angels, or maybe just luck. She had skidded at an angle off the side of the glacier into a patch of moss only about 100 feet down from us, below our visual range. Ken and Tim quickly move to finish crossing the ice and climb down to the ledge on which she stands frozen tightly to the ground. They grab hold of her, remove her pack and pull her gently to safety.

"MY GOD, WHAT ARE WE DOING?" Shaking and crying, Jean screams that we were all fools to take her on such a treacherous path and refuses to go on. We let her scream. We are all trembling, feeling helpless and wishing we had not come. Paula holds and calms her sister.

"I quit. I'm going home," insists Jean. "But we have already come so far and this is the longest stretch of ice" Bashir tries to assure us. "We have to stick together no matter what," we agree. "If we turn around we will have to go right back over it," reminds Ken.

So after a long break with some fearful and serious disagreements and discussion we decide to forge ahead much more carefully, keeping closer touch with each other, wondering about our sanity.

Time is relative. I think life is measured more by experiences than by a calendar. The most intense experiences usually do not last many days in calendar time. But the memory and the lessons expand that time to be more significant than months or even years of daily routine. After a year of living in a very foreign country my views on many aspects of life have changed. I feel a little older. A little wiser. A little more capable. More likely to dismiss the small problems of life because of having had larger ones to deal with.

Once, a long time ago, I was listening to a radio talk show. A 98-year-old woman was asked how she would change her life if she could. I remember only two things on her list of responses. First, she said she would eat more ice cream. So I now always have at least three kinds of ice cream in the fridge. Second, she said she would have more real problems rather than imaginary ones. I really liked that one.

I find that by getting more involved in life, by taking risks, by seeking new opportunities I have a lot more real problems to solve and I am more likely to not sweat the small stuff. I find it amusing to see how easy it is to make mountains out of molehills when there are no real mountains to climb. I think it is instinctive for most humans to try to make their lives better by solving problems. It is the types of problems we choose to solve that make us who we are.

The trail did indeed get better and we hiked on for a few more hours to pitch camp near some stone foundations that may have once been a village. Bashir finds a nice flat rock for a bed.

Bashir on break

June 8, Day 6

The creamy white body of a Himalayan Griffon Vulture soars effortlessly in the updrafts drawing expansive circles in the brilliant blue sky. A golden marmot scurries behind the rocks. This sunny side of the mountain has less snow and easier terrain. We have left the herders behind that last glacier and enjoy the solitude.

It begins as a beautiful day and we are eager to enjoy the sun and serenity of these majestic spaces. But the weather deteriorates quickly. Clouds loom overhead, and a freezing drizzle mixed with a little snow and sleet makes the slippery ice underfoot even worse. My raincoat takes a few nasty tears when I trip over some rocks and I hope the first aid tape holds it together.

"The bridge is out," announces Bashir as we stand in the rain and stare at a raging glacial river before us. "Jane will carry us," teases Ken to lighten the tension. Bashir says he knows of a detour we can take. It will be a longer route and we will not be able to go over the mountain pass today.

Putting one foot in front of the other, misty sleet freezing us to the bone, wondering why we are doing this and trying to feel optimistic that it can only get better, the journey starts to lose all reality. Finally after too many hours of plodding, getting more difficult with lower oxygen at high altitude, we arrive at the base of the mountain pass that we will climb tomorrow. The remnants of an old stone building stand in a flat spot along the trail, oddly isolated in these barren mountains, too high for anyone to live. Parking our packs next to it, we waste no time setting up camp to get out of the freezing mist.

Camp before Babusar Pass

"How about hot soup for dinner?" I offer. "Do you think we can order out for pizza?" Tim asks. Ken sets up the camp stove for me to prepare dinner as the rest of the crew erects the tents in the intermittent drizzle. A full steaming bowl of hot Ramen noodles mixed with cans of beans and spinach never tasted so good. Even Bashir, usually preferring his chapattis, gratefully accepts the hot meal scraping the bowl clean. We eat together, knee-to-knee squeezed into our small blue and white domed tent which envelopes us in a dry cocoon out of the cold wind and rain. Sitting cross-legged on our sleeping bags we discuss our summit of Babusar pass in the morning.

The rain has stopped and Ken steps out for a moment to stretch in the dim light of the misty evening. "Hey, come look at this," he says flinging open the tent flap and urging us outside. "Is that two people up there on the side of the mountain?" We are out in the middle of nowhere, have not seen any other people since early yesterday and there are no villages on this side of the mountain. Bashir told us that two men died on this mountain pass just three weeks ago by getting caught up there at night and freezing to death.

High above us on the foggy mountain, trudging through light snow are two men in black western clothes. Without coats or packs they look dazed and lost, as they head slowly up the trail toward the pass. We yell to get their attention but they seem to be disoriented and faltering. Ken, Tim and Bashir take off up the icy hill to get them.

Two young Pakistani men in black leather jackets. They are soaking wet and carrying only motorcycle helmets and a paper bag of cassette tapes. Their teeth chattering loudly and their clothes almost frozen, they are dazed and can barely speak as our men lead them into camp.

"I just can't believe this! Who are these guys? Where do they come from? Just what the heck are they thinking?" asks Paula as we gather round to find out.

Someone had told them they could ride a motorcycle through this area and over the mountain and so they had tried it. They left their bike with no gas and a flat tire back where the bridge was out and had gotten soaking wet while fording the river. They were trying to hike through the mountain pass before dark.

Ken and Tim help them take off their wet, frozen outfits. Bashir stokes up a fire to warm the men and dry the clothes. Paula makes them hot soup. We squeeze eight people into five sleeping bags and two very small tents; crowded, but warm and alive.

The next morning, after a hot oatmeal breakfast shared with our strange new, unprepared, friends, they are convinced by Bashir to turn around and go back the way we had come, avoiding another river crossing, to retrieve their motorcycle and forget hiking any further.

About a week later, we came across them again, still on holiday, driving around the area on their motorcycle. This time they were so joyous to see us they could not contain themselves. After thanking us profusely for saving their lives they promised to bring their families to see us in Lahore; which they eventually did.

Our rescued friends near Babusar Pass

June 9, Day 7

We start early, climbing with the sun that glows dimly through the misty cold clouds clinging to the mountainside. Bashir leads us slowly and patiently upward through the fresh powdery snow along a fairly clear trail. Somehow the path seems safer than it is as the steep ravines below us are obscured in fog. With great gulps I suck in more oxygen from the thin air for my muscles that are starving for it. One step after another, each is a struggle. High altitudes are especially hard for us sea level inhabitants. Bashir is not as bothered by it. This mountain pass climbs close to 14,000 feet and can be quite dangerous and even deadly for those sensitive to altitude.

We have headaches and our bodies resist but it is still exhilarating, even though it is treacherous. Perhaps because it is so treacherous. We have everything we need on our backs. We have overcome many physical and mental hindrances. We are going to make it.

"Come on, this is it. The top is just around this boulder" Ken has come back down the trail to re-assure me and join him in the final ascent.

At a place where few others have come we really are at the top of the world. It is hard to believe we made it. We sit on the rocks, take

At the top of Babusar Pass

pictures, and giggle in our success. It is Sybil's birthday so we hold up 41 fingers in honor of Ken's sister. In our light-headed exhilaration we stare across the very tops of the spectacular Himalayan Mountain range. An absurd feeling of homesickness overcomes me as I turn around to consume the experience. I want to make sure it becomes a part of me, as I may never see it again.

Screams. This time of joy and laughter and play. Going down this mountain is much more fun. The air is clearing, the sun peeking through the clouds. The slope is gentle and filled with enough snow to slide down. We take off our torn raincoats and use them for sleds.

"I bettcha I can beat you to that black rock down there. Here I come! Watch out below!" We gleefully slide down the mountain and into the green pine forests below.

"Bashir, we will miss you! Thank you so much! I have written a letter of recommendation for you." Tim hands Bashir the note as we all shake hands and thank him. Now that we are through the pass, we no longer need a guide. After spending so much time with Bashir we have become friends and are sorry to see him go.

"Thank you," he smiles shyly and accepts our payment along with a well-earned tip, a pair of lightly used, tough woolen socks and some extra food for his journey home. As we wish him a safe trip back to Naran, he turns and disappears back up the mountain.

The down slope of Babusar Pass

"OK, I'm ready to get there now," I say for the second or third time. Here at lower altitudes and out of the snow, the path downhill is rugged and rocky. I usually prefer going uphill. Downhill is tougher on the joints and easier to fall. My boots must be just a bit too small as my toes are jamming into the tips until they feel bruised and each step hurts.

We finally hike into a small village that should be the end of our journey. We try to hire a jeep here to carry us the rest of the way, but there has been a landslide on the road and they say it will not be cleared for weeks.

"It is only about an hour to hike to the landslide," offers a shopkeeper where we stop to buy some cookies, and the sweetened condensed milk that Tim loves to drink straight. The estimate is off. After two more hours of painfully jamming my toes into my boots, with all the others helping to carry my gear, it is getting near dark and we have to pitch camp for the night on the roadside, hoping to reach the landslide in the morning.

Our driver, Ayub, must be getting worried as he was supposed to pick us up yesterday in Chilas from the end of our journey.

June 10, Day 8

As the sun rises we pick mulberries off trees along the road to the tune of sweet-voiced birds while leisurely hiking toward the avalanche. It will probably take quite a while to clear even with all the villagers working on it, and so we linger and enjoy the morning.

"There is no way that huge mess of torn mountainside is going to be cleared anytime soon," Ken exclaims as we round the corner at the site of the debris. The pile of rocks and boulders across the road is much larger than expected. One of the workers suggests we climb over it where a local transport jeep will pick up passengers to take them to work. It takes about thirty minutes for us to pick our way over the massive pile of rocks with our heavy backpacks.

After about an hour of sitting under a tree downside of the avalanche, surrounded by curious village children, a large Jeep pickup truck finally arrives. This is the local work "taxi" as a lot of men and their tools can be carried in the open bed lined with benches. We load into the truck along with four workmen, our gear beside us. It is comfortable enough for an hour's ride down the mountain, but we aren't aware that we are just the first stop. After two more stops we have twenty-eight people squeezed on this oversized pick-up. Maybe more, as I can't even see into the cab. Maybe there are some in the glove box. And it isn't just people, it's workmen with their broad axes and machetes crunched so tightly beside us on the thin benches we can't move. Tough looking local workman in their shalwar-kamis and turbans, a couple of them in western jeans, an older man with a broad, toothless smile all conversing in Urdu. There are turbaned men standing, bending, crouching in the center, three or four sitting on and clinging to the roof of the cab and a few standing on the back bumper. Sharp metal broad axes, shovels and other tools are stuffed under the benches and between our feet, shifting with every curve in the road. And this steep mountain road has plenty of curves. In a now very top-heavy vehicle, we hold our breath (what there is left of it) as we round the corners, leaning over steep cliff sides that disappear into a river far below.

We have to stop at a river crossing to douse the overheated truck engine with water. The driver simply lifts a large clump of mud from the river and sets it on top of the engine while the rest of us pile out of the back to stretch and take a break. For ten minutes vigilant officers check our foreign papers and ask a few questions at a police checkpoint. All the time our fellow passengers are cheerful, smiling and happy to have us with them, regardless of the extra trouble we are. I love their 'can do' attitude. Taking risks that do not seem to bother them, these friendly workmen were perfectly willing to pile all five of us on to their already crowded vehicle.

"What a ride! I've gained new insights as to what constitutes a taxi drive." Paula says as we disembark

"No problem," Ken says. "I just plain gave up worrying and decided to enjoy the last moments of my life before we headed over that mountain to a sure death. After all, if it is their day to die, then it is the will of Allah, and possibly our day to die too."

As we enter the town of Chilas at the end of our taxi ride, we shake hands and thank everyone, for indeed, it has not been our day to die.

"There it is!" Tim sees it just down the road and runs ahead. We spot our white Toyota van with embassy license plates sitting in front of a local café in the main street of the small town. Ayub is so thrilled to see us he jumps for joy and kisses our hands. We are two days late. He had not wanted us to go and had worried the whole time that he had totally lost five teachers on his watch.

Swaggering with the confidence of mountain climbers we drop our heavy packs to the floor, grab a seat at the café, plop down with big sighs of relief, and have the best cold orange sodas we ever tasted.

"You were born with wings, why prefer to crawl through life?"
  - Rumi

Trouble on the Trail (see map p. 82)
More Karakoram Adventures - Summer 1988

Piercing echoes shatter across the stillness of the wide valley, bouncing between the mountains, rumbling the earth, shocking us from our reverie. "Oh, my God. Look! Do you see that? I can't believe my eyes." Tim shouts jumping to his feet and pointing to the largest mountain in our view.

Relaxing on the sunny hillside perch of a small village hotel we recuperate for a couple of days between adventures. Our hike through Babusar Pass and a bit of food poisoning from a cheap meal has worn us thin. Tim, Paula, Ken, Jean and I sit lazily reading and chatting on blankets spread on the grassy knoll in the afternoon sun, admiring the expansive Himalayan views. The stunning snow-covered peaks of Mt. Rakaposhi shimmer in the distance. With its white outstretched arms embracing the green valley tucked precipitously below, it is one of the most resplendent mountains in the Karakoram Range. It is not the true height at over 25,000 feet, but the sheer drop of 18,000 feet that makes it so dramatic.

Even as we watch and remark on the elegant white snowline against the bright blue sky, we can't believe our eyes as a huge chunk from the very peak of Rakaposhi cracks away in a massive cloud of white. The thunderous sound shakes the earth as a huge avalanche, tons and tons of snow, ice and boulders barrels down the steep slope, engulfing the entire side of the mountain and obliterating the hillside paths all the way down into the valley.

"Boy, I'm sure glad we aren't on that hike today," reflects Ken. "That looks like one icy grave." We consider the ever-present dangers of mountain climbing and the risks we are taking, deciding not to go that way any time soon.

"Sure, come along with us," invites Paula. After ditching the Rakaposhi trek, we decide on a driving excursion along the Silk Road of ancient lore. With plenty of room in our van, two college students, one from Pakistan and one a Brit working with Afghan refugees, join us from the hotel to take a three hour drive up the KKH (Karakoram Highway) to

106

China. Past hours of rocky mountain fields dotted with clusters of yellow wild flowers, on the winding, steep, rocky road obviously prone to avalanches, we work our way to the border at 16,000 feet. A small herd of longhaired yaks graze on the thin alpine vegetation as a few fuzzy, golden-red, Himalayan marmots scuttle between rocks in the sparse landscape.

The Kunjerab Pass through the high mountains between countries was once part of the ancient Silk Road taken by Marco Polo. It is still used to export goods between China and Pakistan, down the Karakoram highway. The border control, where we must leave our passports, is 2000 feet lower than the true border, a no-man's land, as you cannot survive long at this elevation. Breathing heavily, getting headaches, slow chugging movements, spouting black fumes, our bodies as well as the van have a hard time functioning on low oxygen at this altitude.

The sign says we are in the Taxkogan Nature Reserve. Over 5,000 square miles has been set aside, more than three million acres, mostly to preserve the rare Marco Polo sheep and snow leopards. At such a high altitude, visitors are also rare.

China border at the top of the KKH

That was our one and only trip to China. We stayed just long enough to take a picture and step into the most populated country in the world in a spot where no one lives.

107

"Ahhhhh! A hot shower! A soft bed and a real toilet, drinking water that does not have dirt and iodine in it, and a comfortable chair to sit and read, I think I am in heaven," I proclaim. The finest things in life depend on your perspective. We plan for just one day in the small valley city of Gilgit, to investigate our options for another adventure. The center of mountain trade for thousands of years, Gilgit has been a host of many cultures, religions and wars along the Silk Road and we hope to find other interesting places to explore.

From our school in Lahore we had heard about the Agha Khan School for Girls in Hunza. It is the first of its kind in Pakistan, offering a secondary education, as a residential school for the girls in remote mountain areas. With directions from local people, and some persistence, we are able to locate it not far from Gilgit. The new campus is just two years old and the teachers and students are excited and happy to show us around. They delight us with their good English, and their studious, well-disciplined attitudes. The science lab is small but fairly well equipped and it is inspiring to see the girls so engaged and working hard for a good education. They will be the future leaders of a rapidly changing culture both in their professions and as mothers.

The women of this country are much stronger than westerners might suppose. They value education and can be quite forthright in their pursuits. Even with their veils and rules, there are probably more influential women in Pakistan than in many western countries.

"Come look at this." Three girls, dressed in their school uniforms of a blue shalwar-kamis and white cotton veils covering their hair, proudly show me the science experiment they are doing with some bacteria in petri dishes.

Back in Gilgit, rough, brown woolen caps and shawls, worn heavy boots and scruffy beards lounge at small rickety metal tables clasping cups of hot, sweet, steaming chai. As we sit and chat in the teashop we try to listen and interact with other local customers. These tough looking mountain men have information about the area we want to hike. The Lonely Planet book says Karimabad is a "Shangri La" area of amazing natural beauty. We heard rumors there was tribal fighting there. What do the locals think?

"Kwais!" "Mish kwais!" ("Good!" "Not good!") After lots of tea and a few widely varying opinions we decide to go and see for ourselves.

Fresh, plump juicy apricots and dark red cherries dipped in cold glacial melt, glittery with specs of mica from the stream behind them, are offered in small plastic bags by little brown hands of enterprising children. Fresh walnuts, almonds and plums are packed neatly in small open boxes beside them. Tall, white-trunked poplars line the dusty roadside where the eager youngsters stand with their treasures for travellers, calling "Hi!" "Welcome!" "Cherreee?" and "Bye-bye."

We drive slowly for the forty miles of narrow winding roads from Gilgit and enjoy the views off the steep roadside. The small mountain village outside Karimabad has just a few buildings and after some inquiries we find a room to rent, not far from the Batura Glacier that we hope to hike. For only a few dollars we have a simple bed and a private space in a shepherd's hut where a glacial creek is diverted into a trough feeding a stream of water right through the bathroom, carrying any waste back out to the garden. Good thing it is June as even now that water makes for a mighty cold bath. Ken washes his hands three times before realizing that the grey on them is coming from the silt in the glacial melt.

Tucked neatly within the gigantic Himalayan Mountains of the Karakoram Range of Northern Pakistan is the beautiful Hunza Valley. Mostly cut off from the rest of the world until the late 1800's the culture, dress and demeanor is uniquely their own with lots more jewelry and colorful reds in embroidered woolen caps and dresses. Women are shy but not as fully covered or isolated as the typical Muslim fashion. "Hi! What is your name? My name is Aisha." A teenage girl carrying some forage to her goats, trying out her English, proudly tells us she is in grade ten in a land where many girls never attend school. Everyone is friendly, welcomes us, and is willing to help us in any way they can.

"Subha bakhir!" (Good morning) An old feeble man in white robes standing below a large cherry tree, points up at the branches laden with fruit as he greets us.

"Un Kilo?" I ask. He smiles warmly, grabs a small wicker basket and picks; giving us cherries to eat as he does so. Shuffling down the path, he unlocks the door of his small shop to weigh them, selling them to us for a pittance. The most delicious, sweet, dark cherries on a cool, bright, sunny morning with friendly people, in the most gorgeous valley I have ever seen. This must be Shangri La!

Immense silence with only the light wind and our own footsteps echoing in this vast icy space of still, cold, quiet. Ear-piercing, cracking, popping, scraping, and groaning of the glacier suddenly moving unevenly through the valley and below our feet. And then again – total, total silence.

We are well above the lush, green valley and much higher up the mountain, past the tree-line and near the ice. Late spring is not usually an easy time to hike here because of the winds but it isn't too bad today. Ken, Paula and I began at five thirty this morning to climb over some steep rocky hills and get onto the frozen flow of the glacier. We walk and listen for hours as we cross ice as thick as the mountain, covered with hundreds of years of dust blown from such distant places as the brown sands of the Sahara and the black soot of Chinese factories. The gravelly moraine does not even look like ice except where deep fissures show the shiny layers exposed below.

This area is known for glaciers and Batura, over thirty five miles long, is the largest outside the polar regions. Glaciers are defined as dense bodies of moving ice. Thick layers of yearly snow accumulations are pulled down slopes by gravity, losing water in spring and gaining ice in winter. About 75% of the world's fresh water is stored in them and over 200 million people depend on the spring glacial melt for their sole water supply. They say that if all the glaciers on earth melted, the sea would rise by hundreds of feet. This very warm, wet world was that of early mammals, a time of pine trees in Antarctica, palm trees in Canada and rapid changes in species around the earth.

Cautiously we make our way, constantly alert for cracks to open up and swallow us. Our destination, the mouth of this monster ice, at the opening at the head of the valley that was birthing this, was not getting any closer. Distance is impossible for us to judge, as there are no trees or buildings or any other reference points. It is amazing how much our visual perception depends on known comparisons. Three hours hiking, getting tired, and we are not getting any closer to our goal. So we turn around to make sure we can get home before darkness engulfs us in a starkly beautiful, frozen, no-man's-land.

Batura glacier

The inn keeper's old knurled hands hold delicious, juicy red strawberries, shiny and cold from a fresh rinse in the glacial melt, newly cut from his small garden, just for us. The streams here are mesmerizing as the shiny mica swirls with a pearly luminescence. "Kwais, shukran," we thank him with our limited words and unlimited smiles.

The rich, silty melt-water flowing down the mountain is the life-source of this idyllic green valley and will be altered greatly by climate change as the glaciers disappear. How will their future strawberries grow with no water? I wonder if he knows of these things.

Breakfast and packing is hurried before we begin on our next big hike. We had interviewed a local guide, a skinny, scruffy, red-haired village man, to lead us and carry a few things but we did not like his attitude and decided to go it alone. Our van driver, Ayub, reluctantly left us once again, with directions to meet us back at the hotel in Gilgit in one week's time.

Full packs on our backs, bright sunny day, and the sky the deep, rich blue only seen at high altitudes; we begin our hike up to the higher Hunza valley on a rugged jeep trail. Although sparsely populated, the beautiful, lush green mountain area has been home to some families for more generations than they know. A simple existence is eked out of terraced hillsides supplied by the nutrient rich waters of glacial melt.

Some say this is the real "Shangri La"; a mystical paradise written of in the 1933 novel, "*Lost Horizons*"; a place isolated and hidden in the Himalayas. Rich with a clean, natural beauty, good crops and friendly people who live a simple, happy, long life, it matches the description. Women with colorful veils smile and wave to us from the fields and children rush to greet us, asking for pens. As teachers, we are delighted to fulfill their requests.

The day grows brighter, the sky more clear and the air more fresh. Our heavy packs go unnoticed with spectacular views unfolding as we climb higher to behold more of the awesome valley below.

A new, simple, wooden suspension footbridge hangs next to the old one. Hundreds of feet long, they speak of no vehicles but take way too long to cross, with hesitant steps on the rickety slats, swaying over the freezing river swirling with silvery mud far below.

Bridge of courage

As we move along the trail hugging the high, dry mountainside, after hiking most of the day, several local boys run across the creek in the ravine and over to us from a village on the other side. We do not seek their company, as we are enjoying the quiet of nature in these mountain trails, but they anxiously try to get our attention.

"Mish kwais," they say - the only words I fully understand. "Not good." Our aggravation and tenseness mount as more keep coming, till there are about 15 of them trying to get our attention as we try, impossibly, to ignore them and shoo them away. With poor local language abilities and no guide we are having a tough time translating their shouts. They are quite insistent and agitated and it seems as if they are saying, "If you keep going, we will kill you." Ken and Tim are desperately trying to get rid of them while protecting Paula, Jean and I.

There is obviously something amiss. Our fears rise up into our throats, more than irritated at this encounter, so we parlay as they swirl around us. It is clear they will not allow us to continue quietly on the path. We decide to go with them as they have no weapons and are obviously pleading with us to come to the village.

Most of the men and boys of the small hamlet stop their work and hasten to surround us under the massive tree in the village center. There are more than fifty of them for a while. No women come, as they keep cloistered around strangers. We are getting more and more fearful about their intentions as they seem quite serious and without the normal friendliness we had known throughout Pakistan. Yet they continue to try to communicate.

A parlay with the locals about trouble on the trail

Bits of English, Urdu and Pashtu with even a few words of French keep flying around as we work at translations. Between Tim, Paula, Ken and I, each of us knowing just a little, Tim knowing the most, we finally get it straight. The elderly men of the group seemed to be calmer, in control, and easier to understand. Finally we decide they are telling us - "If you keep going you will BE killed." There are tribal and Sunni - Shia conflicts ahead on the trail and their angry bullets have found innocent people passing by. The villagers do not want us to hike into this dangerous zone.

Not good. We are risk takers but not fools. They convince us. Hike abandoned. Our adrenaline lowers as immediate danger subsides and we shift gears.

Now what? There is no place for us to stay in the town and the people do not really want us anyway, as we might call wrath upon them or even just get in the way. Finally we talk the only jeep owner in town to take us for a two-hour bumpy ride down the rough trail and back to Gilgit where we will give him a bunch of money. Although not happy about it, the villagers all want to get rid of us and so he acquiesces and climbs into the driver's seat.

Back in Gilgit we return to the hotel. After a brief break we immediately head into town to scout out other hiking possibilities. We run into the two college men we had taken to the China border. They are having dinner in a small restaurant with a scruffy, bearded, Canadian man with the tops of his fingers all missing. The Canadian, Mario Blasevich, is a true mountaineer who has climbed most of the major peaks of the Himalayas with professionals, has been to this region before and is looking for someone to hike with. He even speaks some of the local languages. What luck!

The trouble in the Hunza area that we had abandoned turned out to be nothing less than a real, full out, tribal war. The small hospital in Gilgit has treated hundreds of wounded and many have died. Some say there are thousands of casualties. Although the city seems calm, a large group of men of serious intent went marching rapidly by our hotel last night and off into the countryside. We are so thankful of the villagers who had irritated us, stopped us, and probably saved our lives. We looked towards another hike that will stay totally clear of this danger.

Mario knows just the place. The Naltar Lakes. So we pack up once again, feeling more comfortable with our new friends and guide.

Safraz, a Pakistani college student, is traveling around to get to know his country and happy to join us. Having studied in California he knows both of our worlds and enlightens us on the history and politics of his country compared to ours. He is also quite an asset to have along as an interpreter with his fluency in local languages as well as English. We chat for hours as we hike. His father owns a lot of land and they are planning to make a real farm out of it. With my degree in agriculture, my instinct to teach, and his need to learn and teach as well, animated conversations energize our steps.

That night, after a beautiful day hiking, warmed with the campfire glowing, singing a few old folk songs and enjoying shared wine along with our new friends, we get the full story.

Mario Blasevich

"OK, Mario Blasevich. Can we ask? How did you lose your fingers?"

"Actually, I have also lost my toes and that is why I have to wear these huge stiff, steel-toed climbing boots. It happened in 1984. Since I was young I have been taking a month off many years from my job in Vancouver as a graphic artist to climb mountains. I have been climbing the highest mountains with professional teams from all over the world. I was with a Spanish team climbing Mt. Makalu, the world's fifth highest peak, and we were ready for the last push to the top. I had chosen to go solo as the others wanted to wait until the freezing strong winds subsided." Mario takes a deep breath.

"Hiking along just fine at 24,000 feet (7400 meters) and catching my crampon on my trousers was the last thing I remember. When I woke up in agony, dazed and half frozen at the bottom of the ravine, the path was about 1000 feet almost straight up the icy, rocky slope. My pants and jacket were ripped and torn through. Pain shot through every part of my whole, battered, tumbled body. I was missing my hat, gloves and a boot and could barely move. I must have hit my head right away and been just half conscious on the way down, instinctively digging my fingers and toes into the icy mountainside as I fell. My fingers were frozen with chunks rubbed off of them, my legs felt broken and torn."

"Luckily, amazingly, I actually landed on our lower path and was able to drag my body along until I came to our abandoned high base camp less than 100 feet away. Just barely holding on, I was able to stay alive for four horrendous days, in and out of consciousness, melting snow for water, starving, until my teammates found me, near death. They abandoned their climbing attempts to evacuate and rescue me. It took another full week for them, along with their porters, to carry me down the treacherous mountain, wrapped in a tent, to a place where a helicopter could land."

"For three long months the tops of my fingers and toes slowly died, turned black, shriveled, and finally fell off. There was nothing the doctors could do to save them. I did not want them to amputate, probably with some deep clinging to an impossible recovery. I lost the top phalange of each finger and the upper part of thumbs and toes. I had to learn again how to walk and to effectively use my hands. No longer able to be an artist, I am now on a Canadian disability pension which goes much farther if I can stay here or in India for four or five months a year. Though climbing with ropes is out of the question, I still love to hike these mountains."

Mario is tough, energetic, incredibly strong, and can hike us into the ground. He taught us a few things about life and backpacking. We did not need to carry forks or plates, as a big spoon and a wide bowl will do double duty. A fishing line and hook can catch a meal you don't have to carry. Never hike alone. Although he liked to travel light, he once carried a small, fresh, sweet yellow melon on his back, all the way from Kashgar, China, to bring as a present to us in Lahore. Live light to be free but go out of the way for your friends.

The whimsical duet of Paula and Jean leading us in folk songs is interspersed by discussions of the fate of the human race. Our evening campfire warmly lights the faces of this multi-national, adventurous crew. The cold, black, night sky is splashed with billions of stars across the Milky Way, and a crescent moon is so vivid it seems I can almost

116

touch it so high in these mountains. Counting shooting stars and wishing upon them as the fire burns to embers, we finally turn to our tents.

What beauty has nature in every tiny niche. The next morning, after a breakfast of oatmeal and dried fruits we hiked up the path to a crystal clear spring-fed mountain lake. Surrounded by aspen trees and green grass it lies in a small oasis tucked into a crevice of the steep barren mountains.

Camp site by a mountain spring

Mario is fishing there with just a line and hook. His porter decides on a quicker method. Using his rifle to shoot just near the fish, he stuns them so they float to the surface. We think it cheating but it sure is good to have fresh, fried mountain trout with our instant mashed potatoes and noodle soup that night for dinner.

The next day got busy with other hikers and locals also attracted to this beautiful spot. One man even brought his donkeys packed with food to sell. We liked it better alone. Our group decides to separate, with Mario and his porter going on to tougher altitudes and the rest of us heading back down to town, ready for a hot bath and a warm bed, hoping we will all meet again someday.

Three days, three offices and lots of sitting and waiting, it takes to get plane tickets back to Lahore on Pakistan International Airlines from the small airport in Gilgit. Without reservations, the system is designed to just put us on a list and wait to make sure no one of importance might want those tickets. Our driver, Ayub, will be taking Tim, Paula and Jean off to Swat Valley but Ken and I need to get back home to prepare for our trip to Thailand and the rest of our summer.

It had only been a bit over three weeks in the Karakoram Range of the Himalayas of northern Pakistan but it seemed a lifetime. Such is the way of exciting adventures.

"Hello! Got any room for a vagabond mountaineer?" the scruffy, bearded man at our door greets us with hugs.

In October, Mario came to visit us in Lahore. After hiking through China and Tibet after we left him several months ago, he was full of stories to tell. He is on his way to India and we invite him to stay for about a week to recuperate. From where he has been, this is a welcome oasis.

Mario shows us some slides and describes his trip. "China is quite dirty and backward in the mountain area above Pakistan. The people are cruder, suspicious and not very friendly. They are very poor and with little food or material goods. The only vehicles are old work or army trucks and most of the roads are just dirt tracks."

Mario describes his journey hiking into these remote areas that we will not likely attempt ourselves. "It was difficult for me to communicate and most people did not like foreigners. At least, they didn't like me. But the Tibetans that I met, a few of them who are still there after the Chinese massacre, were very friendly."

The American Club across the street was Mario's favorite place to visit with us. After months of strenuous hiking in the Himalayas he happily indulged in steak, French fries, beer and a game of darts three nights in a row. Adventure is wonderful but we all love a bit of home.

William

"The secret of happiness, you see, is not found in seeking more, but in developing the capacity to enjoy less." — <u>Socrates</u>

Closing his eyes and facing the ceiling in thought, he stands quietly before us in his freshly pressed cream colored shalwar kamis, arms crossed behind him and feet spread wide. It is time for the evening report of what William our house manager has bought and done for us today. It is not our idea. It is his. He insists we keep a book to account for every rupee we give him and how he spends it. He cannot read or write but has a top-notch memory and reports on the exact prices for dozens of items purchased each day. "Twenty rupees for rice, thirty-two for lentils, seventeen for mangoes, thirty for sandal repair," William continues his litany, brow furrowed in concentration and twitching his fingers as if everything is recorded there.

William came with the house. Teachers come and go in school housing and we can choose to re-hire the house servants or not. As a minority Pakistani Christian he is proud of it and makes sure he is trustworthy

William juicing pomegranates

and hard working. He has offered to work seven days a week for us but we told him we liked our privacy and on weekends would only be needed if we had parties or other events.

As our "cook" he is also the house manager who supervises our four other servants. Chowkidars who guard our compound twenty-four hours a day are supplied by the school. Shariq, the mali keeps our yard and gardens in perfect shape with just a few simple hand tools. Malik, the sweeper, comes to brush away the dust and leaves from the porches and driveway on his daily route through the neighborhood. The dhobi picks up the laundry, washes, irons and returns it in a day or two.

In 1988 the total salaries of all of our servants together cost us less than $120 a month. Everyone told us we were paying too much but we felt responsible to give people jobs and a decent wage. We were quite rich in their eyes and being able to employ so many on our teacher salary was a wonderful symbiotic opportunity, a win-win for all of us. Looking back, we probably should have paid even more.

Our servants in Pakistan and in other countries were special for us. As members of the hard working class they were windows into a culture different from that of our professional friends. Speaking both English and local languages they were not only good translators but people we could ask about all kinds of little daily things like where to buy matches or the meaning of showing the soles of your shoes. William would often go along on shopping trips to help find things and even bargain for us. Many servants were used to being treated like poor trash and preferred working for Americans who generally had more respect for them.

"What would you like for dinner, MemSaab?" William inquires politely before we leave for work. "Can you please make some of your favorite local recipes?" I answer as I give him some rupees to buy groceries. "Not too spicy though. Ken likes it without so much chili-pepper," I request.

We sit down about 6:30 to the neatly set table hungry and ready for dinner after a long day at work. After quietly setting the meal before us he retreats to the kitchen and keeps an eye on us through a window in the dining room door so he can remove the emptied plates and bring desert when we finish.

"Is this the vegetarian dal bhat (curried lentils and rice)?" Ken asks as he licks and fans his lips from the spiciness. "Yes and try the eggplant and potato, I think you'll like the hint of cinnamon along with the garlic and turmeric." I answer, pointing my spoon to the red and brown ceramic bowl at the middle of the table. We take servings from a plate of freshly sliced cucumbers sprinkled lightly with vinegar and individually rubbed with fresh garlic, and grab a piece of fresh hot naan (a delicious chewy flat bread). We savor each carefully prepared bite, served as if we are royalty.

Dishes are immediately washed and stored and leftovers put up. William doesn't take short cuts and works hard all day to find all the little things that can be done to make life easier for us. Freshly boiled water is always available, kept cool in the fridge and sitting in a pitcher in the bathroom. Rooms are kept spotless and shoes polished. Purchasing food and household needs while insuring other servants are doing their jobs properly keeps him busy.

William refers to Ken as "Saab" (mister) and to me as "MemSaab" (Mrs.) and in his quiet respectful way asks each evening if there are any special jobs or meals we might like. "Can you make some vegetarian Italian food?" I ask hopefully "Yes, of course, MemSaab," William replies with a slight bow. Without the benefits of any cookbook, William makes noodles from scratch topped with a delicious concoction of fresh veggies, cheese, garlic, tomatoes and olive oil that would make anyone think they were dining at a fancy Italian trattoria.

Once Ken said to him "William, you are not a cook". William stepped back surprised, waiting for a reprimand. "You are a Chef!" And they both broke into wide smiles. We wondered why he did not work in a restaurant until realizing he was making more money at our house. He is worth every rupee and more. We are lucky. It is hard to trust someone who has access to everything in your home when you are not there and you have to be careful and picky about whom to hire. It is best to get recommendations from people you know. The school had told us that William was one of the best but we still felt uneasy and worried at first. Not all servants are good ones and several of our friends had trouble with theft and other issues. After a few months we grew to know and trust each other. Yes, we are lucky, especially for the affection we have developed for William and his family.

With a wife, four girls and a baby on the way, William's family has a place to live in a small concrete building behind our house and enough money for food and essentials. We help them out a bit by paying for uniforms and books to keep the girls in school. The oldest girl is in grade seven and the three year old, cute bouncy Rima, is still at home with Mom.

William's family quarters is just one room of a white-washed concrete duplex built as servant quarters behind our large house. There are two double beds in the room to sleep the family of six with a few shelves and some boxes under the beds for all of their belongings. Red-flowered wallpaper adorns the neatly arranged stainless steel dishes displayed on the ledges built into the high walls. The porch, freshly painted blue, is their kitchen with a small red two-burner gas stove and a couple of shelves stocked with cookware. The cost of simple necessities is low and living in the room provided by the school keeps expenses down. Their real pride and joy is the strong relationships of their family.

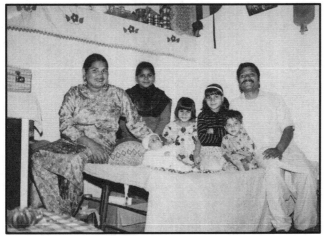

William's family

It is sometimes hard to understand why someone who has so little continues to have more children. Once, when I was very sick, probably malaria, I sat out on the back porch for a full week just watching the birds and William's family. Slowly it dawned on me. The instinctive drive to reproduce is quite strong and it is very easy for most young women to get pregnant. Many women in Muslim countries are not allowed to have careers other than mother. They have very high birth rates. If I had no other career choices I would probably also have many children. We all need a purpose in life to fulfill and motherhood is respected everywhere. Sons and daughters are often the only retirement system that can be counted on. Children are their wealth in more ways than one.

A small woman dressed in ragged but clean clothing is on our back doorstep crying. William rushes to get us and to interpret what she is saying as she sobs in Urdu. "My husband, Malik, who sweeps for you, has been hit by a car. He was riding to work on his bicycle and was run over. He is badly injured and we cannot afford hospital."

"Don't worry, we will help. How much money do you need?" Ken asks.

"One hundred rupees," William translates. A few days' pay for our sweeper, about six dollars for us.

Although they say it is not necessary, to make sure Malik is properly cared for we help both our sweeper's wife, Nadia and William into the back of our school van to go down to the hospital. About a fifteen minute drive away is a 'public' hospital for the poor with many beds lined up in one large room. Malik, a tiny dark man bound with white gauze wrapping his forehead, torso and right leg, is a bit pale and frightened but overjoyed to see us.

I check over the clipboard hanging on his bed to determine what his doctors are doing for him. "It looks like they are taking good care of you. They have put a splint on your leg, bandaged your sores and given you antibiotics for your wounds," I reassure Malik as William translates. The doctor comes by in a typical white coat to greet us and answers our questions in English. "He was scraped up, his leg twisted and his back was hurt and badly bruised but nothing is broken and he should be all right in a couple of weeks with some rest."

It is natural for Ken and I to share in this short visit to do what we can for this man. We feel responsible for those who are close to us. Just our attention and a few rupees made a difference in how he was treated and how his family could survive while he recuperated. If he loses his job, without work it will be disastrous for the family. There is no social security and little welfare. Those without jobs may starve to death.

It took three days in the hospital and about two weeks for Malik to fully recover as we continued to assure his wife that he would not lose his job and we would pay his salary and hospital bills. It felt quite rewarding to be able to help someone near to us who was so much in need.

It amazes me how people can live in such simple conditions and yet find happiness. Perhaps they have something to teach us.

Those in poverty usually need to form strong social bonds to survive. Scientific research shows that beyond basic needs it is not material consumption but good relationships and having honorable purpose in life that make us happiest.

Perhaps sharing our resources to take only what is required and to focus on social bonding and providing decent jobs we could tackle some major global problems. And be happier for it.

William's boy- first birthday

"It's a BOY!" William exclaims, smiling broadly from ear to ear while handing Ken a cigar wrapped in blue cellophane. William is ecstatic. I think he would have continued to have children until they had a boy. Male children are social security in old age. Marriages are arranged and the girls usually go to live with the husband's family. Girls must even bring a dowry with them to get a good husband so lots of girl children can mean financial problems for parents while boys bring more security and wealth. Educated girls fare much better and if they have a good career they can also care for their parents. Countries with poor education and no social security systems are essentially propagating large poor families.

"You won't believe my visit to the hospital. I got the full royal tour," Ken reports as he arrives home. He had gone to the maternity ward to check on Mom and new baby boy with his lab coat on from school. Thinking he was an American doctor he was shown around the place like a visiting dignitary. "It was reasonably clean and neat but very simple, with about a dozen patients per room. I didn't see any nurses. Family members were at the bedsides feeding their loved ones. The x-ray machine looked like a dinosaur; probably one of the first ones made and most likely putting out way more radiation than necessary. But the doctors and administrators did seem to care about their patients and are doing the best they can with what they have."

When it came time for the baby to be born we offered to pay the medical fees. For three days in the maternity ward, doctor bills, medications and care for mother and baby the whole bill was a shocking 1,190 rupees. About seventy U.S. dollars. I would think that basic hospital care could be far more affordable around the world with a more simple approach such as this.

First birthday of William's son in our yard

As is the custom, when baby boy reaches one year old it is time to celebrate. Too many babies die young so people wait. We purchase all the food for thirty-five with about thirty-five dollars as our contribution to the party. William's brother's family arrives at dawn to help cook up a feast. All of our servants pitch in to turn the backyard into a festive picnic banquet.

Swaying to the music while slowly uncoiling from a wide wicker basket a cobra is enchanted by the sweet harmony of a flute. The snake charmer sits on the worn blue carpet of the back porch as he tempts his poisonous pet. His companion opens another basket to display his venomous sand viper with its beautiful sand-colored patterned scales.

The turbaned snake charmers add a special element of exotic excitement but we ask them to move to the side of the patio so we can keep track of the children.

A dancer in a sleek red dress moves provocatively in tune with the snake-charmer's flute. The 'lady' is a man made up like a woman because women are not allowed to dance in public. A wreath of rupees, a traditional way to give presents, rings William's neck as more money is tacked on in generous family fun. The money will contribute to raising and educating the baby.

Cobra and Viper on our patio

Curried mutton and rice, green peas, spicy cauliflower and potatoes sit before us we fill our stainless steel plates and cups to share in the good fortune of William's family. "Rice, rice" little Rima tries out a word of English pointing to the dish on the table that she can't quite reach. "Here, I'll help you." Ken responds as she waits patiently with her plate held high, dark eyes wide in expectation. She sits close to him and curls up like a kitten in his lap to fall asleep after the meal.

We have had other servants overseas but none were as good as William. Hard-working, intelligent, reliable and honest, he took pride in his work and in his relationships. We all serve others in one form or the other and I can only aspire to live such a useful life. I have recently heard that he is near retirement but still working for international teachers in Lahore. One day I hope to see him once again and deliver him this book. We hope he and his family are still well and happy.

"The purpose of life is not to be happy. It is to be useful, to be honorable, to be compassionate, to have it make some difference that you have lived and lived well." — Ralph Waldo Emerson

*William with currency garland
for his baby boy*

Guns on the Frontier (see map page 37)
Darra, Pakistan, 1988

The sharp crack of gunfire rings out randomly around us as Ken holds a grenade in his hand.

We are in Darra Adnan Khal, a small town on the border between northern Pakistan and Afghanistan, tribal in nature and ruled by neither country. For generations the community has been known for their traditional techniques of arms manufacture. With China, Russia, Afghanistan and India all close-by, along with tribal grievances and violent religious trends, there are plenty of customers.

"I can't believe they are selling a rocket launcher. That thing has a range of about 5 miles, and fires 12 high explosive projectiles in 10 seconds. It is a Chinese type 63, called 'the poor man's rocket launcher' that can even stop tanks." Having been in the U.S. army, Ken can identify most of the wide variety of weapons and tell us what they are used for.

Ken & Paula with rocket launcher

With his beard, blue eyes and suntan, dressed in a brown shalwar-kamis and Chitrali hat he looks very much like a local. And with his energetic, engaging smile, he is quick to be welcomed by the gun dealers. Americans have been supplying Pakistan with weapons for years to fight the Russians who have been trying to take over from the north, so we are heartily taken in.

"How do you like recoilless rifle?" a shopkeeper points it out to Ken in broken English.

"Looks more like a cannon, or maybe Godzilla's machine gun to me," I quip, walking around the seven foot long, tripod mounted, Russian 82mm artillery piece. "Obviously made for serious business."

Foreigners are usually not allowed here but we got in on a slack day after several hours of drinking tea and chatting with the authorities in Peshawar. Forbidden cameras hidden beneath our shawls, dressed in local clothes, Tim, Paula, Ken and I slipped through the border patrols with our driver in our large white van, looking a bit like a local bus. The short main street in the village of Darra is lined with small shops selling a little food or a lot of guns and not much else.

"Is that a grenade? I ask the elderly man in the white turban, pointing to the little metal pineapple hanging on the wall. "Aiwa, yes" he answers as his smile spreads above his grey beard. The shopkeepers / arms dealers get a kick out of Paula and I asking so many questions. We see no other women in the streets and suspect our presence is a rarity. In this frontier town filled with guns, these men are quite the gentlemen and even pose for our pictures. Showing off their artistry to admiring eyes brought on animated conversations in broken languages.

Ken checking a rifle bore

Machine guns, pistols, missiles, handguns, rifles, grenades, anti-aircraft rockets, you name it. Every variety, every name, they will make it for you. They will sell it to you. Antiques? Be ready next week. Want to try them out? Gunfire erupts frequently. Frayed and broken telephone wires, awnings with holes, empty cartridges in the streets. Ken asks if they even let people try out the missile launchers. "Sure! Just 15,000 rupees! Cheap, if you consider that it can shoot down a helicopter."

A handmade leather holster and a pen gun were our only souvenir purchases. We figured we could send them back in our shipment to America without trouble. The pen pistol looks exactly like a fat black ballpoint pen with a deadly point - a 25-caliber bullet. We have never fired it as they are known to backfire easily, but it looks cool.

The gun dealers want to know if we rich Americans have brought any weapons with us they can copy and encourage us to come back with some.

Although it all sounds quite sinister the atmosphere is more like a craft fair. Everyone is friendly, laughing, joking around, and offering tea or hashish, drawing in the buyers like they are selling toys, while periodic gun fire cracked all around.

Shop keepers in Darra

After we returned to Lahore by train, some other teachers heard about our exploit and ventured out to follow in our footsteps. Our friend Roy, an elementary teacher at the school, flew to Peshawar with his son Tory and were able to finagle a taxi driver to take them into Dara. They also bought a pen pistol as a souvenir. His teenage son, not thinking much about it, had it in his carry-on bag when he checked into the airport. Security went nuts. Roy took the blame. He then spent about 36 hours in a Pakistani jail in Ralwalpindi, sleeping on the filthy concrete floor with a blanket that looked as if it came from the garbage dump. Dirty water. Not much food. A hole in the corner for a toilet.

Carrying weapons on board a plane is serious business these days. The pen gun seemed like a joke to us but it was clearly not very funny to the airlines. The police wanted to make an example of him to show that Americans were not exempt from the law. We had a special woman at our school, Ayesha Musslahuddin who was very well known in elite circles of the country. It was most likely her persistent phone calls and influence that led to Roy's release in a few days instead of years.

The Lahore newspaper printed the story of the American teacher who had been arrested for carrying a gun onto an airline. Even in a city of about five million the press seems to thoroughly enjoy writing about any sign of trouble at our American School.

I wonder about our fascination with guns. It is animal instinct to protect ourselves but it seems to be more cultural in their wider acceptance and use. They give us a power that should not belong to us emotional, aggressive creatures. Countries like Germany, Japan and Switzerland have strict regulations and fewer gun violence problems, perhaps because they learned the hard way. When our children begin to fight we do not give them weapons. Why do we think that giving weapons to adults or nations will work any better? Giving our children guitars to play with instead of toy guns might be a good start. Learning to say "lets talk" instead of "bang-bang?"

Around Lahore American School
Pakistan 1988

Fatima's tilted over and bobbled to the ground. Faisal's looked promising but was too heavy. Arno's wavered and began to lift but couldn't quite make it. Finally, amid lots of hot air and wild cheering, Kasim's began to rise slowly above us.

Chemistry class was studying the properties of gases. Hot air rises as the molecules zoom around, pushing each other apart and becoming less dense. Thus students tried their hands at designing hot air balloons with the criteria that they do what they can to make them work. "They will probably work best if they are very, very light and large enough to hold lots of hot air," I instructed. Although given an example plan from a magazine, the students were free to build it however they liked to stir their imaginations and learn more about different materials. They would get extra credit if it actually rose above our heads.

Chemistry class experiments with hot-air balloons

A few weeks later chemistry class heads off on a field trip to a local pill factory owned by Umar's uncle. "Look at me, Mrs. Cundiff. Don't I look like a real scientist now?" asks Amer. "Yeah, maybe Dr. Frankenstein," answers Zully. We don white lab coats and hats and promise not to touch anything in the ultra clean environment. We learn about the different active chemicals and fillers produced to make the pills. Each pill has to be perfectly formed and labeled for it must stay in tack for years in a bottle. Although there was lots of good chemistry the students mostly remember wearing their doctor coats and being in a real laboratory.

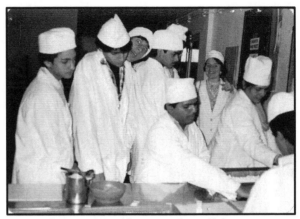

Chemistry students at the pill factory

It is always a challenge to find good scientific experiences that the students both enjoy and learn from. Each school has different possibilities to explore and the students themselves often have excellent ideas. The effort is worth it. Twenty-five years later they still remember.

Twice a week after school we leave our work behind to take horseback-riding lessons at the Lahore Polo Club. I have never ridden such beautiful, well-trained animals. My sisters, Christie and Mary Lisa had horses and I have ridden many at different stables but was never very good at it. These Thoroughbred polo horses were so well trained that I had to learn from the animals themselves how to ride. The British had brought the sport to the subcontinent generations ago and it was now a pastime for the elite of Pakistan. It was a pleasure to ride so smoothly, harmonizing with the movements of this elegant animal.

Since the polo grounds were almost on the way home, we also went there to run a few miles on the racetrack that surrounded the grounds. As long-time runners we like to get out at least three times a week and it is not always easy to find a path that is comfortable. When horses were not using the track, we were welcome and really enjoyed the wide-open, tree-lined space with no traffic.

One day after school, Sam Sloffer, our school athletic director and friend, was doubled over in pain. He called and asked us to go to the local hospital emergency room with him.

Having to go a hospital in another country is always scary. Medical training of doctors ranges from very poor to quite adequate and it is hard to know the difference. With my degrees in biology people often came to me for advice before and after going to a doctor. I carried the *Merck Manual of Diagnosis and Therapy* with me and would dive into the 1300 pages trying to help them figure out what was wrong.

The hospital doctor was quick with his answer for Sam. "Appendicitis." He needed immediate surgery. Yikes!! At least it should be a common, simple procedure. Should be. We were quite taken aback when the doctor asked us to write down the operation materials he needed so we could go and buy them for him. Scalpels, disinfectant, IV drip, sterile gauze, antibiotics and even suture materials were scribbled quickly on a list. So we ran to collect the stuff, downstairs and over to the main building which had a large pharmacy.

As Sam was being rolled off into surgery we were informed by a staff member that he would need to stay in the hospital for at least two days to recover. There was no real nursing staff or cafeteria and a family member or friend was expected to bring all food and drinks and to sleep in a cot near the bed to make sure he was OK through the night.

Luckily, Sam made it through the operation and recovered successfully. We take our advanced medical system in America too much for granted.

A month ago we went to visit the Lahore Zoo. Established in 1872, it is one of the oldest in existence that is still running. There were lions and tigers and bears, of course. Lots of monkeys, birds and a few giraffes. I love zoos. Even though animals would be better off in the wild, I find it enjoyable to get close contact with amazing creatures without getting eaten.

We had just left the reptile house when we heard a ruckus of squealing behind us. One of the zookeepers is emerging from the same building, causing the sightseers to scream and scatter. With gaping mouths and wide eyes we watch this man carrying arms full of live snakes wrapped around his arms and each other. Cobras?? Cobras!! We can't believe it as he sets them in the grass right in front of us. Cobras!! The crowd gathers near, jumping closer and then back, in and out and squealing. Small children are in this circle and no one has a hold on them.

Cobras loose at the zoo

I guess it must be time for the snakes to have their afternoon in the sun while their cages are cleaned. Their keeper is enjoying the attention of the crowd. He grabs a slithering tail and pulls on one of the snakes to rile the rest and get them to raise up to display their elegant scaled hood.

I take pictures and wonder how many children are killed by cobras sunning at the zoo. The cobra bite can kill in less than ten minutes. Their main diet is rodents and they do not attack humans unprovoked. Still, over 10,000 bites are reported every year in Pakistan alone and most are lethal. Local people have a terrified fascination of these regal creatures of the reptile world.

Cobras sunning

One of my students once came to class holding up a tiny jar containing a worm less than an inch long. "Mrs. Cundiff, my gardener told me this is a cobra. Can you tell me if it really is?" She said her gardener had fearfully captured it and told her it was a baby snake. I explained cobra babies came from eggs much larger than that. And showed her the worm under the microscope.

Ken invites his astronomy club students to a night on the flat rooftop of the high school. We cook up some popcorn and turn the telescope to focus on the rings of Saturn and the moons of Jupiter amid lots of "ooohs" and "aaahhhs." The boys enjoy the evening out but the girls did not come, as they are not allowed to attend mixed-sex parties.

Astronomy on the roof at LAS

"William, what is that bear doing in our front yard?" Arriving home from school last week there was a huge blonde bear laying in our driveway. We thought perhaps we were dreaming. We had to park the van on the edge of the road, carefully tiptoe around the sleeping monster and go into the house to ask William what was happening. "Saab, the bear has passed out and the owner does not know what to do".

We had watched this beautiful golden animal they called a Himalayan Honey Bear, leashed to his master, doing tricks just a few days before at the local market down the street. The temperatures were warm and the air was humid and dead still. I suggested that the bear might have heat stroke and would need to be cooled down and given lots of water to drink.

Himalayan Honey Bear in our front yard

William, the owner, Ken and our gardener all dragged and pushed and shoved the partly conscious bear inside of our gate under a huge shade tree, next to a garden water spigot, against the cool stone wall of our yard.

It took two full days of hosing down and watering the bear before it got on its feet again. We advised the thankful owner to keep him here another day for recovery. Mom was staying with us and reminded me that I should take a picture. Life is always such a surprise in Pakistan that this seemed a normal part of our routine.

If you ever get really bored, just move to a foreign country.

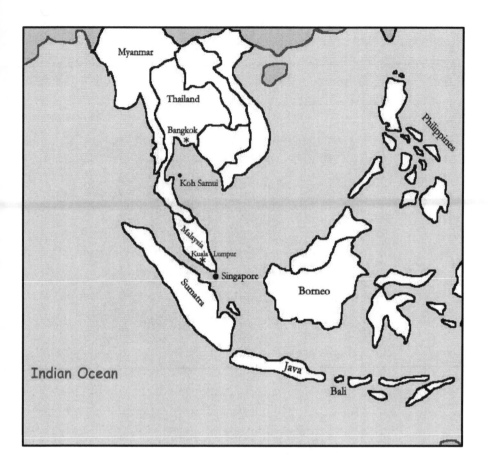

Down-Under
The Long Summer of 1988

We need to establish our foreign residency for tax purposes, so we decide not to go home to America for our first summer overseas. Besides, there is way too much to see in this world and we are just getting started.

After three weeks hiking across ice in the Himalayan Mountains of northern Pakistan, we fly from the top of the world to a sea level summer from Bangkok to Bali. Worlds apart in culture and topography with more than a month to explore.

Mom is still the only one adventurous enough to take off work for three weeks and throw herself into our vagabond life without question –

for the second time in one year. Being close to retirement she is more concerned about missing out on travel than losing her job. We meet her at the Bangkok airport just hours after we arrive from Lahore. "Hi Ann! Swatdee khap!" Ken bows with hands folded, welcoming Mom with the traditional Thai greeting. After hugs all around he pins a purple orchid on her pink cotton blouse as I offer a chunk of freshly cut sweet mango from my clear plastic cup.

We catch a taxi to our hotel rooms in the historic center of the city, not far from Wat Phra Kaew, the Temple of the Emerald Buddha. "Mom, you'll be able to get rid of jet lag much faster if we go out walking," I try to convince her. "Sunshine and exercise are the best way to re-set your biological clock."

Bangkok temple

"But it's two o'clock in the morning according to my watch," she responds yawning.

"Here, drink this iced coffee while I change your watch for you," Ken offers.

"OK, I'll try," she rolls her eyes, smiles, drinks deeply and is ready to roll.

Golden spires touch the bright blue sky, shimmering in the warmth of the summer sun. Orange robed monks hold out begging bowls to collect their daily meal in the market. Round faces smile from under wide straw hats as women sell fresh vegetables from tables on the sidewalk near a temple. A golden Buddha reclines in a shrine on the street corner, surrounded by today's offerings of burning candles, incense and tiny trays of local sweets.

Two dark-eyed little girls in matching blue cotton shorts and white blouses sell chunks of yellow jackfruit in clear plastic sandwich bags. "Yes, please, I'll take one. How much?" I ask. "Five baht," she smiles as I hand her some coins and try this delicious tropical treat tasting something like a crunchy banana mango.

Exhaust fumes from 3 wheeled, 2 cylinder tuk-tuks carrying people in heavy traffic compete with the mouth-watering smells of squid roasting on curbside hibachis and luscious ripe mangoes for sale. I am sure the connoisseur could identify a country by the symphony of odors alone.

Tourist sites are interesting but it is daily life we often enjoy even more. For an hour or so we just wander through local markets and sit on benches to watch the characters flow by. Grabbing my hand, a toothless old woman in a wide straw hat smiles broadly and gives me a fresh yellow flower for buying a bag of cut, sweet pineapple from her basket. A small boy offers to carry my backpack as we stroll along but is happy enough to shake hands, smile and ask me how old I am to practice his English. It always seems easier to connect with the very old and the very young as they are not so caught up in their important lives.

"This place looks promising," Ken remarks as we stand in front of a small Thai restaurant. "Seems filled with happy local customers," I respond. "How about a short nap at the hotel and dinner here?" Mom suggests as we give in to an afternoon break.

The beautiful temples, markets, parks and people of Bangkok keep us busy for a few days before we decide to buy tickets for the night train south. I love night trains. The swaying motion and mesmerizing clank of the steel rails take us to new destinations while we dream. Hot and humid here in summer, we plan to focus on beaches as we move south, through the four countries of Thailand, Malaysia, Singapore and Indonesia, going below the equator, to the islands of Bali. We have a basic path in mind but no reservations or tickets and will enjoy flexibility to discover and explore, to linger or to move on. We each carry only one soft suitcase and a backpack. Summer is not high tourist season so travel should be fairly easy.

The whistle blows and our night ride screeches to a halt after traveling over 400 miles down the narrow trunk of southern Thailand. Leaving the train at Surat Thani we catch a taxi that takes us to a ferry station on the Gulf of Thailand, about twenty miles from the city. We follow instructions outlined in the "Lonely Planet Guide for Thailand." It is a three-hour boat ride to Koh Samui. An airport is under construction there but right now the island is still isolated and toured only by persistent travelers.

"I think I can afford my own cabin here," Mom decides. Not quite tourist season makes for heartier welcomes and fewer crowds. Our $5 a night bungalows sit right off the beach where the calm blue waters of the sea supply fishermen with tons of squid each night. Mom chooses her own tiny cabin with a porch, thatched palm leaf roof and running cold water.

Covered in coconut groves and bananas, the island of Koh Samui is a beautiful small, hilly, coral atoll surrounded by reefs. The people are laid-back and friendly, their Buddhist religion teaching that anger and aggressiveness are not acceptable. It has been a hippie hang out and tourist destination for many years because of the tropical, out of the way, cheap, light hearted life. We are glad the airport is not yet complete and simple island life still reigns.

"Do you see what I see?" Ken asks. During our sunrise beach jogging we pass a man taking his young male water buffalo for a run in the sand. The leash didn't look very strong. He said he was getting the animal in condition for the upcoming buffalo fights. Hundreds of eyeballs stare up at us from the sand between our toes where the island women squat in their straw hats in the early morning to clean last night's catch of squid. Screeching sea birds dive down to savor and fight over the delicacies. We will enjoy their fresh calamari at dinner. We finish our run with a cold shower in our cabin and meet Mom to walk across the path to breakfast. Fresh mango, pineapple and coconut are served with cereal and iced coffee under the palm trees.

Koh Samui transport

"Just hug a little closer, now, and don't touch that muffler!" Ken instructs. "OK, please, just drive slowly!" I implore. For just four dollars a day we rent a small Honda motorcycle, putting aside our fears to put our trust in Ken as a good, experienced driver. I like motorcycles only where roads are empty.

There is little traffic on this fifteen-mile long island. An impenetrable tropical jungle climbs a mountain peak at the center. The three of us chug all around, visiting other beaches, coconut plantations, temples and water buffalos.

"Thai massage?" Mom and I can't resist the soothing hands of the two women who come to kneel by our beach blankets. Lazing on the beach, swimming in the heat of the day, touring in the late afternoon, sitting down to delicious Thai food in the evenings with no set itinerary make for a pleasant, whimsical vacation.

Each little set of bungalow "motels" has their own simple open restaurant under a thatched roof. They compete for customers with food quality, low prices and an evening video movie on their TV. Afternoon walks include comparing chalkboard menus to decide on evening dinner and entertainment. Thai shrimp and calamari dishes can't be beat but my favorite foods are the delicious tropical fruits and drinking fresh coconut milk right from the nut with a straw.

Cleaning squid on Koh Samui Beach

After about a week of paradise we catch the ferry back to the mainland and jump on the next train south into Malaysia.

Kuala Lumpur and Singapore are both very modern, westernized cities — quite different from the more historical life of Pakistan. Starkly new and modern contrasts with classic and restored, both in architecture and in culture. One day in KL we ate in six different food chains. We rag about chains till we are without them for a long time. I never thought how much I could appreciate the clean, efficient dependability of A&W, Kentucky Fried Chicken, and Swenson's. It's been a year since we've had this good ole 'home cooking.' We can understand the menu and even drink the water. But one day of fast food is enough and we head back to the local places to enjoy delicious, and more nutritious, Asian cuisine.

Throughout the summer we hired taxis to take us by the American International schools. We never know where we might want to take a job. Bangkok, Kuala Lumpur and Singapore have much larger schools than Lahore and look like pretty nice places to live someday.

Singapore is quite a port. The city/country is immaculate with its clean streets and sidewalks and always a garden in sight. We arrived this morning on the night train from Malaysia. Thousands of semi-truck

Architecture in KL

beds, stacked like cracker boxes fill long city blocks on the waterfront. Hundreds of gigantic ships are anchored as far as a mile off shore.

"Can we get a drink at the famous Raffle's Hotel?" Mom asks on the taxi ride into town from the train station. "It is the refuge of many famous authors and home of the Singapore Sling party drink."

"Sure, Mom. We'll check it out and enjoy a drink. But the room prices are probably much higher than we can afford." I lament.

Their prices would have been too high, but a wing under construction and off-season attendance allows us to bargain for a beautiful, large, open room with white wicker furniture, overlooking the gardens. Mom even joins the evening floorshow as a Singapore entertainer tries to teach her a native dance on stage. Travel without reservations can be quite good as hotels are often willing to give big discounts on rooms that have not been claimed for the night. It sometimes pays to check the fancy places and make them an offer.

Bus pass in hand we ride around the tiny country in three days visiting the Japanese gardens, museums and China town.   We understand why there are so many rules in Singapore. A melting pot of global nationalities, they try to limit the import of nasty habits. Chewing gum is illegal and there are fines for honking horns and not flushing city toilets. After the less organized life of Pakistan I find it a bit inhibiting.

A travel agency in downtown Singapore is able to get us tickets on the next flight out. After a short three-hour plane trip, we reach the Indonesian island of Bali.

"Mom, do you remember that hauntingly beautiful song *"Bali Hai"* from the classic musical *"South Pacific"* you used to play at home when we were kids?" "Of course", she answers as we both chime into singing the first few words. Bali is, truly, another paradise. Well, at least it seems like paradise once we get away from the airport cities of Kuta and Denpasar and ignore the persistent sales pitches of wandering street merchants. It is easy to get immersed in the magical life of this tropical, animated, culturally rich island.

With a tall thatched roof, carved wooden beams, porch facing a volcano and straw floor mats, our cottage in the cultural town of Ubud, is perched in beauty. The grounds are a jungle of large, bright tropical flowers; orchids, frangipani, bougainvillea, and water lilies in a pond are overseen by a pet white egret. Breakfast is included in this $12 a night room. Banana crepes topped with coconut, fruit salad, boiled eggs and hot tea is served outside on an elevated terrace surrounded by the garden.

Intricate carvings covered in flowering

Temple food offering

vines surround the doorways.   At first we think every building we see must be a temple. Tiny flowers, bits of fruit and a pinch of rice in a small tray made from a palm leaf, lies at the feet of strange wooden beasts that guard the front of every gate and door. These daily offerings to the Gods also feed the many small, stray dogs. Women carry full trays of festive foods to the temples. It seems like every day has some little celebration going on.

We decide to stay in Ubud, a cultural village of central Bali where artists abound. Each night we attend a Balinese dance drawing tourists from all over the world as well as just as many natives. Notices are posted in our guest-house and gatherings are on the patios in front of temples.

In the Barong dance, an animated, lion-like creature with a huge red head, chomping jaws and long body with two men inside, meets mice and witches and various other critters. Twenty musicians play on long red xylophones and resonant brass gongs as dancers act out their parts. A wild masked man moves and jumps to the chanting of 75 men as he chases very young girls in a rhythmic trance. He spins into a frenzy before hopping wildly into the burning pile of coconut husks, kicking them towards us, stamping on the flames in the Fire Dance. Their hands spell out stories, their faces carry exaggerated expressions, and their wooden masks are of mythical creatures and proportions. It's obvious that they love these performances. So do we.

An active volcano sits in the middle of Bali surrounded by black lava last erupting in 1974. It takes us three hours to climb to the top. As we strain to summit, Mom gets spooked and hugs the ground. Close to the rim, the path is only wide enough for the width of one foot as the steep sides slip down into the steaming pit of the crater. "What's the matter, Mom?"
"I am afraid of heights!"
"No you aren't!" I insist. "At least you never were afraid when we were children."
"Yes, I always have been, but I never wanted you to know because I did not want you to fear height too." She sits clinging to a rock,

Active volcano hike

and watches us as we scamper around the steep rim. After the Himalayas — nothing to it! I'm glad I'm cautious but not afraid and appreciate my Mom, who taught me well.

The intensity and vigor of an earth still in formation is overpowering and we can feel the still seething inferno venting hot misty gasses through cracks in the hillside as if it could erupt again any moment. We do not linger long. Sliding downhill through the slippery black ash makes the descent especially difficult. Not a minor feat for Mom, almost 60 and afraid of heights. "Here, Ann, take my hand, take small steps and go slow," says Ken as he pulls her close to stabilize her frightened movements. We all slowly slip and slide to the bottom of the mountain where Mom finally collapses with relief. "You saved my life," she says to Ken, squeezing his hand tightly. "Now can I kiss your daughter?" he replies laughing. "Saving lives is tough work!"

Dancing in a Bali street

Life seems vibrant and happy here. Every day men and women wear flowers in their hair and children have small parades in the streets, practicing dancing with colorful costumes. A volcanic tropical island with its rich soil and water can provide a year–round supply of fish and fruit ripe for the taking. Homes and clothing do not need to be as tough as in colder climes. As long as the population does not outstrip the resources there will be good reason to be happy, wear flowers and dance. It seems a great contrast to the desert countries of the Middle East where food and water are daily struggles and strict religions have sprung up to guide tough lives.

Mom, disappointed to have to go back to work, leaves us on the beach in Bali, buys a ticket to Bangkok and flies back to the States. It was great to have amazing experiences with someone we love. We will share these memories forever.

After another week of hanging out in Bali we figure it is about time for us to move on, so we fly back to Malaysia, heading towards Bangkok by train with about fifteen days left of summer vacation. The Cameron Highlands captures us for two nights while we explore a true tropical rainforest. Wandering through extremely dense vegetation we hike paths that seem desperate to disappear back to the wild. We decide that the hills we climb are actually mounds and mounds of snaking roots waiting patiently to devour us if we slipped through those dark, black holes between them. Ferns more than eight-foot tall and huge vines wind upward under the shade of the tall canopy above. There are surprisingly few visible animals or insects. Maybe because of the cool mountain heights, maybe because they are quiet and elusive, or because the biodiversity is so rich that there are lots of silent predators.

There is a story about Jim Thompson, founder of the Thai silk industry, who mysteriously disappeared right here, in this very spot of the Cameron Highlands. Some say he was kidnapped, some say suicide, others say he was claimed by the forest. We are carful as we walk alone on the dark winding paths.

"I am, sorry but your bungalow has gone up to six dollars a day as tourist season is starting," the caretaker informs us. "Oh, I'm not sure we can afford that," Ken answers in jest as we turn to head right back to the same cabin we had before. We decided that our limited funds would keep us happier back in Koh Samui to finish off our vacation before catching our return flight from Bangkok to Pakistan. We spring for the six bucks and enjoy another relaxing week of a simple island life.

Even though the summer was definitely memorable, it is great to be back "home" in Lahore, safe and sound, good food on the table and our very own bed. School starts next week and we've both got new courses to design. Pre-algebra for Ken and Medical biology for me. The science department needs a new elective and with so many of my students wanting to be doctors in a country with poor medical education I think I'll try to help them get started. So I will attempt to design a simple, practical course from my "Family Medical Guide" that I brought with me and teach human physiology, good nutrition, and some basic, practical medicine.

The summer of 1988 was filled with adventures and the only year we did not return to America. Although it was exciting to live overseas we missed our family, friends and home far too much to stay away for so long. In other years we came back to our own home and eighty acres outside Gainesville, Florida during our summers. With the money we saved from teaching in tough places and living below our means, we occasionally took a whole year off between countries to recuperate and enjoy home family and friends.

Fossils, Kids and Politics   (see map page 37)
Spring, 1989

After the trouble we had last year with the high school boys buying guns in a village, we decide to try something different. It is our second 'Week Without Walls' at the school and we are allowed to design it ourselves. This year the students will sign up for a field trip program, instead of just being assigned by grade level. "What about a field trip to find fossils? There are supposed to be some interesting sites in the north." Ken asks. "It would be nice to take some serious science students and not just those who are out for trouble making," I reply. The school thinks it is a good idea to have a science trip, so we put it on the program list for the students to sign up.

Nine, ninth grade, freshmen boys, all of them students of Ken's physical science class, sign on for our trip. His idea of fun, humor and daring science activities really attracts them and they are excited to go with us. There are eight Pakistani and one German boy along with our driver and us. The entire high school has left, going in all different directions for a 'Week Without Walls'. We will be gone for four and a half days.

Leaving school at 8:00 AM, swerving around camel caravans, ox carts and political rallies we use the van horn as if it will clear our way. It is great to be out on the road again. We are headed north out of Lahore into the salt range of the Punjab that records 600 million years of geological evolution.

Pakistan still amazes me. The ancient scenes are timeless. Such extremes. Women in brightly colored shalwar-kamis thrash bundles of rice by hand in the fields as a jet soars overhead. What are we doing here? I wonder constantly of the status of Homo sapiens in the universe. Layers of rock showing hundreds of millions of years of life are incomprehensible. Are we really so advanced, or do we just have more technology to pursue our animal instincts like gathering stuff and curiosity?

It takes us 5 hours to reach our first fossil site. Exchanging Walkmans for geologist hammers and chisels we strike out for the hills.

The Himalayas are at the boundary of two large continental plates that, still in motion, have pushed an ancient seabed up to the tallest mountains of the world over the past fifty million years. Some of the layers were deposited deep in the Indian Ocean more than 500 million years ago. Harboring layers of limestone, remnants of fossilized sea life can be found in certain seams throughout the area, all the way to the top of Mt. Everest.

"Look, Mr. Cundiff! I think I found some fossils!" cries Umar as he runs up to us with a chunk of rock.

"I think you may be right. What do you think, Mrs. Cundiff?" Ken defers to me.

"Cool! It looks to me like tiny mollusks, or snail shells," I explain while

Looking for fossils

closely examining the specimen. We check our guidebook to fossils and decide. "They are small, shelled ocean critters called Foraminifera. They must be well over 100 million years old to be pushed up this high in the mountains." The other boys gather close to see, and then run off to make finds of their own.

"This looks different. What do you think of this, Mrs. Cundiff?" asks Hasnein as he holds another rock before me.

"It looks like imprints of coral embedded in the rocks. Can you believe it? Here, high in the Himalayan Mountains, over 600 miles from the sea," I answer. The students are thrilled. Ken and I had hoped to find some larger remnants of this ancient seabed but are quite happy the boys are excited about their discoveries.

After an enjoyable few hours of fossil hunting, it takes longer than expected to reach the guesthouse and we have to drive about 45 minutes in the dark through the mountains. The road is only wide enough for one vehicle and roads at night are treacherous. Many truck drivers think they save on gas if they don't turn their headlights on; at least until they have a wreck. We spend a lot of time pulling off the road to make way for the semi-like Lorries coming at us head-on.

Dinner is the pits. It looks and tastes like leftover rice with dried up meat and peas from last week dug out of the coals. I eat a few bites and then opt for a banana we brought along. I think I may be headed for a banana diet weekend. This rest house is definitely not on our must-return list.

Students ready for a fossil hunt

A few nights before our field trip we went to a presentation about local politics at the Cultural Center in Lahore. It was quite interesting. This will be the first time in about 18 years since they have had open elections for the Prime Minister of Pakistan. Most people do not believe voting will be fair with 30 different parties running. They are sure, no matter what, 29 will claim rigged ballots. There will be trouble. We hope not too much. There are posters everywhere out here on the roads, plastered all over any wall standing. Each party has a specific symbol and there are lots of pictures for those who cannot read. Our young students are animated and talkative about whom they think should win. Most seem to prefer the PPP or Pakistan People's Party. More than likely, a few of them are related to some of the candidates.

Day Two.

We drive around the countryside looking for more fossil sites. Dark layers in the mountainside may contain deposits of ancient sediment and we stop to look where there are no homes around. The weather is perfect and the boys are having a good time. Climbing around in the hills is fun in itself but we don't find more fossils. Stopping for lunch in a small busy town, the kids find some food stalls for samosas and other greasy fried stuff. Ken and I eat bananas, oranges, "digestive biscuits" and peanuts; foods that are packaged and fairly healthy.

Back at the rest house we have a minor confrontation. Two cars block the gate and a group of picnickers wants us to wait until they finish eating before moving. They think they are too important to care about us. We think they are pretty inconsiderate and a lot of yelling ensues. Luckily it ends without physical conflict and they finally pull out of the way. It is harder to deal with confrontation in this culture not our own. We try to understand but sometimes miscommunicate.

Ninth graders at Khewra Salt Mine

"Look what we found!" announce the boys, running down the hill behind the rest house. "I think they are something like the mollusks we found before," proclaims Ismail. We did not expect to see them right in our backyard so it was even more fun. Very tiny spiral like shells are imprinted in the rocks held in their hands. "These fossils could be up to 500 million years old. We have to identify the strata to tell for sure but the shapes are common for really ancient organisms," I explain as all nine of the boys gather round. "Let's go find more!" shouts Sharif as they all bound up the hill with their geology hammers.

The view from the guesthouse is stunning and takes some of the pain away from the lousy food. Perched on the edge of a high hill we overlook a lake, the lush green valley, a small village and the peaks of the Karakorum Range of the Himalayas in the distance. A large flock of rose-ringed green parrots fly across the bright blue sky. Acting much like hummingbirds, some large orange moths flit between flowers in the yard. Two peacocks strut across a roof on the hill below us. Water buffalo graze at the edge of a clear mountain lake in the valley. Turbaned cooks make a one-star dinner for us in the kitchen and wasps nest in the corner of the porch where we sit, enjoying each other and the pleasantly cool evening.

Day Three.

Ken sets the telescope outside at 5:30 AM, before dawn. Without TV, after a few fun card games, we had sacked out last night before 9:00 PM so the early morning time feels good. We can see Mercury, Jupiter, Venus and the Moon in the dark sky of the mountains. The boys love it. Saad stares amazed at the Milky Way, an expanse of stars he has never been able to see in the city. Amin is excited over how Ken uses the flashlight to point out the constellations of Orion, Cassiopeia and Pleiades. (Over twenty-five years later Saad still recalls the clarity of the Milky Way and Amin remembers that night as he uses his own flashlight in the sky to show his sons the very same stars.)

After a breakfast of hard-boiled eggs and French bread with fig jam, we drive for about an hour to visit the Khewra Salt Mine. This second largest salt deposit in the world was supposedly discovered by troops of Alexander the Great in 320 B.C. when their horses were found licking the stones. It was formed over 800 million years ago as an ancient sea dried up, and the continental plate was pushed into the mountains. It still produces over 350,000 tons of salt per year.

The salt mine director welcomes and takes us for an amazing tour deep into the mines. Hiking along the rails with hot electric wires hanging low above our heads and bare light bulbs very sparingly placed, we are glad to have our own "torches" or flashlights with us. Solid crystal walls of ancient sea-salt in translucent shades of pink, creamy white and grey glow eerily in the dim light. A huge cavern has been neatly carved out with arched entrances to the tunnels. Several of the boys run their licked fingers over a wall to taste and verify the salt. The mines have been worked for 700 years with over 80 miles dug through the mountains. Salt, the dried up sea of millions of years ago, surrounds us underground in a crystal palace.

Hasnein, Sherif and Amin lead the pack as they dive excitedly into the dark tunnels with beams from their flashlights bouncing from the crystal walls as I try to pull in their reins to keep an eye on them. We pause to admire a mosque built inside the vast cavern, made of salt blocks with walls just high enough to separate a prayer space from the work tunnels.

"Is this mosque actually used?" asks Helmut.

"At prayer time, whenever miners are near, they come to bow west, towards Mecca. The direction is symbolized by the crescent moon and star carved into that salt wall over there," points our guide.

Out on the road again, a Hindu temple, crumbling and green with moss, over 1000 years old, is too intriguing to pass by. It lies isolated, perched atop a barren hill, overlooking a pool of the "Tears of Shiva". Since partition between India and Pakistan most of the Hindu shrines are left to decay. Walking through the ancient arched passages, only wide enough for one, climbing the steep staircase to the top, I can still feel some of the reverence emanating from the ages when this was a great center for Hindu Pilgrims. It is a sad reminder of the separation of Pakistan and India, tearing so many people apart because of religion. If only we could all share and appreciate the whole of human heritage. Our mostly Muslim boys, enjoy exploring the old stone temple and ask why it has been left to decay.

"In a small town off the main road their lives a man called Mr. Rajeed who has some old coins and other artifacts from the region," proclaims our travel guidebook. So, along with the boys, we decide to check it out. After lots of directions, a few wrong turns and a drive into a very simple and poor town we park under a big mulberry tree and set out on foot. Through narrow dirt alleys with old brick walls lining the path, following a young boy, we finally come to a gate. "Is this the home of Mr. Rajeed?" Atif speaks to a small child in Urdu who runs to get an adult. A middle-aged woman, seeming to know just what we are here for, appears with a key. She motions us closer and, with a broad smile, opens the crude wooden double doors, which guard a very compact personal museum.

This unique and unassuming couple has been collecting from all kinds of people from all over the world for many years, enjoying and sharing the simple generosity of their guests. Books, hundreds of matchboxes, pictures, fossils, artifacts from near and far. While his wife steps out to prepare us a snack, Mr. Rajeed tells us the stories.

Mr. Rajeed's museum

"This is an 1873 British gold coin, found in the dirt by a hiker who came to see me several years ago". "An American visitor gave me this old U.S. two-dollar bill that he kept in his wallet for good luck". Strange wooden shoes, pottery from Japan and even a wind chime hand-forged in Africa; he enthusiastically describes the story behind each precious piece. His wife appears, generously offering tea and cookies for all. He chats with us in English and Urdu, patiently answering all of our questions.

When we are ready to leave Mr. Rajeed will accept nothing from us but a promise to send him something for their collection. They refuse to sell anything, saying that this is their life. To collect and to share with others brings them more joy than money. My favorite lesson of the trip.

On the road passing through town, there are political rallies with hundreds of men, in a party mood, gathering to hear speeches, to pass out leaflets, stick posters to everything and ride around calling from loud speakers in cars. Everyone is so excited to be taking part in the upcoming national elections. Even the smallest villages are campaigning. I am not sure how well democracy works in a country where people are so religious and are even told who to marry. "Who will you vote for?" I ask a woman at the rest house. "I do not know because my husband has not yet decided'" she answers.

Day four.

As we head back to school we drive through the valleys traveled by the armies of Alexander the Great, looking for the spot where he may have buried his beloved horse, Brucephalus. The giant, black, fiery steed with one blue eye, tamed by Alexander himself, is one of the most famous horses of history. Although we do not find that particular grave we do a little more fossil hunting and successfully collect some more of the ancient corals. We pass by more political rallies on our way, to end up back at the school about 4:30.

Ken and I are happy all went well. We enjoyed our nine boys, and none of them bought any guns like our older students did last year.

Our boys are tired out, ready for a home-cooked meal, anxious to show parents their fossil treasures and tell stories of lost stallions and bright stars.

Lockdown on Campus

A loud terrifying explosion rocks the classroom, rattling the windows and shaking the floors and our bodies to the core. "MY GOD, WHAT'S THAT??", "SHIT!!!" With wide eyes and adrenalin rushing, the students and I fly out of our chairs in hyper alertness, not quite knowing what to do.

It is the last class of the day, in those days before anyone had practiced for such a thing. They all hush and look to me for guidance. "Everybody! Come here! Duck down!" I order them to the front of the room, between my desk and the wall, away from the windows. They rush to huddle. This is not a drill.

No more explosions come and in just a few minutes I order them to stay down and not move as I carefully venture out to find out what's happening. A million thoughts flood my brain. This country has been perpetually at odds with India for generations and Lahore is not far from the border. War is always a possibility. Fundamentalism and unrest has increased recently and there has been trouble. Even Russia might take a swing at us. What is happening??

I run into Ken, Mr. Dubash and Ms. Rana right outside my room, in the hallway. Mr. Dubash volunteers to find out what's happening so we can return to stay with our students.

"What should we do?" asks Shandar and Khuram as they huddle together with the rest of the frightened teenagers. Let's just stay here, away from the windows and behind my desk" I respond, trying to remain calm and hoping to protect them.

The four acres of school grounds are surrounded by thick concrete walls, over ten feet tall, with large shards of broken glass embedded in the top and only two gates, both heavily guarded. There are about 500 people and several large, separate buildings for classes on campus and we hope and pray that no one is hurt and the barriers have not been breached.

Although it seems like hours, Dubash returns in about fifteen minutes to tell us that there was an explosion just outside of the south wall of our school, not far from the elementary building. We are to stay put while our security officials check into it.

"Do you know about the Indo-Pakistani war of 1965?" Shezad asks me. "There were a lot of bombings around Lahore."

"Yes, my uncle's home was bombed and my cousin was killed responds Shariq. "Many people we know had family hurt and homes damaged."

The "all clear" comes in about thirty minutes, time enough for sharing adrenalin driven conversations of other scares, and atrocities, thankful that we are OK and anxious to get home to loved ones.

Dubash returns to tell the story. Apparently there was a small shop where fireworks were made and the place blew sky high, damaging our compound wall behind our elementary school. They were not sure yet of the details but there was no attack directed at us. We should forget after-school activities today, leave campus and go home.

The next morning as we drive into school we pass near the explosion site. The road is blocked off and a small shrine; a stack of bricks with a Muslim symbol on top strewn with flowers, stands alone near a pile of rubble in the quiet, early day.

On campus, we gather together for a school-wide assembly and are asked to pray for the neighboring family. The father had been blown to pieces while he was making fireworks. Apparently he and his son had been making these explosives right against the school wall for years as a small business. There were many little shops along the narrow road and no one at the school had known the nature of their enterprise. The son had just stepped out for lunch and so it was only the father who had died in the explosion. No one knows exactly what caused it.

Even though the school work crew scoured the campus for debris from the blast, this afternoon one of the children found a thumb on the elementary playground. Some students claimed they saw bloody pieces hanging in the trees.

Each morning for three days we see additional shrines built for more of the body parts that were gathered. We have discussions on campus about attacks, safety and awareness of those around us who are not so worried about dangerous business.

We can build walls around us but we cannot control our neighbors. We need to get to know them and what they are doing.

Mysterious Plane Crash
And a New Government

"What the hell is this all about??" exclaims Ken as we step off the plane from Thailand, ending our long summer vacation in August of 1988.

Automatic rifles are no longer hanging loosely from the shoulder but held taught and ready on the tarmac. "This must be serious," Ken continues. "We have not listened to the news in weeks. Something big must have happened."

The Karachi airport is filled with heavily armed military. Welcome home. While waiting anxiously in long lines of heavy security, we gather from the broken conversations around us that Pakistan's President Zia was killed in a plane crash yesterday. There is much speculation that it was not an accident.

Disturbed and unsure of the consequences we hurry to contact our politically savvy Pakistani friends at the school as soon as we arrive home in Lahore.

Not only was Pakistan's president killed but several notable Generals as well as the American Ambassador. 30 people had died in the crash of a C-130 military transport. We had met Arnold Raphel, the U.S. ambassador to Pakistan at an embassy party just a few months ago. This intelligent, friendly man had been chosen for this post because of his knowledge of the area and his way with diplomacy. He is now dead.

Expecting fear and tension, we are quite surprised that the local folk are basically taking the news as just another turn in their history of violent politics. It is unbelievable what people can get used to. General Zia-ul-Haq had forcefully taken over the government in a military coup in 1977. Alleging corruption, he executed the democratically elected Ali Bhutto, leader of the PPP (Pakistan People's Party). Thus this mysterious plane crash brought up lots of suspicions about politics and revenge.

Perhaps it was the U.S CIA, as they did not favor the military government of Zia. Maybe the KGB because Zia was aiding the Afghan war against U.S.S.R. Possibly the backers of the Bhutto family for

159

revenge and to get the PPP back in power. Some say the Israelis did it. Perhaps just equipment failure. Who knows? I sure don't.

"It seems as if a bid for presidency is pretty much a suicidal choice," remarks Ken in the teachers lounge. "I have to hand it to anyone with such strong convictions."

"Some people compare our politics to a phonograph record that does 33 revolutions per minute," jokes Dubash. "It often seems to be more about power and money than conviction."

Election Day

After the plane crash in August, the Senate took power with the promise to hold national elections in 90 days. The country prepared with great fanfare. Thirty different political parties rose out of the masses to raise their flags and posters, pass out fliers and have rousing marches and rallies.

Voting banner in Lahore

Today is only the second time in history that Pakistan has held open national elections. Posters and banners are hanging from every pole, tree, street sign, building and even phone wires. Pamphlets drop from airplanes and are tossed into car windows. Each political party has their own symbol, especially important for much of the population who cannot read. Only two or three of the parties have any chance at all to win but that does not stop the rest from trying.

Excitement is high and we find the first noisy crowd to pass by our house a bit scary. Only men campaign in public, but everyone seems to be having a great time waving flags, chanting, yelling, clapping and even dancing down the streets to get people to join them.

So far things have gone remarkably well. A lot more police and military are out to keep the peace. Even huge political rallies have been no problem. Several teachers at the school are campaigning for the Pakistani People's Party, lead by Benazir Bhutto, daughter of Ali Bhutto, who was killed by order of General Zia. Benazir is for more democracy and women's rights.

One might think that a woman in a Muslim country could not possibly win an election but her family affiliation is even more important than her sex. Since Pakistani women were given the right to vote in 1947 they have become a force in themselves. But not all women are as educated and confident as our teachers at school. "Whom will you vote for? I ask a woman selling vegetables in the market, as a group of men campaign joyously through the street. "I don't know," she sighs. "My husband has not yet decided." She is the third woman that has given me that reply.

Some of the parents of our students are running for other political offices that will change with the new government. Most worry that even though much care is taken the voting could be rigged against them.

"What do you think? Asks Tim, "Should we risk it?"

"Let's do it!" Ken responds for both of us. The American embassy warns us to stay at home and not go anywhere near downtown Lahore on election day. So Tim, Paula, Ken and I pile into the van at dawn and head straight into the midst of it. We can't resist the embassy tip. Too exciting.

At seven A.M. it is uncommonly quiet in the usually bustling center of Lahore. All businesses have closed for this national voting day. As we drive through the streets all the colorful posters and banners testify to the diversity of those running for office. A picture of a farm with sheaths of corn, a bearded man with the Koran in one hand and a

Kalashnikov rifle in the other, a pair of reading glasses, an umbrella, a saw, a horn and even a bicycle party.

Teams of volunteer workers are hurriedly assembling tent polling booths on this legal holiday. Party information stands are giving away free bus tickets for people to travel to their assigned voting stations, as some will need to journey quite a distance. Everyone is required to have an ID card. Some say these rules were made to keep the poor from voting. Sound familiar? One of the teachers at school said that in the last vote she was on three different lists and even though she only voted once it was recorded that she had done it twice. They say it will be better this time.

"American Press!" "Welcome!" "Come here to see!" We are waved over to join the set-up crew as Tim pulls his rather large video camera from the van. We do not correct our mistaken identity as the "press" and take advantage of the tour. They are very excited to show us their voting booths and take us through all the steps of the process as Tim continues to film them.

There are separate tents for men and women so that women in burkas need not show their faces to men during identification. Voting directions are pictorial and easy to understand. The election sheets carry both the names of the people running along with their party name and symbol to help those who cannot read. We cannot read either as it is written in Arabic, but the pictures say a lot.

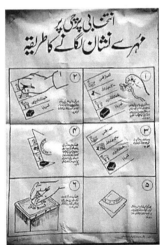

Voting procedure

Political party symbols

162

The poster man with the Kalashnikov rifle in one hand and the Koran in the other would not get my vote.

Vote for me or else!

Benazir Bhutto was elected the 11th Prime Minister of Pakistan and served for two non-consecutive terms from 1988-1990 and 1993-1996. As a member of the Pakistan People's Party or PPP, she promoted democracy, free market, education and women's rights. She was the first woman leader of a Muslim country. Under allegations of corruption she left the country in 1999 but returned in 2007 when President Musharraf withdrew charges and granted her amnesty. She was assassinated in a bombing in December 2007 after leaving a PPP rally in Rawalpindi where she was running for the 2008 national elections. Benazir was the recipient of the United Nations Prize in the Field of Human Rights.

Ma'a Salama – Goodbye Pakistan

"I object to violence because when it appears to do good, the good is only temporary; the evil it does is permanent." - Mahatma *Gandhi*

Salman Rushdie. Boy what fervor over a book. It was quite frightening. You would think he had killed thousands of people. Combining fiction with history his novel, *The Satanic Verses*, was a Booker Prize finalist. It also lead to thousands of Muslims in several different countries rioting because of the "blasphemous" depiction of the Prophet Mohammed. 40 people were killed and over a hundred wounded in a riot in Bombay alone. Most Muslim countries banned the book. Ayatollah Khomeini, ruler of Iran, issued a fatwa, calling for all Muslims to try to kill Rushdie.

Religions can be pathways to God and playgrounds for the devil. Fanaticism is often linked to people who are poor, powerless or disenfranchised. It is rare in countries that have a good economy, low unemployment, high education and strong social and health programs.

Attacking American embassies around the world over a book written by an Indian man living in England? We are warned to be on the alert for trouble.

Our phone rang quite late at night. "Hi, Ken, its Richard Eng." Our superintendent during our second year in Lahore sounded tense. "The Embassy says to pack your bags and get prepared for a possible emergency evacuation." We organized our valuables, secured our passports, packed a suitcase and got ready. We did not sleep well for a few weeks.

What I found surprising was the position of the educated, and westernized Pakistanis. Although they did not agree with the death edicts of Khomeini or the riots, most did take the Islamic stance that the book was evil and should not be published. Perhaps it is evil. I did not read it. But we certainly don't have to believe what a book says and freedom of speech is important. At least important to Americans and true democratic nations.

The Satanic Verses hit number one on the New York Times bestseller's list from all the publicity. The radical attack on Rushdie and innocent others drew worldwide attention and made the book quite popular around the world. Riots continued to break out globally throughout the spring.

The book has become the most controversial book of modern times and remains banned in many countries to this day. Iran continued to call for Rushdie's death and in 2006 proclaimed that the fatwah would remain in effect "forever".

Leaders of floundering countries often try to focus their people on outside enemies. It is an age-old tradition to which America is not immune. Perhaps we should be solving root causes of insecurity instead of fighting over religion.

It is getting near Christmas of the second year of our two-year contract and we have to decide if we want to teach here again next year. Our contract will be up in June and the school will need to hire this February for the next school year. They really want us to stay but we are already getting itchy feet and I want to finish my PhD at University of Florida before my credits are no longer valid.

The situation for foreigners in Pakistan is deteriorating and we are feeling more threatened. If someone can blame and kill innocent people over a book written by a total stranger living in another country, there is no limit to their wickedness.

Enjoying a pleasant social evening over at the Marr's house, we are just chatting about the day, lingering at the dining-room table. A knock at the front door draws Tim to answer. The outside security guard is standing at the entrance with a folded note in his hand. Tim opens it to see a blank piece of paper.

A loud crash of shattered glass comes from the other room as we watch a brick tumble across the floor towards the table, terminating our relaxed discussion. "My God, what is that?!?" cries Paula as she jumps and runs to the living room. The large plate-glass window is scattered in shards across the floor. No doubt the note to Tim was used to draw the guard away from his post. Tim and Ken run outside to look around but don't find the perpetrator.

We can pick up the glass but it is much more difficult to pick up the trust.

There were also a few incidents of vandalism at the school and it is possible that some of our students might even be involved. So far nothing really bad. So far. We have met, taught and worked with some wonderful people in this country. It is too bad that the violent actions of a few can have such an impact.

We turned down our renewal contract and began to get excited about going back home to family and friends and living at our farm in the country near Gainesville Florida. Having not been home for almost two years, we were really missing it. We were ready to enjoy the last few months of school and prepare to head back to America for at least a few years.

It was early spring, our last semester at Lahore American School. We had all our plans made and our hopes set on moving back home when Gene Vincent, our former superintendent from our first year in Lahore called from his new school in Dhaka, Bangladesh.

"I've searched the world over and have not been able to find good teachers like you." He says with a sweet, persuasive voice. "I know you're planning to go back to school in Florida but would you even consider working in Dhaka?"

"No, we've made up our minds, we are going home for sure. We think. Unless you make us some kind of offer we can't refuse.

He did.

And so we went round and round trying to make a very difficult decision. Go back to our beautiful quiet, nice, clean, sophisticated, educated, modern Gainesville; or continue our adventures in Asia.

Gene said the American International School in Dhaka has high academic standards, a modern campus and the students are studious and diverse. Bangladesh, being the most disaster prone area of the world, is highly populated with foreign relief agencies - a good group to work with, as they are very global and altruistic.

The country is mostly Muslim, previously part of Pakistan when they separated from India at the time of Partition. Bangladesh gained its independence from Pakistan in 1971. The people, with their more Asian culture of quiet humility, are not so religiously strict or as violent as Pakistan.

The climate is similar to South Florida - wet and warm all year. Tropical fruits, birds and flowers will fill our yard.

OK, it was the also the paycheck increase for each of us that really turned our ear and took the stubbornness out of our decision. Gene almost doubled our salaries. Not only is teaching in Asia interesting, but it can also be fairly lucrative, at least for an educator.

Anyway, this has certainly changed a few things. The summer will be a whirlwind of visiting family and friends in America. We will be busy buying and preparing for a new big adventure, and hopefully, spend at least a couple of weeks back on the farm, renewing our sanity.

Even though we were hired to teach in Pakistan, I believe that we learned far more than we taught. It is truly an experience that changed our lives. Every day was something new, different people and a different lesson. We will miss all of our students and friends we leave behind. We will not forget them and what they have given to us.

LAS graduating class

Bangladesh

Water Water Everywhere.
Arriving Bangladesh, August 1989

"Travel is fatal to prejudice, bigotry, and narrow-mindedness."
  - Unknown

The sun reflects brightly off the wet mosaic below. Narrow rivers dissect an expansive patchwork of green rice paddies. Ribbons of roads on raised mounds tie together small clusters of buildings. It is still monsoon season and I wonder if our plane has pontoons, as I don't yet see a patch of solid ground big enough for a runway.

"It looks like a big shallow marsh down there with a few small islands, quite different from the deserts of Pakistan," Ken chats, as he strains to lean over me to get closer to my window in the plane. "The captain says we should be approaching the airport but I don't see it or the city yet," I reply. We hold hands, talking non-stop cheek-to-cheek, noses to the glass, as we try to envision what our new life will be like in this wet, warm, populated country.

The land of Bangladesh is a tropical paradise. Almost. Lush with brilliant red, purple and pink bougainvillea, swaying coconut palms, productive banana trees, thick green grass and twirling, hefty philodendron vines climbing all the way to third story open decks. If you can overlook the throngs of poor, ragged, skinny, starving people the noisy din of construction, animals, and traffic in the trashy, crumbling streets you might believe you were in Eden.

It had taken about 48 hours to get to Dhaka. Our flight from Florida had been one eternally long day. By traveling west with the sun following us, we left Orlando in the morning and arrived at our overnight layover in Thailand before the sun set. After 22 daylight hours of eating, napping, squirming in our seats, jumping up to stretch and zoning out watching movies and one stop in San Francisco, we finally arrived in Asia, the other side of the world.

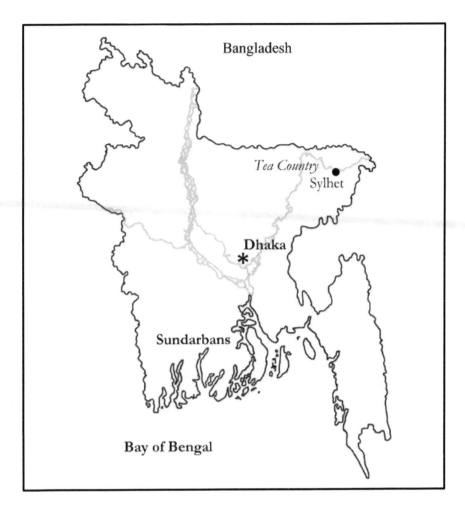

Having been here just one year ago, this layover is our second taste of Thailand and we love it once again. As a Buddhist country, it has a very different philosophy and culture than those we have known so far. I still recommend it as my favorite country to visit. It has friendly people, tropical beauty and is exotically different from America.

When the airline offers a choice of hotels we choose to stay near our favorite place, Lumpini Park in Bangkok. The Crowne Plaza Hotel brings us purple orchids on our pillows, some fresh tropical fruit, cookies, coffee and a beautiful view overlooking the park. The room is free, compliments of the airline, as we wait to catch the next flight to Dhaka. We are happy to have an overnight in Thailand before flying the last two hours of our journey.

"Pretty classy," I remark while donning the cozy terrycloth robe provided in our room after my hot shower. "Not bad for a free airport layover." Ken peels the bumpy flaming red outer coat off a litchi fruit picked from the plate on the dresser. "Try this, it's delicious," he says as he pops the small round fruit like a big peeled grape into my mouth. He knows how much I love fruit and the sweet tangy flavor makes this tropical gem as tasty on the inside as it is pretty on the outside.

Rising before dawn with jet lag we figure we might as well get moving with first light. The best cure for jet lag is exercise in the sun so we tie on our sneakers to join other early joggers on the Lumpini Park paths at 5:30 in the morning.

This 142 acre manicured park with its small lake and long paths winding through deep green tropical trees is a lot like Central Park in New York, a haven for the public surrounded by the bustling noisy city. Lushly green and freshly wet from last night's rain the sweet smells of Frangipani flowers and ripe fruit fill the air. Local people are beginning their day while we run, moving slowly in unison through Tai Chi poses in the foggy tranquility near the lake. As we jog, walk, sit and tour our way around the park we soak in the smells and sights, lingering as long as we can before we have to catch our flight. Eating bananas and mangos we sip a cup of iced coffee at a small outdoor café while watching people enjoy a bit of nature before the heat of the day shoos them into the shadows.

Before we know it, we touch down once again. The flight from Bangkok to Bangladesh had only been about an hour's difference in time but a pronounced difference in culture. Crowds of people gather just outside the huge glass walls at the entrance of the beautiful, new Dhaka airport. Security is fairly tight just to keep out the homeless. We have a bit of trouble locating our friends who should be here to pick us up but finally see them peering through the huge plate glass walls waving at us, as they do not have tickets to enter.

Gene Vincent, our headmaster and friend, his wife Terry and the whole Sloffer family (Sam, Linda, Ty and Monica) have come to pick us up and ease our arrival.

Two years ago Gene hired the Sloffers and us for two year contracts to teach in Lahore. He left Pakistan to be the superintendent in

Bangladesh one year ago only to hire all of us once again to teach at the American International School of Dhaka this year. In international schools where adventurous people move around the world and take new jobs, it is common to meet up with old friends.

The Sloffers have been in Dhaka for just a few days. Driving through noisy traffic and waiting in the heat and the crowds for hours is an effort not to be forgotten and to pass along to those who will come next year. As newbies to the country and as friends we are excited about making discoveries together with trusted shoulders on which to cry and to laugh. Smiling from ear to ear we meet and receive a welcome kiss on each cheek, a generous hug and vigorous handshaking, the traditional greetings of overseas travellers. Although this is a Muslim country we can already feel it is not as strict as Pakistan.

We were placed into a big dark house we did not like. The servant, who had come with the premises until we decided otherwise, was as gloomy as the house. A busy street in front was noisy all night long. The yard next door was a nexus for teenagers playing soccer. "The last teachers who lived here did not seem to be happy with it. You are welcome to move if you can find a better place." Offered Gene as he showed us around. So we took him up on it and began to look immediately. Dhaka is considered a hardship post with a generous package. Along with good pay they provide housing, a vehicle and a yearly trip back to your home of origin. Some schools provide only a salary and a one-way ticket.

Our freight, coming directly from Lahore, was supposed to be delivered to Dhaka the middle of August, arriving before us. It was not here. After arranging an international call to our Pakistani servant, William, we got the bad news. Our 42 boxes of stuff were still neatly stacked in the back room of our house in Lahore. It took a few furious conversations with the shipping agencies and some help from the school to get it moving our way.

This means we will be without most of our things for about two more months. Having only what we brought in our suitcases, most of our clothes, schoolbooks, kitchenware and treasures that make a house a home are in those boxes. Shipping things is always a double-edged sword. It is so nice to have your own stuff instead of buying everything you need in a new country but there is the clear possibility of losing boxes. Or even the whole lot of it. Or having 42 boxes there instead of here.

The school sits on about five acres in a suburb of Dhaka. Quite international, it is populated with children of embassy and aid agency personnel from over fifty different nations. In a place where student diversity is so high and many are new arrivals prejudice, cliques and racism are almost nonexistent. I was talking about the biological classification system in my seventh grade life science class the other day and the importance of scientific names. I asked them to come up with different common names for "horse". With all the languages that the children spoke between them we were able to list 14 different names for *Equus ferrus*.

One class of biology, one chemistry and two classes of seventh grade life science are my assignments. I haven't taught young seventh graders. The students are quite cute and energetic but boy are they slow to learn the science, as they do not have the background of older kids. I am learning more patience, flexibility and fun hands on experiments, expanding my own educator skills.

One of my seventh graders has Down's syndrome. He comes every day with his nanny who sits with him in class. An older, sweet, quiet woman, she keeps Randy under control when he gets too rambunctious. Many of the other students have grown up with him and are really good at taking care and watching out, helping to teach and guide him. Randy is bigger and a bit older than his classmates, always sweet and happy and quite excited about learning. I would not have thought that such a child would be an asset in my classroom rather than a hindrance. He seems to bring out a responsible attitude in his classmates that predominates over pre-teen impishness.

Ken is teaching earth science, physical science and computers. There is no physics class offered this year as the high school is new and there is not yet a grade 12. He is working with Macintosh computers that are different for him and therefore challenging and time consuming. The school is in the process of constructing a whole new building for the newly added high school sections as the student body increases. Unfortunately this means that we have to share the one and only science lab for the next two years. At least it is a large room with plenty of working space. Just our luck to be here for the beginning of construction. We "get to" help design the labs but we may not be here long enough to reap the benefits.

It is Thursday, the end of our first full work week and we have chartered a riverboat with some of the other teachers to celebrate. The river is one place in this city of teaming millions where the atmosphere is relaxed and you can just float along, watching the hectic, busy life of Bangladesh go by without the involvement. It is worth the hour drive to get from our home to the boat docks.

"Ahhh! Finally, we get a break from the city and our work. Jane, move over! I am so ready to just sit here and relax and watch the river." Ken lets out a big sigh as he plops down next to me on the blue vinyl boat cushion.

Fishing boat in Dhaka

"Here, have some wine. I got it from the commissary and I'm betting you could use it," offers Linda as she pours some for us. Here in this Muslim country our boat has no wine goblets but plenty of small old-fashioned flower-printed teacups. "Here's to having a smooth school year. A year of fun without the mayhem," Ken toasts as we raise our teacups in a rousing salute.

The river life in Bangladesh is so natural and eternal feeling, as life on water has always been. Dhaka is on the east bank of the Buriganga River (meaning "Old Ganges"), and near a confluence with other major rivers that bring water down from the Himalayan Mountains out to the largest delta in the world and the Bay of Bengal. It is also one of the most densely populated places in the world due to the rich soil, tropical climate and all that guaranteed fresh water. An evening on a charter-boat is just the thing to get away from the crowds.

The ingenuity of the simple design and function of transport on the river is celebrated in a book called "The Country Boats of Bangladesh" which we have purchased to learn more. Only a few boats have motors but almost all have sails. Tall masts with a billowing rectangle of muslin hoisted high above the water are simple and effective. Small dark men hold the rigging, dressed in simple sarongs of just a length of material wrapped around their waist. They deftly catch just the right amount of wind to maneuver through the narrow, busy rivers. Chanting in unison a group of men sitting in rows pull strongly on their oars to move a barge upstream against the wind. School children crowd on the edges of a large motorized riverboat, hanging over the side as a loudspeaker blares local music and their teachers shout above the noise on some sort of field trip. An old white-bearded man and a half clothed skinny young boy shift a tattered sail on a rotted wooden skiff as they stick close to the shore for safety, trying to catch their family's food for the day.

Dhaka houseboats

Land and homes are expensive to own or rent in this country of flood zones and high population. There are many poor families who, unable to afford land, build and live on small hand-made boats tied up anywhere they can. The "houseboats" are made of trash they find in garbage bins and barely provide a simple shelter to protect from the rain. No bathroom, laundry room or kitchen. Those are for the river to provide.

We've been out on the river three times already. Once as a full orange moon rose quietly over the still black water. As the sun set, I was sure it was Moses I saw riding atop a passing boat who stood alone, tall and stately with a long wooden staff, his white robes and long white beard waving behind him in the breeze. Our eyes met briefly in a deep timeless connection of sharing the moment. We both nodded in acknowledgment, ships passing in the night.

During the first week of school each grade took an overnight field trip to get to know each other better. With grade ten I travelled down the river and away from the city to a rambling old plantation home. We rode on one of those small creaky wooden skiffs that looked like it would safely hold six as fifteen piled on. One just breathes deeply and hopes that it's not your day to swim in the murky river. I am not afraid of the water. It is the contents of the polluted brew that concerns me. These teensy microscopic unknowables. The clue they say is to try to hold your nose shut if you fall in, keep your mouth closed, scrub really well when you get out and hope your immune system does its job. I plan to stay out of the water.

Our tippy skiff pulls up to the tattered dock at a small island village, a scene right out of National Geographic. Next to a small hand-built adobe hut a woman in a bright green sari is squatting near a small open fire cooking a meager dinner of watery dahl bhat (lentils and rice) for her large family. "Salaam alaykum, Shagotom!" As poor as she is, she smiles happily with a missing front tooth and invites us for dinner - all fifteen of us. We thank her graciously and say that we have just eaten. Luckily we have a translator with us who says this properly.

The villagers gather around us in a relaxed atmosphere of curiosity. Some of the boys of our group, Richard, Saquib and Aziz join in a nearby field for a game of soccer with the island boys. Simple worn benches and wooden stools are brought from the houses for us to sit on in a small open community area in the village center. A few of my students speak the local language and translate for us. "Who is the oldest and the wisest?" asks Alain. Carin and Nicole want to know who is newlywed. "Can you read and write?" Shama queries a young boy. "What do you do for a living?" Himanshu politely asks a sinewy-legged middle-aged man.

Most are farmers growing their own food with little equipment and working hard. Long days to make less than twenty dollars a month from their excess produce. Their children go to school but some of them have bloated bellies and sores that are not healing. They seem happy and quite proud of their families and their small mud thatch homes with hard clay floors swept so clean there is not any dust on them.

Teacher's ferry ride to a riverside village

I have heard people say that they could not live like this, destitute and diseased with little hope of a better future. But humans have a deep survival instinct and with our amazing minds we can often find happiness in the depths of difficult circumstances. Here in a fishing village of Bangladesh or the slums of Detroit or even in a terminal cancer ward, people often cling to what makes us happy and lightens our burdens. It is important to remember we have this ability and not worry so much about tough times. Our human species will keep on going. We will manage. We always do.

This overnight trip with the tenth graders is a great way to get to know and understand each other as school is just beginning. Although

English is the second language for many of them their international diversity and the liveliness of youth make for a fun evening playing cards and sharing conversations about where each has come from and what they are doing in Bangladesh. Most of their parents work for aid agencies. Alain was born in Belgium but has been in Dhaka for most of his school years. Hesham is from Egypt, Nicole from the Netherlands and Richard is from Canada. Saquib and Sayera are from Bangladesh. Havard is from Norway, Stafano from France, Himanshu from India, Mats from Sweden, and Shama and Ty are from America. I feel like I am at a meeting of the United Nations of teenagers.

After a few weeks of real estate searching and dealing, Ken and I finally settle into a fairly new, large and spacious home. It is only one mile from school, across the street from a local elementary school and near an open field with a small river running through it. It is fairly quiet in the evenings and on Fridays when kids aren't there. But on Saturday mornings when the local children are in school while we are not, it can get pretty noisy. We get a nice view of the river and have set up a running route that keeps us fairly near to it, getting the pink and orange reflections of the rising sun to greet us at 5:30 AM when we start our day. The house has three bedrooms, three full baths, two verandas and a wide-open living / dining room. We really love the extra light from all the big windows that look out onto our yard with litchi, pomelo and red-flowering flame trees. A tall wall surrounds the property shielding us from the view of the homeless who build shelters against the outside of our enclave. There is a convenient staircase up to the roof where it is open, flat and airy, a good place to sit in the warm evenings. Another teaching couple lives just a few houses down the street.

Our first servant at the other house did not make the grade because of his pushy and demanding personality. Still, it is difficult to fire someone who may be out of work for months or even years. When we told the school we needed a new servant, about 20 people showed up to apply the same day. We panicked, sent them away and decided to go through friends. We hired Anthony, a young 25-year-old man who had been working but was no longer needed at another teacher's home. He is very nice and can even read the notes and recipes I leave for him. But he is young and not quite as industrious as William, our cook and head servant from Pakistan.

The school provides guard service for us. 24 hours a day someone is walking around the house to make sure no one climbs over the walls. They say that theft is a bigger problem here than in Lahore and also it is good to give people jobs when you can. It is better than just handing out welfare.

The street scene here is quite different than Pakistan. Mingling odors of sweet jasmine, rotting garbage, fresh fruit and animal manure fill the humid air. Bicycle rickshaws are everywhere, over 100,000 in Dhaka alone. We pass hundreds each day on our way to school. Skinny small men with bulging leg muscles petal hard to carry everything from two or even three people to refrigerators or TVs on their small carts. Cars hustle around them as they try to stay to the side and maneuver around puddles or throngs of walkers who cannot afford the 15-cent ride.

Small herds of cows or goats are lawnmowers for the city grazing on the medians and roadsides. Scruffy dogs roaming through the garbage or protecting the houses watch us warily as we jog through the narrow streets, occasionally having to jump over a sleeping, homeless person wrapped in a discarded torn blanket.

There are more women out in public here than in Pakistan. Only a few wear a burka or veils over their faces in the traditional Muslim way and so we get to appreciate more smiles. It feels important to be able to see the faces of strangers. Smiles can make the difference in how we treat each other.

In the early mornings women stream through the streets in their brightly colored saris on their way to work in the garment factories for a few dollars a day. Now I can see why products from Asia are so cheap in America, as we pay these hard-working people so little to make them and then wonder why they stay so poor and we stay rich.

There are very few machines of any kind, since it is better to pay people than to buy a machine that will break down anyway and parts are nonexistent. About twenty men are digging up a parking lot down the street with pick axes, mixing asphalt by hand and dumping it from barrels to repair a neighborhood store front. When we moved our furniture from the first house it was done on an open flatbed cart with only two wheels pulled by one man and pushed by another. Two heavy beds, three couches, several tables, many chairs, a refrigerator, everything went on just three trips. For weeks there has been a crew of people breaking up bricks with hammers across the road. There is no rock in this land of silted runoff at the foot of the Himalayas so people actually make bricks and then chop them up to use as rocks. Dry, weathered, bony hands work endlessly through the stifling hot summer day, trying to stay under the shade of their umbrellas. They barely make enough money to buy food much less buy what they need to be healthy.

Making rock fill from mud bricks

Some modern products are quite difficult to find here. There was not a Styrofoam cup in the city when I needed it for a chemistry experiment nor any Corning-ware plates to use in our imported microwave. But we are allowed to receive packages through the U.S. Embassy mail pouch so I will probably be searching through catalogs for 'necessities' and have them shipped to us, slow but sure. It is nice to have use of the U.S. embassy commissary even if it is over a thirty-minute drive away and quite expensive. I have also learned to reduce my 'necessities' list as I see millions of people who live without.

"Have our tickets been booked yet?" I ask Linda as we sit down to lunch in the teacher's lounge. "Yes, Sam made sure of it yesterday. The school is arranging it through the same tour agency that they use for the eighth grade field trip to Nepal each year. They are booking both our flight to Kathmandu and the one into Lukla where we will start our hike up towards Everest. They will even have some porters lined up for us."

We have already set into motion reservations for our three-week Christmas vacation. As long as the political situation with India and Nepal does not get too bad we hope to go hiking up towards the Mount Everest base camp with the Sloffer family. From what we read it will be cold, steep, rigorous and also amazingly beautiful and exciting. There is a large Buddhist monastery along the way where we hope to pause for a day or so.

We have made some new friends here in Dhaka already. Every week there is something fun to do. Dances, parties or just small get-togethers. Since everyone has servants it is easy to throw parties. Last Friday we went to the British club for a dance. It was fun being in England for the evening. Lots of beer and some bloody good blokes to hang out with. There are at least six different international clubs, all expats (people living outside their own country) are welcome and fees are minimal.

The language here is Bengali and related to the Urdu and Arabic spoken in Pakistan. We can already understand the main greetings, the numbers one through ten and the word "backshish" which means, "Give me money".

I have been coerced into being student council adviser. It has just been three years since the school added the high school onto their elementary and the eleventh graders have not had older students to learn from. They tend to have big ideas with little foresight. I thought we might be in line for our first canceled school dance from poor planning but they worked hard, proved me wrong and were able to pull it off. I am very impressed with their abilities and worldliness. Almost all of them are international travelers and I often overhear conversations about global issues, even among the younger students.

It is still monsoon season and every day we don our raincoats and wade through muddy puddles and across flooded streets filled with the pollution of the city. We are still waiting for our 42 boxes and worried about our freight, as we have heard stories of people losing many of their boxed treasures to flooding. "Don't worry, coaches Mr. Assef, a Bangladeshi in our administrative offices. "Today will be the last day of rain because it is a Hindu feast of the Rain Goddess and it doesn't rain anymore after that. Tomorrow will surely be sunny". I love his attitude. I am ready and waiting for that sun and the cool, clear days of fall.

Nations and Pirates
Nov. 1989 Bangladesh

"Chew quietly your sweet sugarcane God-love and stay playfully childlike."
- Rumi

Leila, a dark haired little girl in a bright red and yellow shalwar-kamis, grabs the out-stretched hand of Helmut, a blonde German boy wearing blue shorts, thick suspenders, knee socks and brown leather hiking boots. Swinging their arms together, they skip to join the others. Today is United Nations Day at school. It is quite a moving extravaganza. The children here represent over 50 nationalities and they have gathered together to proudly fly their country's flag as they parade around the school grounds. Most of them are wearing their own colorful native costumes.

A few Americans are wearing cowboy outfits, some are in blue jeans, one is dressed like a pilgrim, and another like a Native American warrior. Less than 25% of our students are American and many of them have never spent much time there.

The sunny day is filled with shows, songs and dances that the children have prepared. Parents and teachers of different nations have helped to organize and rehearse. Even a local Russian school has come to participate.

"Oh, you have to taste this," Ken croons as he offers me a spoonful of Malaysian pudding. A delightfully international culinary experience is spread before us for a massive picnic lunch, cooked and served by a kaleidoscope of moms. At wooden tables and on blankets spread on the ground, hundreds of students, faculty and parents enjoy the feast.

I love the kimonos of the Koreans most. The little Netherlands girls with their braids, puffy starched colorful dresses and the handsome Arab boys in their starched white robes and red checked head cloths are pretty cute too. OK. I love ALL of them! Unfortunately, I forgot my camera.

Wouldn't it be nice if all schools could be this global in perspective? If each person could revel and join hands in the participation of songs, foods and dances of others, then how could they go to war? If we really want world peace we must guarantee an education where all young children learn to appreciate all the other children of the world, regardless of nationality, skin color, sex, religion, disability or anything else. Learning to celebrate differences rather than denounce them. Isn't it even more important than math or literature? Celebrating differences. It is an evolutionary fact that diversity is the key to success of a species. When life changes, as it does constantly, diversity always allows different individuals to shine. Different minds see different angles and solve different problems. We really need our diversity in this accelerating world culture. Studying, celebrating and encouraging global diversity could be a core subject every year, every school, around the world.

It has been more difficult to get into the local culture here in Bangladesh than in Lahore. There are very few native Bangladeshis working at the school, unlike Pakistan. Dinner invitations or easy ways to connect with the local culture are lacking. But we do have a friendly, diverse international contingent at the school and it is fun to get to know the French, British, Australians, Germans, Koreans and Canadians. Most are involved in working with aid to this poor country. They are here to bring money and to help train and set up businesses. They say it is a black hole of need that seems to suck in all the help they give, while gasping for more. But recent reports indicate that the birth rate is dropping, a sign of a more educated and healthy society.

Social life between foreigners (ex-pats) abounds here, as we all have servants to keep our homes clean and meals prepared – similar to Pakistan. So we meet at the clubs, go for boat rides or think of some crazy things to do.

Today we have been invited to an international "boat race." About a hundred people of all ages and persuasions are gathering for fun at the home of the British ambassador. The eight wooden boats for the race were especially chosen for their sink-ability. Leaky, heavy and falling apart. Each of the eight teams has an appointed captain and a theme with some costume.

With a black rag tied round his head, an eye patch, a plastic sword and a colorful cardboard parrot attached to his shoulder, Ken is with a dashing pirate crew. I decide to watch and cheer from the shore.

Boat numbers are drawn from a hat and come with one bailing bucket and six oars. Turns out the bailing is far more important than the oars. The captain isn't shy. "Bail like mad, mate!" "We're a-fallin behind!" "She's sinkin fast and we'll be in that putrid, hellish water before ya know it!"

Ken the pirate

The waters of this lake are not for the squeamish. Lakes here are really just depressions in this huge delta, filled with monsoon rains and the run-off from shanties without a sewer system. We saw a rotting dead goat floating here just last week and watched homeless people use the edges as a toilet. The climate is warm year round and lots of not-so-nice things can grow in warm water. Even though we boil all our drinking water, we have gotten nasty pustules on our skin from washing with water straight from the tap. Parasites and diarrhea are a common topic of conversation. I have a bottle of iodine soap to add to Ken's bathwater when he gets home, to kill the creepies.

"I think we've had it mates." Calls the captain to his crew. Sure enough, Ken's boat is sinking ever so slowly no matter how hard they bail and row. Soon they are all going down under and they actually have to swim in that nasty dark caldron. But, not to worry, as soon as he gets to shore he grabs a beer and flushes out his ears and face and drinks the rest down. If it doesn't kill the bugs at least it lessens the blow. You can't be a germophobe and live in Bangladesh.

There is a hose to rinse off, towels to dry, changes of clothes and lots of howling laughter.

The yard is covered in carpets and small lights are strung everywhere. Beer in a keg, wines and food on the table, a dance floor on the deck and even a small band make for a grand party as the evening settles in.   But the most fun is all the engaging conversations of people who have lived in exotic places, seen many amazing and terrible things and are not much afraid of silly little risks like dirty water.

Pirate race in murky waters

Tea Country Thanksgiving
Nov. 1989

"Have you got the turkey?" I eagerly ask Sara Ann as she drives up with Merrick and Maya. "You bet! Do you have the sweet potatoes?" she smiles back at me, as she opens the cooler to give me a peek inside. "And we have the pumpkin pies!" chimes in little Aliya, as she tugs on her mom's hand, dragging Patty over to join us.

As the rising orange sun casts its golden glow across the red bougainvillea on a warm Thanksgiving morning, nineteen of us load into a small school bus. We are eager to head out of the city and into tea country in the northern hills of Bangladesh, at the foothills of the Eastern Himalayas.

Our crew includes six teacher families and two drivers, one for the small Coaster school bus and one for the van full of luggage and food. And most importantly we carry a complete, Thanksgiving meal and lots of thankful smiles and fun.

We planned our trip over popcorn and drinks at the American Club. Yes, Dhaka has an American Club. In fact, most big cities around the world have one. They are social places for citizens living overseas who just want to get together to share experiences and a bit of home. We can always get hamburgers, French fries, chocolate chip cookies, popcorn and beer. Everyone speaks English and is glad to see us. We can take a deep breath and relax a bit without worries of cultural problems. Ken likes to play squash on their court and we come often to hang out with friends.

"I'll make some calls and find a place to stay," offers Sara Ann, who can speak Bengali, the local language. Sara Ann Lockwood, our administrative secretary and good friend of everyone at school, sets up a rest house for us just south of Sylhet in Sri Mongal. Tea country. Bangladesh is a small, very densely populated place but there are tea plantations and a few bits of forest in the north where we can get away from the bustle and back to some nature. It is in the foothills of the Himalayan Mountains not far from the border with India and the famous

Darjeeling tea companies. The area boasts some of the best tea in the world.

Teacher families headed to a tea-country Thanksgiving

It is especially fun getting to know more about our diverse new Dhaka friends on this trip. We are all Americans who have lived in other countries, driving through Bangladesh to celebrate a traditional American Thanksgiving.

Our friends the Sloffers and the Vincents were with us at Lahore American School in Pakistan. It is common for teachers to move together as they recommend each other in job interviews. We have lots to share with them in this new school and country.

Chris and Marcia Copping both teach English and social sciences in the high school and are bringing their six-year-old Nathaniel and three-year-old Julia. Although we see them almost daily we have not yet gotten to know them well but we are already enjoying their enthusiasm and adventure.

Richard and Patty Sonnet have been here in Dhaka for two years already. They adopted their two beautiful, dark brown baby girls, Aliya and Jasmine from a local orphanage. Quite an adventurous couple who have already lived in Romania, Patty is an excellent librarian and Richard a great elementary teacher. (We eventually taught with them again, years later, in India.)

Sara Ann and her husband Merrick grew up in India as the children of missionaries. Merrick works as an engineer and inventor for Bangladesh Rice Research Institute. He is currently working on a sterling engine that can burn various materials to generate power for rice thrashing machines used in remote villages. Sara Ann also doubles as a physical therapist and was able to help me recover after a shoulder injury last month. Sara Ann and Merrick's pretty daughter, Maya was also adopted locally and is in my seventh grade life-science class.

Ahhh! The green, green, tropical countryside, rice fields, and some wide-open spaces. We just have to get out of the city. People are great but millions of them crushing all around us triggers an escape response. With a long Thanksgiving weekend and the air beginning to cool, it is time to stretch our wings and see a bit of our new country.

Miles and miles of rice paddies border the narrow road. Small plots in various stages of production are all hand tended. It takes almost an hour to get totally away from the six million people of Dhaka. We drive along a narrow road dredged up out of the mud. Just a very long mound about 20 feet wide and 10 feet high, it is the only area outside the villages that remains above water in monsoon season.

The wet rice-paddy landscape is punctuated with small villages that are elevated on 'islands' and connected to the road. Only a few one-room stalls are the 'stores' in these poor communities.

Men in just a dhoti (white cloth around the groin) are wading in and moving mud from fields to mounds. Women in dirty saris once colorful, are shoving new rice plants into the mud. Little girls swing buckets of water from one plot to another and call playfully to the young boys who ride the water buffalo, pulling plows behind them. Everyone we see is consumed in rice farming. A young girl in a yellow western t-shirt, holding a blue plastic bucket of mud in one hand, smiles and waves as we pass by.

"Hurry up girls!" Richard waves to us from where he stands by the van. "Here they come." We thought we were far away from people when we stopped the bus to have a short break and use the bushes on the roadside. We barely had time to finish before people began to arrive, running from the distant village. They quickly surround us to see who we are and what we might be doing. We feel like their entertainment of the day. They just stand quietly, quizzically, staring and smiling at us weird-looking strangers until we leave, waving good-by. You will never walk alone in Bangladesh.

About four hours driving away from Dhaka the rice paddies and villages finally give way to hills, trees and tea plantations. Tea with caffeine (black or green tea) grows best where there is a long growing season and it is not too hot or too cold. Most plantations are in the mountains near the equator and tea thrives here at the foot of the Himalayan Mountains in Bangladesh and India. The round bushes are neatly trimmed and kept about one meter high with nice paths for the pickers. Sporadic tall trees keep the tea lightly shaded for best production and the whole area looks like a manicured garden.

The good place to stay had already been booked so we have to stay at a cheap rest house near some tea orchards. A beautiful spot but meager conditions. Our group is a tough one and we make-do.

Our accommodations consist of four whitewashed concrete rooms in a row. Each has only simple cots for beds and a small table. We have brought everything else we need. As we prepare our Thanksgiving meal and set up tents for more 'rooms,' we begin to draw some visitors who seem to arrive from out of the jungle. I think we are the afternoon matinee for the locals as they gather at the gate of the fenced-in yard to watch us.

With only a two-burner camp stove on the concrete porch floor and a cold-water spigot in the yard for our kitchen, we prepare and thoroughly enjoy our big Thanksgiving meal, complete with turkey and all the trimmings. "Where did you get the pumpkin for the pies?" I ask Patty. "From the commissary, along with the condensed milk. Probably more than a few of the ingredients for this meal came from there." She answers. "Yeah, I got the canned green beans and mushroom soup for the casserole there too," Terry adds. "Don't matter where it came from, it sure tastes like Thanksgiving," Sam says as he smacks his lips, asks for more dressing and passes around the red wine, thanking all of us for this delicious meal.

A small group of men, women and a few children stand watching along the fence near the gate. Staring at strangers is an uninhibited pastime here. The villagers have never been told that gawking is impolite. It is uncomfortable and frustrating that we cannot yet converse with them so we just smile and wave. We share some of our food, thankful that we have so much.

This tea plantation belongs to the family of one of our students so we are invited for a full, red carpet tour from fields to tea bags. We don our straw hats and sunglasses, swing our cameras over our shoulders and head to the hills after our boiled eggs, bread and fruit breakfast.

Local women do the leaf picking and are paid by the basket-full. There must be at least fifty of them hard at work just in this one orchard. Dressed in worn colorful saris their thin bodies bend over to run their toughened hands through the tea bushes. Leaves are gathered one by one, using both hands to pick as fast as they can to fill the tall straw baskets ever so slowly. They line up to have each full basket weighed and collect their chips to be turned in later for the day's wages. Tea grows well here, high enough in the hills to keep it fairly cool year-round. Hand labor is very cheap and gives work to many. We enjoy drinking cheap tea around the world only because these women work for us for just a few dollars a day.

The leaves are dried and packaged inside a small "factory" which is just a big concrete block drying room with an office at one end. Even as we approach the building the rich leafy aroma delightfully overpowers our senses. Inside, the manager scoops a kilo of tea for each of us right from a mound of the highest quality, freshly dried black leaves.

"Look at that roof. Now that looks like a real tropical home," I point to Ken as we approach the house of the plantation owner. A high, two-feet thick palm-thatched roof spreads across the entire house sticking out over a long, wide verandah with couches and a marble floor.

The plantation manager invites us all into his home for a curried chicken dinner and, of course, some deliciously smooth homegrown tea. The rooms inside are typical of other upper class homes we have seen here. The dark red heavy drapes, lots of knick-knacks and big blue stuffed chairs are comfortable and homey. His cute little girl peaks shyly from behind the black velvet couch. Wearing an orange dress with layers of ruffles above her blue high top sneakers and white knee socks she giggles and hides when I smile at her.

After giving us each of us a kilogram of high grade beautiful black tea, the owner and his wife even offer to put us up for the night if we are uncomfortable in our meager accommodations. "Thank you so much for your generosity," Sara Ann replies for us. "But we are just fine roughing it and now we even have some of your fresh gourmet tea to enjoy for breakfast."

With only one dim light, a couple of cots and nothing else in our concrete room, we hang out on the porch around a lantern enjoying each other and playing Pictionary as the evening ends. The stars twinkle in the beautiful dark night sky with the hum of crickets, frogs and the evening birds. The jackals must have gotten wind of our food as they bark periodically, moving closer, howling mournfully in the blackness of the night. A perfect time for sharing stories of ghosts.

Tea pickers stand in line to weigh-in

Father Donnelly, a Catholic missionary priest, and Sister Mariam, an Irish nun, join our group the next day to take us up into the hill villages for a cultural hike. Sara Ann and Merrick know them well as they have also lived in this area. Veterans of over 20 years in Bangladesh, the missionaries are storybook characters. So full of love for the people they serve it is quite a pleasure to listen to their life tales and to watch them speak with their local village parishioners. Father Donnelly was in this north hill country before roads were built and before the war to separate from Pakistan. He has seen and experienced much, right along with his people.

They guide us on a two-hour drive up into the mountains where we hike through some forest then up into an isolated village. Here lives a different tribe, the Casas, who are primitive but Christian. Rather gentle

192

and shy they bring out tables, chairs and their best "china" from every hut to serve Father and his guests tea, cookies and fresh papaya under the trees in the village center.

"Is that what I think it is?" asks Patty. "Looks like it to me," chuckles Richard. The village children gather round at a discreet distance to watch us. Some of the younger ones are blowing up balloons, but on closer inspection we confirm that the family planning crew has been here with free condoms. No wonder they still have so many children.

Casas village children with "balloons"

The Casas tribe grows and harvests betel nut and makes paan for a living. The cured product is chewed and spit out for its mild narcotic effect. They even offer us some to taste. Kind of bitter but not too unpleasant, it gives me a buzzy feeling as it stains my mouth and teeth dark red. It is known to be addictive and cause cancer but I think it is still legally sold here. I know I have seen many red-toothed smiles among villagers all over the country.

On our way back to Dhaka we have to use an overcrowded ferry to cross a wide river. We make sure to get out of the parked car, leave our heavy packs behind, and stand near the jam-packed edge in case we might have to swim away. These ferries are infamous for accidents and drownings. Often ferries just sink from overloading. Occasionally a bus with bad brakes will drive on board and drive right off again into the murky depths at the other end. Most of the people cannot swim and whenever a boat sinks there are many deaths. It seems strange that they live for generations in a land of water everywhere and never learn how to swim.

Successful ferry crossing

Thanksgiving is a special day to celebrate all that we have. It is especially poignant when we live with people who have so little.

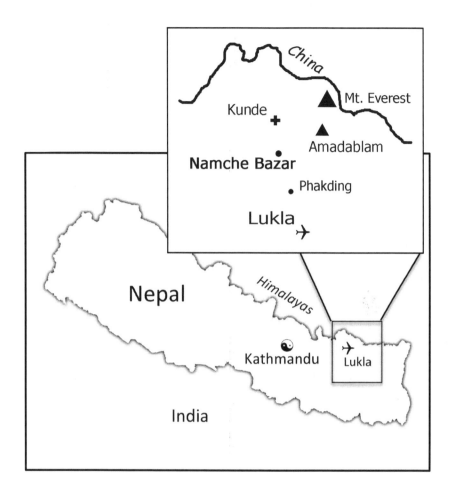

Toward Everest
December 23, 1989 to Jan 1, 1990

"No matter how sophisticated you may be, a large granite mountain cannot be denied – it speaks in silence to the very core of your being"   - Ansel Adams

"Hey! – Tim! Paula! I'm up Here! Woo-hoo! I can't believe it. Come on up! The Sloffers are here with us!" Hanging over the balcony I shout and wave wildly before bounding down the stairs to hug and welcome them.

195

We had just been debating with Sam and Linda over how to go about finding our good friends Tim and Paula Marr who should be arriving from Pakistan and may not know where we are. Spotting them in the street as I look out our fourth story window solves the problem.

Yesterday afternoon we flew from Bangladesh with Sam and Linda Sloffer and their teenage children Ty and Monica. Our handsome young Nepali agent dressed in slacks and a red flannel shirt met us at the arrival gate in the airport holding a welcome sign with our names in large black letters. Behind him stood the Sloffer's cousins, Chuck and Betty who also just arrived from a U.S. military post in Belgium.

We are all staying at the Blue Diamond Hotel in downtown Kathmandu, Nepal. The Blue Diamond offers hot water and clean rooms right in the middle of the bustle of the tourist haven of Kathmandu for low prices and enough beds for all. It suits us.

"How are things at LAS (Lahore American School)? Is everybody OK? What is happening with fundamentalism? Tell us everything!" asks Linda as all ten of us crowd into our tiny room, piling on the bed, sharing the one stuffed chair and standing in the corners. It is great to be together again. We love them all like family from forming such a tight relationship when we were all in Lahore. Unfortunately Tim and Paula don't have as much time for the holidays as we do and cannot do the Everest trek with the rest us. We will spend a couple days all together and then go our separate ways.

"We still like the school, the students and the teachers, but political problems and dangers are increasing," answers Tim as he curls his long legs under him on the bed. "More American families are leaving the country these days and other international folks continue to depart as fundamentalism and violence increase," adds Paula as she leans up against Tim. "One of the new teachers recently had their van shot at as they drove home from school. She got a bad scratch on her neck from shrapnel but was OK. Several bricks were thrown over the school wall a few weeks ago and we think it might be some of our own students. There have just been too many incidents. We are thinking of starting a family and want to go home. We have decided this will be our last year in Lahore and have turned down a new contract."

"Well, I'm glad we left on a pretty good note, and especially pleased that you could take a break and meet us here in Nepal for Christmas," I reply as another round of hugs and laughs begins and we ask more questions about our friends and students we left behind.

The streets below soon beckon our adventurous crew to explore so we dive down the narrow stairs to get immersed in the amazing life of Katmandu.

The air is smoky with exhaust from small engines and the burning of trash to stay warm. Sweet smells of gardenia garlands mingle

Namaste

with pungent odors of incense and curry. "Namaste," comes the friendly greeting from a toothless smile of a wrinkled old man as he offers the traditional bow and praying hands. Wearing native clothes mixed with western ones, the Nepalese people are laid back, friendly and a little shy. The narrow cobbled alleys with little vehicle traffic are easy to stroll through to observe the daily life of this fascinating culture. A hippie haven for many years, there are little coffee shops and even a small western used bookstore where travelers can make an exchange. Explorers come to climb the mountains, to pursue Buddhism or yoga or just hang out where life is cheap and simple, the people friendly and the scenery marvelous even if it isn't so clean and orderly.

Finely carved arches of dark wood surround a small old doorway that opens into a family courtyard. Mother in a long scarlet cotton skirt and blue-buttoned blouse is pulling and fluffing soft white flax fibers. Father in a plaid sarong and a light beige jacket winds the flax to spin it into thread with his wheel as their children gather pieces into piles to use like we use cotton. The father smiles, waves, and allows a photo.

Babies are crawling around everywhere. The birth rate is high. These tiny tots, dirty from matted hair to crusty toes, wear only little T-shirts partially covering naked bottoms. They play in the muddy streets and garbage with a black string tied tight around their unclothed waist to ward off evil spirits. Good luck with that.

Shrines are tucked into little crannies in the walls, black from centuries of burning incense, strewn with fresh flowers and spice offerings at the base of Buddhas and Gods or saints I do not recognize.

The tourist industry thrives here and many Nepalese make their livings this way. Exotic trinkets of brass, bronze and cheap silver lie on blankets in the market streets with wrinkled old women or men in their traditional, colorful dress calling us to buy. T-shirts and wool clothing are embroidered with fiery red dragons and blue and white mountain scenes. I love this stuff and will fill my bags before we depart. Such fun gifts! OK, I must admit that much of it will end up adorning my own place.

"Look, I give you good price." A lady follows me around with a really cool dragon necklace that I love but she has not come to a price I love. She keeps following and asking and I walk away doing other shopping for close to an hour. We finally settle on a price and I get this dragon face made of bone and adorned with turquoise and coral that is supposed to keep away evil spirits. I wear it often and have not yet seen any evil spirits so I guess it works.

Processing Flax

Sweaters in the daytime and light coats at night are comfy here in the valley but they say it will be much colder up in the mountains. It is January in the Himalayas after all. So we find a place to rent some real mountain clothes. Apparently some of the mountain climbing expeditions leave equipment behind and the locals can make some money by selling or renting it. Each of us who will be hiking find a huge parka and thick gloves for about five dollars a week.

"Is anybody interested in visiting the Monkey Temple with us?" Tim asks. "I think we'll pass and take the kids to the bookstore," answers Linda. "We're game!" Ken and I agree.

Monks and monkeys, prayers and pilgrims. Perched on a hilltop in Katmandu is the Swayambhunath or Monkey Temple. We visited it last January, on a brief trip from Pakistan for a teacher's conference, but today we just really feel like going again. We have learned to follow our instincts.

Prayer wheels

A hill with many many steps takes us up to a small plateau overlooking all of the Katmandu Valley. Monkeys approach cautiously for food while playing and climbing over the shrines and swinging through the drooping shade trees. Nepalese pilgrims are spinning lines of wooden or metal prayer drums as they walk around in worship. A short monk in an orange robe with a nametag spins an individual prayer wheel in his hand, making himself available to anyone who asks. Inside these prayer drums carved with devotions are thousands of prayers written on thin paper and curled tightly. Spinning the drums sends all of these prayers to God.

The monastery is busy with pilgrims, tourists and monkeys but not too crowded. Tim, Paula, Ken and I roam around quietly, taking pictures, feeling the good spiritual vibes, and just hanging out, for about an hour or so.

We are about ready to leave when we hear faint, rhythmic music coming from somewhere behind the shrines. "Do you hear horns?" Paula asks as we sit on the steps of a monument feeding crackers to the monkeys. "Yes, and it sounds like drums too. Let's go check it out," I answer.

Stepping quietly through the wooden double doors of the large temple at the back of the monastery grounds we move up to an altar. Hundreds of burning candles shine their golden light at the base of a large Buddha sitting in lotus position. The sweet sound of music and chanting draws us around the altar to a long hall where a monk beckons us to come toward him. The orange robed man pulls open a curtain to unveil an amazing scene.

One of my favorite movies that I have seen many times is "The Golden Child" with Eddie Murphy. It is filled with a combination of humor, spirituality, magic and irreverence that is quite fun. Anyway, the scenes from Nepal are magical but real and this must be one of them.

Before us lies an inner sanctuary of chanting, bald, orange-robed monks. Two lines of them sitting cross-legged on long low, cushioned benches face each other, with a shrine of the Buddha at one end and two ten foot long horns stretching down the center. Two young boys on each end keep a slow steady beat on huge thundering drums. Older monks with brass symbols alternately play or chant while the deep sound of the melodious horns vibrates within our bodies.

Sliding quietly behind them, close to the wall of the narrow room we find some cushions to sit on and settle in. With long deep breaths the slow beat of the

Monkey Temple

chants, horns and drums begins to re-tune my body as I meditate. It feels exhilarating, intense, ancient, and immediate. There are about fourteen monks, the four of us and a few other pilgrims.

At one moment I am with them only. And then I can see them superimposed with the Sufi qawwali chanters we knew from Pakistan, the Hindu mantras of the gurus of India and the Christian hymns of the church choir. All use chanting to call their minds and bodies to pay attention, to try to see beyond the physical, to reach a state somewhere in tune with the universe. All of the human race, fascinating in its diversity, melds into similarity.

December 25.

For months we worked with Sam and Linda planning this expedition to hike the trails toward the Everest base camps during our three-week winter vacation. We arranged to travel Nepal together with the help of a Nepali trekking agency Sam had organized through our Dhaka school. Although we usually like to travel on our own, the logistics of mountain hiking and flying in this country requires the help of local agents and guides. Our agent has arranged for our airline tickets and hired a guide with some porters who will meet us in Lukla to hike.

Our trekking group consists of thirteen. The Sloffers – Sam, Linda, their son fifteen year old Ty who is also in my biology class, and thirteen year old, Monica. The Wilsons - Chuck and Becky, cousins of Linda in the American military coming from a post in Belgium. One guide and four Sherpa porters will meet us in Lukla.

It is Christmas day and we are waiting at the Kathmandu airport for a small eighteen passenger Twin Otter aircraft. With two props it is built for short take off and landings. The sky must be absolutely clear to fly because "there are rocks in those clouds," according to the pilots. Their lives and ours depend on how they maneuver through the clouds and mountains. Sometimes people wait for weeks. We are very lucky and we only wait a few hours to get the OK to board.

Linda and Jane disembarking in Lukla

We are flying into Lukla in the Khumbu region of Nepal; the staging point for most expeditions heading to Everest. The airport, at 9,100 feet has one of the most dangerous landings in the world. Holding tight to our seats we oooohhh, aaahhh and gasp as the plane shifts altitudes and moves between the breath-taking mountain peaks. These small planes cannot fly above them and the drafts between them are like riding a bronco. There is no door between us and the cockpit. We watch the spectacular mountains loom before us right out the front window as the pilots work to keep the aircraft stable. Boy, what a ride! After 35 minutes of stunning mountain views, breathlessly gasping and gripping the seat at each shift of the plane, we dive almost straight down onto a rocky, unpaved, short mountain airstrip. Braking hard to keep from slamming into the mountain smack in front of us, we finally land safely on the ground in Lukla. There is a burnt-out wrecked plane on the edge of the runway that missed its mark on a recent unsuccessful flight. We are eager to step out of the plane and feel safely grounded. "Whew! Best hundred bucks I ever spent!" Ken exclaims as he jumps out of the plane.

Above Lukla, surrounded by mountains

Ahhh! The air is fresh and clean, chilly and perfect. The afternoon sun shines brightly on the white snowy peaks surrounding us. We are really here, a lifetime dream, to hike with the Gods at the top of the world. Mount Everest here we come!!

Our guide meets us at the plane with four Sherpa porters. Wonderful people, the Sherpas are gentle, quiet, friendly and helpful.

Their life consists mostly of hiking. The mountain trails of Nepal are too steep, narrow and uneven for other forms of transport. Yaks are used to carry certain things but it is safer to walk than to ride them. They are difficult to own as they require forage and it is hard enough to grow food for people here on these rocky slopes. The people walk and carry everything with packs or straw baskets that strap across their forehead and hang down their back. Eighty pounds or more they can lug up the steep slopes and most of Sherpas weigh little more than that. Everyone starts to carry as soon as they can walk.

Our trek agent and the hiking guide have been very helpful. They are also setting up a simpler trip for the AISD eighth grade class trip this spring, and have been especially accommodating. You cannot get a flight to Lukla unless an agency books it for you. The agent reserved hotel rooms and set up a guide and porters. So when we arrive at the Lukla airport the Sherpas carry our gear up a short hill to a café where we re-pack for days of hiking in the Himalayas. We get organized and ready to set off on the trail right away.

"How heavy is your pack? Here, give it to me," Ken grabs my backpack and tries it on. "Feels heavy."

"It's fine, I can handle it," I respond stubbornly.

"Maybe, but that's what we have porters for. Give them another ten pounds. They can carry it and you will be able to climb a lot easier."

I give in and hand over some heavy bags of nuts and dried fruit. We adjust our packs, giving most of the weight to our porters, keeping some water, food and clothes we will need during the day. We aren't camping and will be eating dinner at guesthouses so we don't have to carry as much as we did in Pakistan.

As soon as our packs are ready, we take off up the trail for our first day's short, two-hour hike to a guesthouse in Phakding. The scenery is awesome. There are tiny villages along the way but mostly it is just snow-peaked mountains and trails. Beautiful, majestic

Sherpa & Jane

and more forested than I had expected. Much of Nepal has been stripped of its trees for lumber and firewood. It is illegal for trekkers to use wood for a fire and in this region it is often too steep to get to some of the trees and so they remain.

"Joy to the World...." "Silent Night, Holy Night......" Tonight is Christmas night. A small simple trekking lodge provides shelter in the quiet, cold, black night of the Himalayas. No electricity. No engines. No indoor plumbing. Wearing huge down jackets we cuddle next to a barely warm wood stove by the light of a kerosene lantern. We sip hot chocolate after savoring a steamy bowl of creamy hot potato soup. Our Sherpa's surround us smiling as we heartily belt out familiar Christmas carols. Outside, white flakes of a soft snow hit the windows and begin to lightly cover the hills. We are in heaven!

"I'm not feeling too great," Ken reluctantly admits when we are getting ready for sleep. We are already over 8,000 feet high or over 2,600 meters and are having some signs of altitude sickness. Ken seems especially affected but doesn't like to show it. Headache, nausea and trouble sleeping might be common after a day of hiking but they are signs to take seriously. Being strong or big or healthy doesn't seem to matter, as it affects some more quickly than others. Coming from a sea-level life in Bangladesh does not help. Acclimation is very important as our bodies deal with altitude. From just outside Kathmandu, some Everest climbers actually hike seven days to get to Lukla to allow their bodies to adjust. Flying directly to high altitudes can cause the brain to swell and kill you. With so many adverse reactions to altitude change we need to pay attention and not push ourselves.

"Are you sure you'll be OK?" asks Linda at breakfast.

"Yeah, we'll be fine. Ken and I will take a day off to acclimate, relax and do a little reading here by the fire," I ensure her. "We'll keep one porter here with us. You guys go ahead and we'll catch up tomorrow at Namche Bazaar."

December 27

After a quiet day of reading by the fire and going for a short walk near the cabin, we are ready to hit the trail as soon as the sun peaks over the mountains in the morning. Ken's kidneys still feel a little swollen but he insists he'll be OK and is anxious to get moving.

We give much of our food and heavier gear to the one shy-faced smiling porter who we share. Pirim, a quiet, strong, stocky young man, will make our six hour up-hill hike today much more pleasant. I'm carrying only about twenty-five pounds on my back while he carries about seventy just as easily. It is a good thing that this path to Everest has guesthouses, as carrying camping and cooking gear up these steep slopes would be out of the question unless we did some serious body building first or hired a lot more porters.

It is a gorgeous hike. Deep valleys and snow top peaks are connected with foot-traffic-only suspension bridges used by the Nepalese people. All carry something on their backs. Moving slowly but steadily, with a strap wrapped around his forehead that is tied behind his back, a young man drags six, wide, heavy boards over 8 feet long behind him. Even building materials must be carried here by backs. There are some yaks but they do not seem to be carrying as much as the people.

There are not enough adjectives to describe the Himalayas. Dramatically shooting above the clouds, glistening starkly white in the sunshine with their snow tops jutting into the deep clear dark blue sky. Being here in the middle of it is overwhelming. Time and reality seem to drop away with each upward step. Sounds only of the wind along with the breathtaking scenery fill me with the relaxed consciousness that I only feel in nature. The troubles of civilization and daily life fall away as we climb into the heavens.

Most villages up here have no electricity or phone. There are no roads, only hiking trails. No vehicles at all. Some have enough electric for lights at night coming from small hydroelectric generators perched in waterfalls in the mountains. Yaks are common but not plentiful. Short furry bovines with tough horns and bushy tales, they seem to be saddled for riders but so far I have only seen them carrying bags of cargo slung over their backs. I think the men can carry more than the yaks. This is the off-season and so there are not many hikers or mountaineers.

"Namaste". The broad-faced smiling Nepalese people we meet along the trail are relaxed, friendly and helpful. Their Buddhist background teaches them to strive to be unattached to the miseries of the world and they seem to have a fairly carefree attitude. Perhaps living a life so close to nature and without TV and other modern entertainments, gives them a good reason to connect with other people.

It seems as if every big curve along the path is graced with a shrine. Individual rocks carved with devotions are stacked in a neat pile and strung with prayer flags blowing their desires to the Gods.

We hike on and off with Brooks, a young man we met on the trail this morning. He teaches outdoor fitness classes and is here on vacation hiking alone. After a strenuous day the three of us finally stroll into Namche Bazaar to meet the Sloffer family and the rest of our expedition at the Thamsaku Lodge.

"Hey, Ken and Jane! Glad you made it! Are you feeling any better?" asks Sam as he calls for the cook to make us some hot tea.

"Not really," Ken confesses. "I was hoping the hike would be energizing, but I'm afraid my kidneys still feel swollen and my headache is worse. Maybe a good night's sleep will help."

Thamsaku Lodge is a simple place hugging the mountainside with no electricity or running water. A funky little place, it is better than expected and easier than camping. They make hot, tasty food and have simple bunks for weary trekkers.

The bottom floor houses the owner's family. Upstairs are the bedrooms, kitchen and eating area with shelves for kitchenware. Walls are plastered with posters and faded magazine pages. A small counter holds simple items for sale such as toilet paper, canned soda, candy, and outdated crackers. There are three "bedrooms". One large room can sleep ten and two small private rooms. Simple is the word. Beds of wood with a thin pad. No heat, toilets or anything else.

A huge clay stove burns all day long in the dining area where we sit and visit. Dinner takes a while. Everybody orders, and then the woman of the house cooks one or two things at a time. Three potato soups are served and then two rice and veggie soups are made and served separately. In the meantime we all sit around the warm stove and chat with the other travelers until we have all eaten and are ready for bed.

Food and rooms are cheap. A big bowl of soup is only 50¢, black Tea 10 cents, and a bunk in a dorm room is only 35¢ but we have our own private room for a big $2.00.

There is no bathroom, just an outhouse and water in a pan. After days of exercise without a shower I feel pretty greasy. I keep my hat on and don't look in a mirror. Handy wipes can only get me so clean. Most of the locals don't look much better with a thin layer of grime coloring their hands and face a shade darker. I guess it helps to prevent sunburn. Nepal is only about 30 degrees in latitude, about the same as Tampa, Florida and everyone is tan from the strong sun and lots of time outside.

There is a hot shower here. We simply ask for a big pot of water heated on the stove, dump it into a bucket with a cup and stand outside on the side of the hut behind a few boards to "shower" as quickly as we can in the freezing cold. The toilet is also outside. We stand over a hole in the wooden outhouse and everything drops over the edge of the mountain. We stop eating and drinking early so we don't have to use it in the middle of the night when a little slip could send us over the side as well.

Cooking potato soup in the guesthouse kitchen

The food tastes good here but there is little protein in it. Mostly rice, potatoes and kale with garlic. But the soup is hot, creamy with yak butter and really does hit the spot. The nuts and dried fruit we have brought with us add nutrition and needed calories.

We meet some interesting characters trekking. This morning a young French Buddhist monk stopped into the guesthouse for tea. He had just been to see his reincarnated lama in a cave higher up the mountain.

"I'm freezing. Do you think we could squeeze into the same sleeping bag?" I ask Ken, teeth chattering as I lay awake on a separate single bed. "We can try. Come on in and get close," he offers, unzipping his puffy down bag as I spoon in tightly against him. But the tapered bag doesn't close and my legs are sticking out and hanging off the narrow bed. I go back to my bunk, put on another layer of clothes, zip up my new thick, down sleeping bag, lay my parka on top and try to sleep. Both of us have headaches and nausea, signs of altitude sickness. We are at 11,300 feet. The Himalayan winter seeps through the walls of the un-heated room as we toss and turn on the rock-hard beds. "I have to pee." Ken insists. "But I can't face going down the stairs and across the yard to the outhouse on the edge of the mountain in the middle of the freezing night." Sleepily I mumble, "I think that's what that big jar in the corner is for."

December 28

Happy birthday Christie! I think of my sister because I miss my family and wish they could join us.

We want to take it slow and spend another night here. This morning we just walked around Namche Bazaar, enjoying the views and smiling at the people as they worked at household chores. Right now it's mid-day and I am sitting with a hot cup of tea in the rest house with my thick down parka on. Ken is dozing off sitting next to the warm kerosene stove. It's snowing now but cozy enough inside. Linda gets Ty and Monica to sit close to stay warm while we play a card game. Wood is very scarce here and it is illegal for foreigners to burn it but locals can and still do. The forests of the Himalayas are mostly gone, leaving only a few trees in steep areas.

Staying warm in the Namche Bazaar guesthouse

After lunch we take another walk around the village and buy some rope, Australian hats, and a toothbrush from Norway. The little stores have some amazing stuff left here from climbing expeditions. A small Korean team comes hiking through town, having just aborted their attempt on Everest. Although skies were clear, the wind was hurricane force and the cold had taken its toll. Two of the mountaineers are wrapped in bandages covering most of their face and hands due to serious frostbite injury.

It is especially bright as the Himalayan sun penetrates right through the thin atmosphere. The sky is intensely dark blue in the middle of the day and the stars at night are magnificent, clear and sparkling. We are getting into a good rhythm of hiking, resting, eating, watching the people, talking, sleeping and just enjoying ourselves.

Most of the houses are made of stones found right here and wood that has been carried through the mountains by people-back. They are usually two or three stories high, tucked into the side of the mountain. They do have some electric lights at night that work from a small hydroelectric plant in a mountain stream. Everywhere there are prayer flags waving and rocks carved with mandalas.

Later in the afternoon we hike out of the village and up the mountain a bit farther to get a good view of Mt. Everest, Ama Dablam and Mount Nuptse. They are all spectacular peaks on the border between Tibet, China and Nepal. I think Ama Dablam is the most spectacular. The name means "Mother's Necklace" and her wide open arms are ringed with a thick white snow flowing down into her enormous lap.

The Tibetan name for Mt. Everest is Chomolungma meaning "Goddess Mother of the Earth". The Nepalese name is Sagarmatha meaning "Mother of the Sky". The British named it Everest after some man who did the geography. A bit egotistical and unimaginative I think.

December 29

Ken is still having some altitude problems but today we hike straight uphill another 2000 feet to a small town that has a hospital staffed with two Canadian doctors and a young woman medical student. The doctors are away for the day so the Canadian intern shows us around. The place was built 25 years ago to serve the Sherpa's of the area. It has an operating room, plenty of medications, a few beds for patients and a kitchen for the patient's family to use to feed their sick. As we arrive, a young Nepalese woman is being helped to leave the hospital by her parents. The intern tells us her story. "About a week ago an older women came in tears to the hospital about her dying daughter. She leads me to her home where three llamas and two spirit doctors are working unsuccessfully to cure her. One of the spirit doctors says, "she is probably afflicted with an evil spirit who attacks women who wash their hair on Tuesdays or Fridays." They won't let me touch her because, "it is bad luck to be touched by a woman before death." After much deliberation and begging to save her life they finally allow her to be carried up to the hospital and treated. With a serious case of meningitis it was a few days of hospital treatment and care before she was well enough to stagger out of the bed leaning heavily on the shoulders of her relatives." The intern shakes her head and rolls her eyes as she sighs in disbelief at her own story.

The intern is able to suggest and sell us a medication for Ken's kidney problem but she recommends the best treatment for altitude sickness is to go down the mountain. "Every year there are a few hikers who get seriously ill and sometimes even die at the heights that we are presently at, about 14,000 feet. In fact you can die overnight even at only 12,000 feet." So we take her advice, turn around, and go back down the trail, back to Namche Bazaar. We did not know altitude sickness could get serious so quickly and are thankful that our ignorance and naiveté has not been fatal. We will not go any higher.

The hike between our rest house and the little hospital is only an altitude difference of a couple thousand feet but it has amazing views of Mount Everest and Ama Dablam. There is no view like it in the world, here at the top of the Himalayas where the air is cool, fresh and thin, the sky so starkly blue and the mountains craggy and snow peaked. I cannot get enough of it and try to savor every moment.

Jane & Everest (left-snow plume)) and Ama Dablam (right)

Immersed in our own thoughts we walk quietly down the mountains enjoying the beauty and mystery of the place. The dark stripes in some of the mountainsides of the Everest range are sedimentary layers that attest to the changes that the earth has gone through. Within the layers are fossils that once lay beneath the oceans and now here they are in the highest places on earth. All things change and all things are possible.

We arrive back at the lodge to greet the Sloffers, who have just returned from the Tengboche monastery up the mountain. We had planned to make that trip with them but changed our strategy so that we could go to the hospital to inquire about Ken's health.

"It was a spectacular hike," reported Sam "but the monastery where we hoped to spend the night was nothing but a black shell." "They said the place burned down just a few weeks ago," added Ty. "Not even our Sherpas knew about it."

December 30

Wrong purpose. Today I hiked with the Sloffers to the Everest View Hotel the "highest hotel in the world," uphill about a thousand feet from the rest house in which we are staying. They carved out a short airstrip nearby where people could fly in to stay and promptly get altitude sickness. It is a gimmick and they say rooms will cost over $300 a night when it is finished, with all profit going to the Japanese owners. It is really very beautiful up there but they will fail because of 'wrong purpose'. Thinking only of money and not the people.

Ken is still sick and we are a bit worried. He is quite an athletic, active individual. Tall, strong and determined, he is not happy about staying behind but we cannot go any farther up the mountain. I don't feel perfect either but seem to be getting better.

Sanitation here could be improved. In the dining room where I am writing, the floor is made of mud and is swept but never mopped after people walk back and forth from the outdoor squat toilet. This afternoon I watched the cook sweep the floor then use the same broom to brush off the counter tops where she promptly rolled out dough and cut up veggies for the evening meal. So far we haven't gotten food poisoning. Everything is well cooked and that helps.

December 31

This morning we rose at daybreak and climbed the hill from our rest house to watch the sunrise on Mount Everest. We did a morning meditation to welcome the last decade of the 20th century from the top of the world.

Our expedition leaves Namshe Bazar to head back down the mountain after four days. For food, lodging and a porter it had only cost about $43.00 for the two of us. Simple but unique and far more interesting than a hotel stay for $300 a night. If I want comfort I can go home.

The rest of our expedition goes ahead to get back to Katmandu more quickly as we linger for another day on down the mountain. Stopping at the same rest house in Phakding where we had stayed on the way up the mountain we meet up with a couple of other travelers.

"Where are you from?" I ask the girl, Bonnie, in light conversation.

"Oregon," she replies as we chat by the fire.

"I know one person in Oregon," I remark nonchalantly. "His name is Zindani Tilchin. He is a chiropractor. Do you know him by any chance?"

Her response totally floored me.

"Yes. Zindani is a good friend of mine and actually, I know who you are! I had read your letter to Zindani that you were coming to the Himalayas and I knew that I would be in the same area so I was looking out for you."

Of course, we struck up a bit of a friendship and stopped to visit Bonnie and Zindani in Oregon the next summer, on our way back home to Florida.

That is my best small world story.

It feels sad to leave the mountains and head back to Kathmandu. Somehow the views here are both expansive and introspective. I feel like I have tested my mettle and have grown, hoping to hold onto these visions from the top of the world.

"He who climbs upon the highest mountains laughs at all tragedies, real or imaginary."   - Friedrich Neitszche

Everest (left) & sea fossil bands on Lhotse Face

Kopan Monastery, Katmandu
Jan 4, 1990

"I have just three things to teach: simplicity, patience, compassion. These three are your greatest treasures." Lao Tzu

We decided that a hotel stay for our last couple of nights in Katmandu might be uneventful. Having asked around at some hippie-hangouts for a more interesting possibility we heard about the Buddhist Kopan monastery on the edge of the Katmandu valley. Storing our gear at the hotel in town we set out in the afternoon for an overnight adventure with just our daypacks. On arrival we were shown to separate tiny cubicles. With just a wooden chair and a single bed of plywood covered by a thin mattress, the sparseness is meant to encourage contemplation. "There will be a lecture after sunset followed by a modest meal," the orange-robed monk informs us.

Monks and nuns come from all over the world to pursue a classical monastic life and education here. Some begin as young as seven years old. Some begin after they have finished with career and family responsibilities at the age of fifty or sixty. Anyone can come for a daily dharma talk by a learned elder and spend a quiet contemplative night or stay longer for meditation courses and Buddhist teachings. To encourage all souls, Kopan monastery is run by donations and you can pay what you like as no money is requested and all are welcomed with open arms.

"Here boy! Come on, fetch!" With a thick furry tail wagging his body, a burly black Tibetan mastiff bows and bounds after a stick as Ken and I play with him in the garden. After a few rounds with this friendly temple guard, Ken takes my hand in his to climb the steep grassy hill behind the monastery as late afternoon wanes. The darkening peaks of the Himalayan Mountains encircle a beautiful view of the setting sun streaking red and orange across the whole of the Kathmandu valley. Just sitting, enjoying the fresh clear quiet air and relaxing we finally head over to the lecture.

An elderly monk wearing black-rimmed glasses sits in lotus position and speaks of absolute simplicity and a life of non-attachment. "The less you own, the fewer your worries." Some monks eat only once a day from a begging bowl, depending solely on handouts. "Simplicity allows more time for focus on learning, understanding, mindfulness and compassion. Pursuing these goals is a higher path than chasing material goals," the monk explains the evening lesson of the day in Tibetan and again in English.

Mastiff temple guards

The simple supper of beans, cabbage and rice is enough to provide nutrition and warm our bellies but not fill us up, and that is the point. A full belly dulls the senses.

"I enjoyed the lecture on simplicity before dinner," Ken reflects as we leave the dining hall and sit on a bench in the garden under the bright moon.

"Simplicity is also an ecological goal." I expound to Ken, as he sits close and listens thoughtfully to my contemplations. "Our earth and our humanity are being destroyed by our incessant pursuit of material goods. More, bigger, better means more factories, mines, stores, trucks, asphalt and energy for every single object we buy. We think it will make us happy, as that is what the advertisers and economists and even governments promise. But every religion, psychologist, and counselor tells us otherwise. With simplicity as our goal we could work less, learn more and have better relationships. Good for us. Good for those around us. Good for the earth and our future." Ken knows all this but listens patiently. "I guess I can throw out all your clothes then?" He teases as he tickles my side. We kiss and head off to our separate evenings of solitude.

As darkness brings emerging stars twinkling in the black sky outside my window, I close my eyes to a restless sleep. I dream of a troubled student who cheats, steals, fights and does drugs. The counselor wants us to throw him out of school. The teachers decide to confront him and lots of conflict ensues. But in the end he learns better ways to handle his energy and becomes a real asset, even saving someone's life. Compassion sometimes requires conflict and always involves patience. It is our job as teachers to help students to direct their energy productively, even when they resist. I have been having some trouble with a belligerent student lately and this dream was inspiring.

I guess a little solitude in a monastery has been more enlightening than a night at a hotel.

The lingering deep, clear echo of a huge brass bell hanging outside the temple beckons us to early morning meditation. Not yet light at 5:30 AM, rubbing away the sleepiness from our eyes we rise and stumble over to the community toilets for a brief cleansing.

"Om Mani Padme hum." "Om Mani Padme hum." With shaved heads, wearing robes of orange, red and ochre, they twirl wooden beads in knurled hands. A simple flute and a harmonium are played to keep our rhythm. The harmonium is a very small organ with about an eighteen-inch keyboard in a

The Kopan Monastery

ten-inch high wooden box with a bellows on the back. It is used extensively in temples in this part of the world, as it is easy to transport and to play while sitting cross-legged on the rug. "Om Mani Padme hum." For almost two hours we chant and meditate during the morning puja. The harmony eventually clears my mind and wraps around and through my heart. The words of the mantra are a prayer to invoke compassion and mindfulness. The Buddhists, above all, strive for

217

compassion for each other as well as for all living things. "Om Mani Padme hum." "Om Mani Padme hum." Some of the youngsters are a bit fidgety but they are trying. The elders seem to be totally together as one. We all chant together. "Om Mani Padme hum." The rhythm, harmony and meaning sink ever more deeply. One with each other. One with the universe. Compassion for all. "Om Mani Padme hum." "Om Mani Padme hum."

We leave the monastery after prayers, riding a motor-rickshaw back to town. We head to Mike's, the favorite breakfast spot of expats, for some whole-wheat pancakes and fresh fruit.

On our last evening in Kathmandu we head back to the hotel through dark and mostly deserted streets after dinner. The Buddha passes by! A great big monk covered in ochre robes from head to toe rides calmly by in a colorful bicycle rickshaw pulled by a skinny, turbaned driver. A smile wider than the street spreads across his round jolly face, as his peaceful presence lights up and warms the darkness. He gently nods and passes on by, seemingly cruising around to spread some light and compassion.

"Did you see what I saw?" I ask Ken, staring down the street wide-eyed. "Yes." We join hands, pull closer and continue walking along with wide smiles, nodding at everyone we see.

"Thousands of candles can be lit from a single candle, and the life of the candle will not be shortened. Happiness never decreases by being shared."
  - Buddha

Tigers, Coconuts and Kids (See map p. 170)
Sundarban National Forest, Jan 1990.

Education is what remains after one has forgotten everything he learned in school. - Albert Einstein

"Pirates? Tigers? Crocodiles? Are you sure you want to take children there? You better take at least two or three armed guards." A British crew had just come back from a two-month geological expedition and warned us of the multiple troubles in the region. They wondered why we would want to take our students to such a dangerous area. Our high school principal, Dave Wallin had read about one-too-many outward-bound programs and insisted that a hardship voyage fraught with danger was just the thing for teenagers. I tried hard to find another trip and worried about the sanity of our leader but I was new to the school and I was not the principal.

Tigers attack over 50 people every year in the Sundarban area. Armed pirates are known to cruise the waters and board ships to steal anything they can and take hostages when it suits them. Crocodiles swim the marshy swamps and can bolt from behind bushes to make an easy lunch of slow-running prey such as tenth-graders with backpacks. But we are going to take the risks anyway.

Coconuts delivered for our trip

We have spent much time preparing for this trip. Months of gathering information, lining up a riverboat and making lists of what to take.

Buying, stocking, organizing and coordinating kept us busy. We were not likely to see potable fresh water for about ten days and the river water would be polluted. Dave wanted to take 800 green coconuts as our sole source of fluids for drinking and cooking and planned to bathe and even wash dishes in the river. The rest of us insisted on bringing our own 5-gallon jugs of clean, pre-boiled water to drink, brush our teeth and rinse faces and dishes. Handi-wipes were a must.

I would have felt much better if Ken were going with us. I have learned to depend on him for his army-trained protectiveness, his mechanical-fix-anything abilities and my partner in solving most any problem together. But we are the only science teachers and he is taking a separate rough trip with the ninth graders. They will be flying to Chittagong and boating to St. Martin's Island to the very south of Bangladesh just off the coast of Burma in a story all their own.

The school facilities director managed to get the American Embassy to loan us a VHF radio so that we can keep in touch with them if anything happens. A couple of marines install it on the top deck and teach Shishir, John and Jason how to use it to check in daily with the embassy. The boys enjoy taking this important responsibility and are quite good and dependable with it.

Important responsibility is something that our youth do not often get enough of. Life in developed countries has gotten so easy that we rarely have to rely on the help of our children. We need to have faith in them before they can have confidence in themselves. Group expeditions are especially good for sharing responsibilities. We also must remember that our children trust us not to put them into serious danger, which is why I question this excursion.

School field trips are a big deal here. 9 to 10 days of traveling with hoards of teenagers is an especially big deal for me as a chaperone. But it is, after all, more interesting than the everyday classroom. So we plan to sail off with the 10th and 11th grade, 25 of them and eight adults on a small old cargo boat into the tropical jungle home of the Bengali tiger. No matter that the river water is saline, heavily polluted and there will be no clean water available. No matter that the captain has no education, does not understand the tides of the Bay of Bengal and is known to get stuck on sand bars. No matter that the seven crewmembers have absolutely no regard for safety or for proper prior planning. We are taking coconuts with us, so everything will be OK. Right? But then I guess none of us live in Bangladesh because it's safe. So we prepare to see what we can see.

"Can we get the captain to add a length of bamboo parallel to the deck at waist height as a handrail?" I ask. The tin surface of the narrow exterior walkway is wet, slippery and curved toward the outside so that we slide to the edge every step we take and will surely lose someone overboard.

Loading the "African Queen"

Mosquito nets are secured around the "windows" that are just framed openings in the walls of the cabins. Although we will be taking anti-malaria drugs there are other nasty diseases carried by bugs that bring more than an itchy bite. An extra "men's room" had to be built. It is a toilet seat set over a wooden box off the edge of the deck with thin plywood walls around it. The girls have their own private wooden hole next to the main cabin decorated with a handful of pink plastic flowers and a can of perfumed air freshener.

Together with the students during classes we evolve our educational program for daily journal entries and scientific data collection before our trip begins. We will take microscopes to see the tiny critters, binoculars for the distant ones and nets to see what we can gather from the water. Each day we are to test for temperatures, PH and salinity of the river, as well as humidity, temperature and visual quality of the air. They are to spend at least 1 hour daily recording the kinds of life they see, using guidebooks for identification. In groups of three of the same sex they are to keep a health watch record noting the heart rate, temperature, and their physiological and mental states. Although science is the overall focus, the trip is interdisciplinary.

The Sundarban National Park is a unique biosphere and tiger reserve in the Ganges delta of India and Bangladesh. Densely covered by mangrove forests the large wetlands area is fed by fresh water and fertile silt of the Himalayan mountain range flowing down into fingerlets of the Bay of Bengal. Home to a wide variety of tropical animals including monkeys, wild boar and a sizeable number of saltwater crocodiles, it is also the largest reserve in the world for Bengal tigers. The man-eating kind. The topography, islands, mudflats and waterways change shape with the monsoons and cyclones of the wet season making navigation difficult.

It is a trip that Ken and I would be more than excited to do on our own, but not as chaperones. I was desperately hoping that all would go well.

AISD Students ready to go!

Wednesday, January 31

Weather is good for our planned departure so we load up kids and gear in the school vans and head down to the river to board the boat after classes are over. By 5:00 PM we are all loaded and ready.

Some of the older boys, Ty, John, Jason, Shishir and Christian had come down earlier with a couple of chaperones to bring all the equipment so we can get going without too much delay.

"Mrs. Cundiff, I think this railing will hold us OK," reports Bjor, grabbing the bamboo to test it.

"The girls out-house has been cleaned and sprayed down with air freshener," Nicole and Shantini shout from the deck.

"The food and coconuts are in the hull below deck," remarks Stefano as he and Chris climb up out of the galley.

The students have all done their assigned tasks and are ready to push off.

Crowded with large brightly painted riverboats and swarming with smaller simple wooden rowboats, the Dhaka port teams with life. Riverfront villagers bathe and wash clothes in the murky water right next to stacks of leaky oil barrels, floating garbage and boat sludge. So much for poor homeless people trying to stay clean. Boats bumping against each other, shouting orders from dock crews, crying seagulls and a cacophony of sound add to the bustle. Up on shore, brick factories spew thick clouds of pollution from tall, dirty smokestacks, reducing our visibility as we begin to boat down the river, away from the city and away from the chaos.

"*Purple Rain*" blares from the kid's boom box on the top of the ship as we all find a spot to settle in on deck, forward facing toward this big adventure. The light breeze, the motor chugging, the comfortable evening temperatures and a lovely golden pink sunset flows across and calms the busy river. Heading out to the Bay of Bengal we relax, enjoy the views and wonder where our journey will really take us.

"I miss Ken already and I do wish I had put something of me in his bag as I just found a little 'I love you' note in my pouch." I confide to Evelyn, another chaperone. "How sweet! I'm sure he misses you too," she answers. "My husband's probably glad to have some free time."

The boat ride is more fun than I expect and we are all enjoying the trip so far. We have a really good group of chaperones and the kids are amazing. Sitting in small groups and chatting, the students are already beginning to take some journal notes as we float along in the relaxing evening.

Evelyn brought cheese, crackers and pate and Maura brought a tablecloth, a big jug of rum and a couple small vases of plastic flowers to brighten the dingy cabins. It is often the little things that make hardship easier and life more fun. There are four women chaperones in our cabin. Maura, the school nurse, Evelyn a PE teacher and Pam a parent volunteer are all tough experienced travelers and teachers.

This boat is reminiscent of the old movie "The African Queen" with mosquito nets, hurricane lanterns and red and blue paint peeling from the old wooden walls. I half-expect to see Humphrey Bogart walking the dark decks at night with a glowing cigar. Very basic and barely floating with a bit of a starboard list, this scow usually just carries large bags of rice and other freight up and down the river.

There is more traffic on the water at night than I anticipated. Most boats are traveling without lights to 'save energy' until other boats come way too close. Right now there is about an 80-foot cargo boat running alongside us on a pitch-black night and all you can see are a few dim lights on the deck. There is not much concern over safety in this country so I take it on myself to worry about everything and alert the captain often. "Don't you see that big boat coming right at us? Watch out for that dock! Aren't you going a little too fast?" Since he doesn't speak much English it's mostly a game of charades from a wacky schoolteacher. I do my part.

Thursday morning February 1

Traveling on this big old boat is a step back in time and certainly in facilities. With no electric or running water small hurricane lanterns brighten our tiny cabins at night and we wash hands and dishes from our jugs of water. 'Cabin' is not quite the right word. Our 'beds' are narrow 18-inch wide wooden benches that line the walls, topped with a blanket. This is after all, a freight carrier. The female teachers have the biggest room with four benches and a small table to fit in the center. I am fairly comfy on an inch thick foam pad that sweet Evelyn brought along for me. Three other cabins are very tiny with only two short benches and just barely room to stand between or lay another 'bed' at night. The students have pitched a couple of tents on top of the boat and usually four or five squeeze into them at night. The flimsy white mosquito netting we tacked onto the open windows all across both sides of the boat has been nice for privacy but not really that important for bugs as they don't seem to be as bad as we thought at this time of year.

We ran aground last night about 1:00 AM on a sandbar. There was tons of shouting from the captain and crew while revving up the engines, but to no avail. "We can't sleep," reported Shantini, Leone, Carin and Shama as they stood in front of the teacher's cabin wrapped in blankets. "OK, come on in then," invited Evelyn. We could not sleep either of course, with all of the hullabaloo, so we sat up, squeezed together with the girls and gathered round to complain, laugh and eat cherry poptarts. The boys could be heard having fun over a game of poker in the tent on the top deck.

As dawn broke we saw that we were still stuck on a spit of land and fishermen were gathering to stare at us here in the middle of nowhere. There is a dead dolphin washed ashore and a faint call from the loudspeakers of a distant mosque to greet us on our first morning on the river with an unscheduled stop.

Saturday, February 3

All day Thursday and Friday we spend riding down the river doing activities with the students. "Group two! Saquib, Stefano, Richard and Carin! Its your time to go on watch," I call from the top deck. For one hour they survey the landscape to share observations and record environmental notes. "Group three's turn to catch critters in the river," I add as Shama, Ty, Alain and Sayera jump up to get the long-handled fishnets. The other groups are preparing food or checking their blood pressure. All of them seem to be involved and enjoying their tasks.

We have to use the microscopes for tiny discoveries in the river. We hoped to be looking at some fish or crabs or something else that we might have caught in the nets but it seems like there are not many big things alive in this murky water. Raw human waste and chemical pollution dumped from boats and expelled by Dhaka, a city of millions, tends to kill a lot of wildlife.

"Come look at this, Mrs. Cundiff! I found a teensy crab under the microscope!" Helena grabs my arm to show me her catch. I am glad she is excited, as I am trying hard to be enthusiastic and positive, even though we have gathered very little in the nets.

We anchored at a busy river port on Thursday evening. Thirty or forty boats of all sizes and shapes bumped against each other, loading and unloading, coming and going and making a racket all night long. Nobody was getting much sleep, again.

Is it just coincidence this beach we plan to camp on is called Tiger Point? Tigers can and do swim. We finally arrive at the small deserted island of our destination late this afternoon about 4:30. The boat has to anchor hundreds of feet away because of the shallow water. The mainland lies less than a mile behind us and the island beach before us slopes upward to the rich tropical greenery of palms, mangroves and scruffy pines. The expansive sea of the Bay of Bengal opens up beyond, stretching to the horizon. One by one we climb down the wooden plank gingerly joining the others in our tippy little skiff to move in groups of eight to the shore.

The wide sandy beach melding into the forest appears to be a camper's delight. It feels so good to be out in nature on a deserted island away from all the people and the city. A couple of fishermen have come by but we are really pretty alone now. Our boat crew sets up the colorful, large shamiana awning for us as a necessity to keep out the tropical sun but there is not much time before it will set. We follow an animal path to the center of the island for a short hike and spot a herd of small, spotted deer. The villagers are not allowed to kill them because they are food for the protected tigers and so the deer are fairly tame and monitor us from the grass and shrub before they scatter.

We have pitched the tents and will spend our days here but we are not sure about the nights yet. The name of the island is a bit disconcerting. The fishermen say there are no tigers here but we have found some unclear large prints in the mushy sand. They could be deer, wild hogs or possibly tiger. They are the size of a very large dog.

"We plan to stay on the boat tonight until we can determine the owner of those large prints in the sand. Anyone who wants to stay with us is welcome," Evelyn, Maura, and I announce to the students. "Or you can choose to stay in tents on the island with Mr. Wallin," I continue.

All but Jason decide to sleep on the boat until we can determine whether there are tigers or not. One lone occupied tent on the shore stands as bait to see if the night is safe.

Sunday, February 4

"The concept of conservation is a far truer sign of civilization than that spoilation of a continent which we once confused with progress."
— Peter Matthiessen

The tent on the beach is still standing and Mr. Wallin and Jason are quite alive and waving us to come ashore. After spending the night safely on the boat we take an exploratory walk around the island to check out all the footprints and decide they are probably boar and not tiger. Although boar can also be a problem we decide to go ahead, take the risk, stick together and camp in the wild. We hope the local fishermen are right about no tigers here.

After our camping breakfast of oatmeal and raisins I gather about a dozen students for a long ecological beach walk. We have split them into two groups so Maura and I can take just a dozen at a time while the other group does camping chores with Dave and Evelyn.

Hundreds of red sand crabs run in and out of holes entertaining us as we pick them up to get a closer look and then watch them run for dear life from us invasive monsters. Shiny brown minnows slither in the shallow pools of water near shore. A few tiny mudskipper fish, stranded from high tide, are carefully placed back into the sea by Sydney, Richard and Carin. "Why are these little fish getting stuck up here on shore; won't they die?" asks Carin as she holds one flipping and flashing, silvery in the sun. "These little guys have evolved to eat all the tiny critters and particles of decaying matter that gather where the forest washes into the ocean and the sea rushes in. They can live out of water for a while as long as they stay wet and muddy." I answer.

Brown kites, egrets, and little mice skitter in and out of their nests and boroughs going about their daily mangrove activities. "This complex system has more integrated parts than we can possibly understand. The thousands of visible organisms we see don't hold a candle to the millions of microorganisms present. It is impossible to determine all the effects of the connectivity," I explain as the kids gather round to see Carin's squirming bulgy-eyed critter. "That little mudskipper eats tiny bugs keeping their populations in check while leaving its waste behind to feed the fungi and bacteria that in turn feed the roots of these plants which give us their oxygen. The kids take notes as Carin returns the fish to the muddy shore. "Mangroves and all marshes are preciously important ecosystems to preserve, as the biodiversity is just as high as rain forests. Tigers are top predators here and important to keep this web of life balanced." We are careful to leave no trace of disturbance other than footprints.

While we were out hiking Shishir, one of the eleventh graders, decided to take our small shuttle boat to go exploring on his own, without permission. "I got to see the biggest monitor lizard I have ever seen in my life and a crocodile that was enormous. Tiger tracks were all over in the mud." And he wondered why he got in trouble and we were upset and praying to get him home alive.

Monday, February 5

The thick mangrove swamps were difficult to navigate but promised new discoveries around each curve of the narrow waterways. Tied to the back of our cargo ship we have carried a small inflatable Zodiac boat with a 40 horsepower motor that can hold about 8 people. It serves as a good shuttle to shore as well as a serviceable vehicle for traversing the shallow, narrow waterways of the tropical swamps. The dense jungle teams with life as bird chatter, monkey howls, insect humming and frog peeping fills the moist warm air. Critters disappear into the murky water, leaving only the swirls to challenge our guesses. It looks a little like the Everglades of Florida except for the tiger prints. A small troop of Rhesus macaques rush through the bush, scurry to the waterfront to grab washed up wild yellow fruits and disappear back into the woods. A five-foot crocodile basks in the warm sun in a small sandy alcove to ignore us. At a distance but quite clearly a black panther moves across a shallow creek, slinking back into the thick forest on the other side. Three otters splash in play while a red-beaked, blue-backed kingfisher hunts for a meal. A pair of turquoise-purple birds dart across the bright blue sky diving down to threaten a wild boar foraging on the shore near their nesting site. All life seems to dance in a harmony of give and take, fast and slow pirouettes, each with its own creative purpose. And we have to be careful not to fit into their food web.

Looking for tigers in the Sundarban

The next morning tiny mammal prints and a few deer tracks are circled in the sand around our tents but nothing big, so we feel just a little better about our decision to camp. I had borrowed a small pup tent from my friend Patty Sonnet and therefor have a private 'room' of my own. The kids are working out little problems and weaving stronger relationships in their shared spaces. After our busy daily schedules the 'lights out' curfew is usually more welcome than not.

This afternoon we are taking six kids at a time to go walking through the island's jungle. A forest guide hired from the National Forest station on the mainland will lead us. We are supposed to have two guides with shotguns in case of a wild boar or tiger attack.

We do not get attacked and we see lots of tropical birds and about eight herds of small wild spotted deer. The graceful females graze quietly with spunky fawns while handsome bucks display tall antlers while guarding their harem.

Like being immersed in a womb, the warm salty water of the sea soaks off both physical and mental grime. Wearing our dirtiest clothes we all go swimming to clean our grimy bodies in the silty water.

Little fish squiggle below our feet in the muddy bottom. The shore in one area is especially muddy with fine, slippery clay.

The "Mudpuppies" of Bangladesh

"Mrs. Cundiff, can we play in the mud?" Eight of the students come running up the beach to ask. It shows just how good these kids are to ask permission for such a thing. Later, they come back totally covered in the dark grey silt eroded from the great Himalayan mountain range and flowing out to this Bay of Bengal. Carin was not too happy with a mudskipper fish squirming and stuck in her matted, muddy hair but Stephano was doing a good job trying to pick it out without killing it.

We laughed and joked, took pictures and then rinsed them off quickly before any creepy crawlies burrowed into their skin. There is more than just dirt in this muck.

I am enjoying lots of fresh coconut water thanks to Dave Wallin. It is actually my favorite drink, containing tons of nutrients and naturally refreshing. We had finally decided to bring about 400 coconuts with us as a source of liquid along with 300 gallons of freshly boiled water in five-gallon plastic jugs. We are all used to boiling water at home as most tap water in Bangladesh has too much bacteria.

I was really quite worried at first to take 27 children into the jungle where there would be no fresh water for 10 days and rumors of pirates, tiger attacks, malaria and crocodiles while living off an old freight boat with no guards and no communication system. But everything is going quite well so far. So far.

"Here's to all of us and the kids who have made this a successful adventure" toasts Mara. The sun has set, our bellies are full and dinner has been cleared away. The kids are all playing capture the flashlight on the dark beach having a great muddy, sandy time while the chaperones taste just a little touch of that rum we have been hoarding. It is our last night on the island and it feels great to relax a little knowing that our greatest fears have not manifested.

Wednesday, February 7

Yesterday we rose early to break camp as the sun turned the sky a golden pink. Our inflatable Zodiac and a wooden canoe, brought to the island by our national park guide, were both filled to the gunnels. We packed our gear to shuttle it to the 'mother ship' that was closer to shore now with the high tide.

Fine sand fills every crevice of my dirty body and I long for a hot shower and a soft bed. But I hate to leave. I will miss the clean air, the quite expansiveness of the sea, the broad beach, walking barefoot in the sand and the solitude. Especially this solitude and harmony of nature. And the students. It has been so nice to make friends with them, get to know them better and enjoy them outside of a demanding classroom structure.

The kids have really been wonderful the whole trip. Most of them are always ready to help out above and beyond what is necessary. Some have even set up all night vigils at ports to keep watch and kept the local, curious people from boarding the boat; which was happening. They have been constantly writing in their journals and collecting data as I set up their projects to count for two test grades. I had to actually make them put down their notes now and then so that they could relax and enjoy the trip and each other.

About six of us board the small wooden canoe with the experienced park guide to travel through the narrow rivers to eventually rendezvous with the big boat taking an ocean route to our next port. Gliding quietly through the Sunderban jungle rowed by a small brown man in a traditional cloth skirt called a lungi we spot several very obvious sets of tiger tracks on the shore about as big as my hand spread wide. A big fat wild boar comes too close for comfort. A large troop of rhesus monkeys rambles along and several three-foot monitor lizards escape into the forest. Diving kingfishers, stately green herons and snowy egrets take wing before us as we negotiate the shallow narrow passes between the mangrove swamps.

Last night we stayed at a guesthouse at Katka Forest station. Herds of spotted deer came right up near the house to get fresh water from a pond. The owner described the scene just two weeks ago when one was killed by a tiger right out in the front yard. Windows have bars on them, as tigers are known to jump right through glass. We walk in large groups. "Everybody stick close together," I remind the students. "They say if we walk in groups only the slowest person at the back will get eaten."

Today is our last day on the boat. Tonight we will spend the night in a small town on the way back to Dhaka. Humanity has taken over almost every corner of the earth except where it is uninhabitable or preserved. So we cling to and relish these last remnants of the beautiful jungle and ancient river where people are insignificant and nature reigns.

Everybody is safe and nothing terrible happened, despite, or perhaps because of all our worry. We learned much about nature in the Brahmaputra River, the mangrove forest of the Sunderbans, and the Bay of Bengal at the foothills of the Himalayas. Nature is our best teacher. We learned about roughing it, taking risks and looking out for each other. A successful field trip we will not forget. A trip that will not be done again at this school because of the dangers. Where nature is so powerful, perhaps it is better to let it reign and keep the people out.

"One touch of nature makes the whole world kin."
   - William Shakespeare

Monsoon Mail
School Days in Bangladesh, 1990

Action breeds confidence and courage. If you want to conquer fear, do not sit home and think about it. Go out and get busy.
    –Dale Carnegie

The streets are eerily quiet today. Only a few rickshaws and an occasional daring car risk an appearance. It is 10 AM on Wednesday and we have an unexpected day off after a frightful morning.

We knew that a hartal had been called; a general strike, a massive countrywide protest over poor wages for transport workers. You are not supposed to drive anywhere during this type of hartal. It is supposed to be a total transport shutdown. No cars, busses, trains, taxis or even rickshaws. But if school were canceled at every little warning of danger we would be making up days until July. Since we are some distance from the central city it is usually safe to drive a mile or so to campus.

"What do you think?" asks Ken. "It's early, we don't have far to go, and the last time there was a hartal it wasn't such a big deal," he continues. "I guess we can always come home if there is a problem." I answer. So we set out at our usual early time of 7 AM in our little white, non-descript Toyota Corolla that belongs to the school.

We are already on the bridge before we see the flaming bonfire in the middle of it. "My God, what'll we do now?" Ken blurts out as he holds his breath to swerve the car and make the decision faster than I can answer. "There's no way to turn around or even back out." A small but angry crowd is determined to stop traffic and is already surrounding us. Almost scraping the sides of the bridge, Ken quickly veers around the crackling fire of trash and logs and leaping flames. Right through the waving arms of the angry group we keep moving slowly, just as one offended striker brandishes a burning post in our windshield, trying to stop us. We carry on, maneuvering around those trying to stop us, not daring to go back. Finally we break through the picketers to the other side of the bridge and down the empty road.

233

"Well, what'll we do now? I ask. "This is more serious that we thought." "I wish we had stayed home."

"We can't go back. At least not until that bridge is clear. I guess our only option is to continue on to school and take shelter on the guarded, walled-in compound," answers Ken

There are absolutely no other moving wheels on the way to school except ours. The normally dense procession of workers, rickshaws and mini-buses is replaced by menacing strikers on the roadside. Since we are so close to school we step on the gas and race to take cover on campus.

An immediate call to Gene Vincent, our superintendent, sets our emergency phone tree into motion. We stop everyone else – teachers, students and staff – from coming to campus. We stay around and catch up on some schoolwork for a few hours until we think we can make a dash for home.

With such a high population of poorly paid and unemployed, unrest is common. One good thing about mobs in this very poor country is the lack of any firearms. Sticks and stones may break our bones but are not likely to kill us inside of our car. Glad we are safe at home now and have the rest of the day off. The minimum wage in this country is only about twenty dollars per month. Next time a hartal is called we will support the strikers, stay home, and hope they get better wages.

Jane & Linda with their Rickshaw Driver

"I counted 52 mosquito bites on my upper body alone," confides Linda in the teacher's lounge.

"We bought a mosquito canopy for our bed," I answer. "It seems like the house is full of them no matter what we do. The netting is a hassle to get in and out of bed, but it looks cool and really cuts down on the biting."

The weather has been pleasantly warm. Just cool enough to wear a light blanket at night and to take a nice walk in the evening. But the monsoon rains are beginning and with the rain comes the mosquitos and other interesting problems.

"This floor seems to be tingling and I just got a shock from that lamp," I complain as I walk across the cold, damp terrazzo in my bare feet. Ken drags out his box of tools and grabs his voltmeter. "Yup, it is actually measuring 80 volts right here between the lamp and the floor. The wiring in the house has probably gotten wet from monsoon flooding." Ken can fix anything and proceeds to attach ground wires to every electrical object in all rooms without carpets. I put on my flip-flops anyway.

I was coaxed into being the student council sponsor this year so we find ourselves in all kinds of activities. Shanthini and Leone are capable leaders and good to work with. Right now they are planning a school-wide pool party to inaugurate the opening of our new Olympic-size swimming pool.

In this very international school much of the students' social life is tied to their classmates. Over half of the kids come in after school and on weekends just to see what is going on and who else is hanging out. They are a really well behaved bunch, and usually entertain themselves with basketball and such. We still have a small high school population with no seniors and only 11 juniors. But it is growing with 27 ninth graders moving up and more international companies moving here to Bangladesh where labor is cheap.

"Yikes! Look how cloudy this is. These test tubes definitely show contamination. This is our drinking water sample?? The broth should be clear but is really milky!" I exclaim to my students as they remove their experimental tubes from the incubator.

Acquiring science supplies usually takes close to a year and teaching labs with whatever is in the storeroom is quite a challenge. Last month I found some nutrient broth mixes that would test for the presence of bacteria in water. So I encouraged my students to design a well-controlled experiment. With my years of research in bacteriology I guided them through the sterile procedures and repetitions of a good, scientific experiment on bacterial growth.

Armed with strict guidelines they each gathered 5 test tubes of different water samples throughout campus, including toilets, lab faucets, and kitchen faucets. Since most tap water in Bangladesh is known to be contaminated, the school cafeteria boils drinking water. They fill coolers that are placed around campus on tables with washable cups. Several of these water coolers were also tested.

After two days in an incubator ALL the tubes except our sterile controls are cloudy with bacterial growth. Yes, even our boiled water that we drink from school water coolers is contaminated.

"Well, most of our drinking water does contain a few bacteria but this quick growth could be a sign of more serious contamination." I explain. "Perhaps it is just a fluke, or maybe some harmless bacteria." After some discussion about possible errors in collection, we decide to test again. This time we will use a few tubes I had found to test specifically for E. coli. It is a species of bacteria found in human feces that can make us sick and is an indication of sewage in the water.

"Look at this!" exclaims Thomas, one of my more serious biology students, as he evaluates his second set of tubes. "I can't believe these samples are positive!"

"Mrs. Cundiff, it looks like ALL samples, including our drinking water have turned from clear blue to milky purple," remarks Shama. "They are contaminated and positive for E. coli."

I think I am more surprised than the students. It opens a proverbial can of worms. The school staff tries their best to keep the campus clean. We take our results to the superintendent who calls the Embassy medical clinic to test and confirm our analysis. Meanwhile, the kids design more experiments to find that the boiled water in the coolers is clean but the plastic cups we use to drink the water are contaminated. They are washed in straight tap water, which usually contains bacteria in

Bangladesh. Most of the thick plastic cups are getting old and have cracks and crevices where bacteria might hide and multiply.

So the kitchen staff decides to buy new stainless steel cups, use a chlorine bleach soak and a very hot dishwasher.

Student and staff illnesses decrease and science class is the talk of the school.

The study of ecology is intertwined with population growth. Biology students learn that all species will increase in numbers as long as there is plenty resources and no other limiting factors killing them off. So the tenth grade biology class sets out to design an experiment about limiting factors for life.

"I can't believe you just did that," squeals Sydney as I grab an escaping Asian cockroach with my bare hands. Ants, caterpillars, roaches, worms and tiny fish came in jars and shoeboxes, starting class off with plenty of excitement. We needed some animals that we could get in high numbers so I gave extra credit to anyone who could round some up. As a class we finally decide to use tiny fish. They can be supplied by a family fish farm, kept in 5-gallon tanks we already have, and won't cause too much squealing.

Two fish in tank one, four fish in tank two, eight, sixteen, thirty-two and sixty-four fish in other tanks. Kids checked pH, temperature, water clarity and nipping behavior daily in their lab notebooks. They made sure there was good aeration and all were fed properly.

They watch them die, one by one. First in the tanks of 64 and 32, then in tank with 16. The tanks of 8, 4 and 2 remain healthy. We study and share observations. They have plenty of food and the aeration is good. The pH did not change much. Behaviors have been mostly the same with surprisingly little fighting, even in the crowded tanks. It was turbidity that was obviously different.

The fish had most likely died in their own pollution. It had been a slow but sure death of too many organisms in a limited ecosystem dumping their waste.

The earth is finite. Humans have overpopulated and our own pollutants are accumulating. Carbon dioxide from fossil fuels is changing the climate and acidifying the oceans. Other unnatural chemicals are building up in our ecosystems and our bodies.

Life in Bangladesh is an immersion in human overpopulation. With 155 million people in an area about the size of Florida, the density is over thirty-two times that of the United States. Once, when we were downtown on a busy Saturday, Ken said he was feeling kind of seasick. At six feet tall he towers above most everyone on the street. He thought it might be from watching the undulating movement of a crowded sea of people moving down the sidewalk before him.

It often seems contradictory that starving and war-torn countries have such high population rates. But living organisms tend to reproduce in higher numbers under stress to make sure the species survives. It is instinctive. Political stability, enough food and a good education are directly related to smaller, healthier families and less cultural strife. These are the goals of the leaders of this country and of the aid agencies who have come from around the world to help.

Just around the corner from our house is a walled-in garbage collection spot where the neighborhood takes trash. I have never seen a garbage truck, yet the place is usually empty. Poor people go in and out all day to collect the waste. For many it is their sole source of food and clothes. All glass, aluminum and paper waste is carried off by hand-pulled carts to re-use or re-cycle for a few pennies. Poor people, as individuals are actually the friendliest to the environment because they use so few resources.

Living simple but healthy with fewer children, and more in tune with the earth, will probably be the goal of our future. Birth rates have already dropped dramatically in developed countries around the world. Now it is important to help countries still under stress.

Beautiful local babies

Monsoon Mail. That is the name the students decided on for the first school newspaper. Ken was asked to be editor-in-chief and design his computer class around it with the new Macintosh computers. He is in love with his new machines even though running a course with them means all kinds of networking, crashing and virus problems. I am still on our old Apple computer at home, highly reluctant to kick in the 3000 big bucks to upgrade.

Monsoon Mail AIS/D

The kids are excited and beginning to interview, write and set pages. Alain, a tenth grade student from France and an A student in my biology class, is also one of our best writers for the paper. Below is an excerpt from one of his articles, "Behind the Scenes in Monsoon Mail".

.....He-Man-Shu, otherwise known as Mr. Math, (Himanshu, from India, is in grade 10) *is busy twiddling his thumbs as he waits for his computer to open the word processor. Our "brilliant" Editor-in-Chief, 'Chiller' Cundiff, exhales his fuming hot air from the depths of his belly down the necks of the innocent students. As he gulps down his seventh cup of coffee, he turns around with a glare in his eye as he screams, "Y'all aren't doing a *&*# thing and this paper is going to press in five days!"....... He turns around like a swirling dervish and you think he is about to knock your head off. You are surprised to find your skull intact and his hand patting your shoulder in a gesture of encouragement. ....*

Ken edited and allowed Alain's unique description to go to press.

The *Monsoon Mail* became the sounding board for what the students were learning. David wrote an article called "Eco-Fallout" asking students to send letters to their respective governments

239

demanding action on environmental conservation. Bushra drew and described the beauty and importance of local birds. Several students wrote short posts in the special "Eco-Alert Bulletin." Nicole, Richard, Hesham and Sayera worked together on a group project discussing possible future planet scenarios for the article *"Utopia 2050"*. I hope someday their utopia of a balance between people and all the creatures of earth will be theirs.

Special Monsoon Mail edition - Utopia 2050

Twenty-five years later, living in different parts of the world, these students are still environmentally active. Shama called me recently to discuss her Oklahoma forestry project on invasive species. Alain works for Johns Hopkins University School of Public Health in Epidemiology, traveling back and forth between Baltimore and Bangladesh, writing and presenting seminars on global health. They still remember the bacteria experiment and writing for the Monsoon Mail.

It is important to involve our young people in the pertinent problems of the day. Not only can we use their help, it is far more interesting, challenging and educational for them. They enjoy and learn more from solving real problems instead of imaginary ones.

Transitions

"I cannot know the future. I have only learned that following my heart and my highest goals has lead me to a life of wonder and happiness." - - me

We stayed only one year in Bangladesh. Although the students and school were quite good, we found the country difficult. Too much disease and poverty and way too many people for us nature lovers. Traveling around the countryside was especially troublesome. In a land of few tourists, we would often draw a crowd of curious villagers who would gather just to stand and stare or perhaps to beg. With a population doubling every twenty years, the din of construction and people was twenty-four hours non-stop. To help block out the racket with some white noise we kept our windows closed and ran noisy air conditioners and fans. We also slept under a mosquito net to prevent the dozens of bug bites we had been getting every night. We rarely slept well.

Ken and I really enjoyed our students and the friends we had made. Many of them like their life in Dhaka. Some have been here for years and have settled in to a fine routine of work, parties and hanging out at international clubs. I guess they are just not as bothered by the intensity of people and noise as much as we are. Having lived much of our life in the countryside before coming overseas, we find city life wearisome.

When we came to Dhaka, I had put aside my desire to finish my coursework for a PhD in science education at the University of Florida. Now once again that came to the forefront. So we decided to leave Bangladesh after just one school year and return to our home and eighty acres that we had kept in Archer, just outside Gainesville, Florida.

My sister, Mary Lisa and her son Christopher have moved out and our house is un-occupied, so it is easy to move in. It is wonderful to be home again visiting with family and renewing friendships. Cindy, the gourmet cook of our family will soon be having our yearly family reunion at her summer home in the mountains. I can fill my own cabinets with familiar food, plant a garden, hike our trails and ride my bicycle down country roads. We can even speak our native language and not be stared at. We sleep soundly; windows wide open to the fresh country air. Only the sounds of crickets, distant owls and the beautiful trill of the Whip-poor-will drifts into our dreams. Everything seems so easy after living in such challenging places.

I enrolled at the University to take courses in research statistics and Ken went back to teach at Oak Hall Private School, where we had both taught just four years ago. He even had some senior physics students who had been in his eighth grade science class. They were quite excited at his return.

Life was comfortingly smooth. For a while.

Here is a good magic trick. When you come back to America from living or traveling in other countries, open any newspaper to find those countries have disappeared. Nobody even knows where Pakistan or Bangladesh is. Woosh! Just gone. Like a lost fairytale, it makes us homesick for our international life.

It was barely six months after returning home when we started talking about going back overseas. We couldn't help it. Life was just too exciting in the fast lane of adventure. Sure there were lots of problems and yes it would be noisy. But our international students were so authentically interesting, daily life was packed with surprising experiences and there was still so much to see and do in the world.

"I sure do miss all the excitement," remarks Ken. "Where's all the danger, adventure and international intrigue?"

"Yeah, and I miss the close community of people, amazing students and new cultures" I answer. "OK, and I miss the servants too."

We talked. We argued. We thought. We laughed at our predicament. We even made long lists of pros and cons. We enjoyed being home. We itched to go off and away again. We debated for over a month. "February is coming soon and we need to decide what to do so we can sign up for a hiring conference – or not," Ken says as he grades his student's physics tests.

"Well, I guess we must be pretty crazy but it sure seems like we want to go overseas again," I answer, looking up from my statistics textbook to see Ken's broad smile.

We called the International Schools Services, signed up, and attended the spring hiring conference in New Orleans. Turning down offers from schools in Madrid and Venezuela we finally got a call from Cairo Egypt. It wasn't a perfect fit. Ken would be teaching more math than physics and I would have mostly chemistry. But Cairo American College had an excellent academic reputation and the country of pharaohs and pyramids sounded totally fascinating. So we accepted.

Our easy routine days step into high gear once again as we prepare ourselves. Things to pack. Languages to study. New people and places to seek out. More adventures. More challenges. There is so much to learn about the world. Yes, regardless of the downsides we are excited, ready and chomping at the bit.

"A ship is safe in harbor, but that's not what ships are for"
- William G.T.Shedd

International children

Egypt

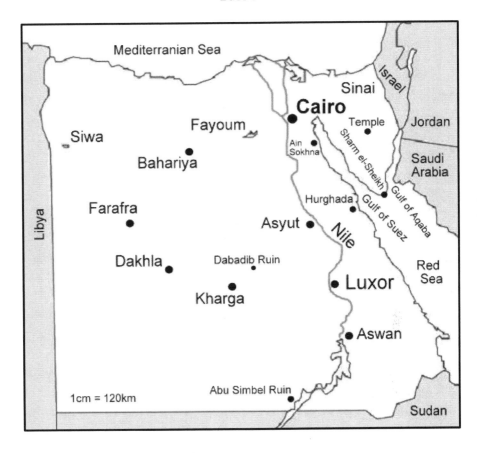

RED SKY OVER CAIRO
August to September, 1991

"When we are mired in the relative world, never lifting our gaze to the mystery, our life is stunted, incomplete. " - Peter Mathiessen

I guess it's in the blood or maybe the stars or perhaps its some viral disease but we do love this international teaching life. The thrill of it begins to grab hold at the airport. It feels so good to be back in the travelling lane again after a year at our home near Gainesville Florida. Stepping into the Orlando Airport international departure wing we are surrounded by people in turbans, saris, robes or sarongs speaking different languages, going all over the world. Just watching them makes me feel involved in a bigger picture. Ken and I smile broadly at each other as we walk to the counter to get our boarding passes. We are in

245

our element.

Cairo American College paid for our flight and our headmaster, Guy Lott asked all the newly hired American teachers to gather in Zurich, Switzerland before moving on together to Egypt. We decided to arrive five days early to enjoy a short vacation.

With bellies full of cheese, bread and chocolate we rode the train to Lucerne to spend two nights overlooking a picturesque river with the mountains above and the old town street life below. A long afternoon stroll on the promenade around Lake Lucerne was so beautiful and relaxing that our plans to fight jet lag succumbed to an unexpected nap on a sunny park bench. Leaning on each other sound asleep and drooling must have brought some chuckling comments from walkers passing by.

Mary Budd Rowe, our major professor at the University of Florida, had invited us to spend some time in the mountain village of Zermatt so we headed up there to do some hiking with her and her friend, Irmgard. Wildflowers were so thick I thought they must have been planted and carefully tended, the green mountain meadows were ablaze with yellows, pinks and reds and the air fresh, sweet and clear. The majestic Matterhorn topped with snow towered above. Brass bells tinkled softly as cows grazed lazily over the next hill. Cool enough for sweaters in the morning then growing into the warmth of August just in time for afternoon picnics. Pretty heavenly.

We have thought of working in nice European countries but the school year goes through the winter, which is a bit too cold for us Floridians. We usually go back to America to be at our home in summer, which is the best time to be in Europe. And besides, we do like the excitement and learning about cultures that are really different than our own. Switzerland is beautiful, neat, organized and very clean but Pakistan and Bangladesh were definitely more exciting and Egypt will be too.

Leave it to the Swiss to design a cable car to the very pinnacle of the Alps. We ride right to the tiptop of the Klein Matterhorn (just slightly smaller and not far from the Matterhorn) to a view so spectacular that I can feel, once again, why so many people risk life and limb to mountain climb. Snowy peaks of Switzerland, France, Austria and Italy, mountain after mountain, they shine silvery white n the morning sun. Joined together like peaks on a chiffon pie as far as I can see, it's as if there are no borders.

I spend my fortieth birthday hiking in the Swiss Alps, with wonderful international teaching friends and role models who are still climbing these mountains over the age of 60. Arm in arm and in love with Ken we were ready to begin a new life once again, this time in Cairo Egypt.

On August 7, we take the train back to Zurich, eager to meet more new friends and begin our next big adventure. Twenty-six excited newly hired teachers and their families gather for introductions and a lovely dinner all hosted by the school as a treat before we begin our new life in Egypt. The meal is followed with a cocktail party with no lack of animated conversations as we get to know our new adventurous friends and colleagues. The next day we board the plane together, getting better acquainted on the five-hour flight into the early night of Cairo.

"Which apartment complex are you assigned to?" Denise and Vicky ask me as I thumb through our welcome packet while we fly across the Mediterranean Sea.

"Fontana, how about you?" I answer, smiling up at our new friends standing up in the row of seats in front of us.

"Fontana too, along with Sheila, Dave and Terri," Vicky replies as she points them out. "Looks like a lot of us will be in the same building."

Ken is over on the side aisle, chatting up a storm with Curtis, Ron and Carl. It's a good thing our plane seats are together because all 26 of us are way too excited to sit quietly.

We can't believe our eyes when we see our household shipment of 38 boxes all neatly stacked in our new apartment. This is a first. It actually arrived as promised, before we did. Our Oriental rugs now grace a worn carpet as we look out over a fairly busy street in the New Maadi suburb, about eight long, crowded miles from downtown Cairo. We're on the fourth floor, in a building of seven floors and 14 flats called Fontana. The long, large living-dining area has three sliding glass doors that open onto a small balcony with a view of city life below. We've been told that on a clear day we can probably see the pyramids from here. But a clear day?

The evening sun sets well above the true horizon. The dusty sky filters the disk so much, that we can look directly into it with binoculars to see sunspots. Heavy desert dust and city pollution makes for beautiful sunsets as the entire western sky glows hues of orange and scarlet and the dark red sun disappears into the smog.

Our first apartment in Cairo

And so we take the bad with the good. We are a 20-minute busy walk to school but the taxi ride is only 60 cents and a hired driver will be ready for us each morning. The school does not provide a car so we will have to buy one ourselves. It is quite noisy here but all of the apartments in our complex have teachers, mostly new ones. We solve our little hassles together while sharing meals, investigating new places or partying.

Because we are new we have been placed in the least desirable accommodations, vacated by other teachers. Whoever called this a residential neighborhood must have been dreaming. We are allowed to apply for another apartment, but only after two years. The flats themselves are nice, modern and roomy but the noisy, busy area has a bus station, a late night open-air theater and a storage area for steel re-bar where trucks load and unload. The owner of the re-bar lives on the top floor and yells orders to the noisy trucks below at all hours of the night. We have stuffed a camping mattress and a quilt into our bedroom window but still have trouble sleeping.

It is nice that our apartment is up high. A fourth story view seems to add a bit of distance to the scene - at least visually. Cairo is not a pretty city. Closely packed high rises with a few trees and lots of noisy vehicles are all covered in layers of brown dust. Getting only one inch of rain a year has its downside. There are some sidewalks but most are broken or covered with debris and so we walk in the dirty street or ride in bumper-to-bumper traffic that knows no boundaries. It is a place where we shower when we come home, not before we go out.

Egypt, however, is beyond just interesting. People are friendly, women are out with the public and there is not much begging. Even the poor seem a little better educated and not so likely to stand and stare. There is so much to explore in this land that has seen civilizations and cultures come and go for thousands of years.

Historically and culturally we have not yet even brushed the surface of discovery. Time and numerous characters have left their indelible stamp on this country. From the Stone Age to the pharaohs to the Romans to the modern day Cairo metropolis, humanity has come and gone and come again. Within the same city there is evidence of many different religions that have contributed to today's culture. Engraved in granite over four thousand years ago the goddess Ma'at holds her huge feathered wings over us as the primordial mother from the heavens. Over one hundred other ancient gods and goddesses are carved into permanent memories in Pharaonic walls. Today, close to 90% of Egyptians are Muslim; predominantly Sunni and the rest are mostly Coptic Christian.

We are living in New Maadi, a district of southern Cairo. It is a dusty walk through busy streets to the market but the local food is good and cheap. I bought all I could carry of ripe mangos, fresh figs, bananas, grapes, cucumbers, carrots, squash and a sweet yellow melon all for about $6. There is a small grocery store about two blocks away and Road Nine, a larger more diverse shopping area, is about a 25-minute walk or a $1 taxi ride. We have been able to find most of the foods we need and can surely make do with fun new ones. There won't be any maple syrup on our pancakes but we can always have a nice glass of cold fennel tea. Maybe the fresh roses only last a few days but, hey, for 60 cents a dozen, have the maid go out and buy some more. No peaches, but flavorful mangos and ripe pineapple can keep us happy.

Kusheri is the most common traditional Egyptian meal. Spicy, sweet, chunky tomato sauce with lentils and garbanzos are spread over a bed of rice shaped pasta called orzo. Topped with crispy fried onions it is quite tasty, pretty nutritious and we have our maid make it often.

The school is first rate. Although it is called Cairo American College they teach kindergarten through grade twelve and use the word college to mean educational institution. An oasis in Cairo, the grounds are well kept with beautiful flowering trees, cactus gardens and a large grassy playing field surrounded by a tall privacy wall. It is often called the American Club of Maadi as it is the center of so many activities of Americans and other nationalities. The eleven acre campus supports over 1300 students, a well-stocked library, a new synthetic running track, a nice gym and a large pool, all of which we will use often. The administrators are well organized and helpful, the students eager to work and the teachers an interesting and energetic crew. The science labs are well built and are generously stocked by Olivia, a medical technologist from the Philippines who will help set up our experiments. Ken and I work right across the hall from each other and share lunch and two planning periods. There are 12 science teachers in the middle and high school so we have more professional interactions and more meetings than previous schools.

"What am I going to do with a class of seniors that have flunked most of their other math courses?" Asks Ken when he finds out he has to teach a consumer math class.

Bruce Kramer addressing high school assembly at CAC

"Well, Bruce (our principal) did say you could invent anything you think appropriate," I answer.

Ken was supposed to teach physics and physical science and the additional math is an extra preparation. He is not overjoyed but flexibility is expected. "Oh well, maybe I'll make the class computer project based," for his own amusement as well as the students.

One of the things we love best about international schools is the ability to design our own curriculum. There are basic standards expected, of course, but it is fun to investigate new ways of teaching and have the school administration's full support.

The first week of our arrival was a blitz of unpacking, local shopping, meetings and introductory socials. Such a rush of new input. The school provided most of our meals the first few days during orientation. A volunteer host teacher showed us around the area and answered lots of questions. Each morning when traffic and heat are not so heavy, we tie on our running shoes to get out early and explore the streets around us. So many new sights, sounds and smells. They say there is nothing better to activate the mind then to be placed in a totally new environment. Every part of our life changes and it is both amazingly exciting and dreadfully stressful. What is safe to eat and drink? Where can I go or not go? Who can I trust? What is he saying and how do I reply? How can I deal with the noise and dirt? How do I appreciate all they are doing for us? How can I thank them for being so patient with me? It will take a lot of effort and flexibility but we will make this our new home as fast as we can.

The high school principals, Bruce Kramer and John Kruk end our first hectic week by inviting the new teachers on a felucca ride down the Nile. As the red sun sets over Cairo, we relax on cushions set around the benches of a long wooden boat as the tall cotton sail quietly pulls us up the same river used by the Pharaohs. Tall reeds of grass surround villagers bathing and washing clothes in the black water. Crowned by date palms heavy with fruit, they work along the banks of the Nile as they have for thousands of years. On the boat we share Kentucky Fried Chicken from take-out boxes with some baba-ganoush and pickled vegetables on the side.

"How is it going in the high-school counseling office," I ask Sheila as she passes me some chicken.

"Pretty hectic with so many new international students to deal with. This morning three Korean students came in who barely speak English so they will have to get some language tutoring along with their studies, " Sheila answers as she settles back against the boat cushions.

"Don't worry about their science classes", laughs Ken, "Koreans seem to be able to speak physics quite well."

"Yeah, give them a week or two and they'll be fine in Biology" says Nick who had taught many other Asians, known for their good study habits and parental strictness.

"Just let us know if there is anything we can do to help", offers Bruce Kramer, our principal.

New high school teachers on a felucca

We've made lots of new friends already. Especially with the new teachers who tend to flock together and are mostly living in our apartment complex. Curtis and Denise from upstairs have much in common with us. Curtis is a lot like Ken as both teach physics, love to scuba-dive, run, and have lots of stories to tell. Denise is petit, energetic, used to be a counselor- social worker and is now teaching third grade. Although they've travelled around a bit, this is their first job overseas. Ron and Vicky are both elementary teachers with no kids (like us) who came from teaching in Argentina. They both have a great sense of humor, adventure and flexibility. Dave and Terri love to host small impromptu parties on the fifth floor and Carl and Jean, Ted and Mogie are all seasoned travelers always ready to join in the fun.

It takes us over a week to get to the pyramids. Early on a quiet Friday morning (the Muslim day off – much like our Sunday) we employ a cab with Curtis and Denise, setting out to see the oldest wonder of the world. So ancient, it is almost incomprehensible to me. It was built in 2600 BC, 4,600 years ago. Almost all of American history that we studied in school is less than 500 hundred years old and World War 1 seems archaic. Time scales seem to give a whole new perspective on what is important in our life. Where have we come from and where are we going? I stand at the base of The Great Pyramid of Giza feeling utterly insignificant. Like millions before me I wonder how such a monument came to be. It is the only one of the seven wonders of the ancient world that remains largely intact. Once it was covered with highly polished limestone that must have glistened like a jewel in the sun. The ancient Egyptians called it "Ikhet" meaning "Glorious Light". There are over 80 pyramids in Egypt but this one is by far the largest. Some say most of these monoliths were built at the height of the Pharaonic civilization when lots of resources were available for a large population of workers.

People at Great Pyramid of Giza

After the pyramids, our driver takes us into the bazaar of old Cairo. Shops are set within painted arched stone buildings, crumbling with age. Brass, jewelry, rugs and souvenirs abound. Merchants call us to view their wares and a few beggars ask for "backshish". We have a brass nameplate made for the door with our name in English and in hieroglyphics with a blessing written in Arabic script.

"Haaappy Biiiiirthday too meeeee,..." Ron sings as his wife, Vicky shakes her head smiling and we all laugh along with them. Last Thursday we celebrated his birthday at the Sheraton Hotel restaurant out on the terrace watching the felucca sailboats slip quietly down the Nile. It is only about a fifteen-minute taxi ride from home and a pasta dinner is just three dollars so we will be back.

There are three ways for us to get away from the busy life of this huge sprawling city of over 15 million people. The school compound, the Nile River and the Sahara desert. A ride out on a felucca sailboat on the river is cheap, peaceful and a sort of TGIT (Thank Goodness it's Thursday) end of the Muslim week and our work week. We've been told that you can be away from the city and into the desert in less than twenty minutes with your own vehicle so we plan to start shopping for one right away. Fossils and artifacts have been "promised" to the persistent desert archaeologist. So we have begun to search for information about ancient ruins in the desert and for a four-wheel drive to find them.

We've got a nice routine down for our running addiction. At about 5:25 AM we run through local neighborhoods about a mile over to school, then four times around the quarter-mile track followed by 20-30 minutes of swimming and then running back home. This hour workout

feels great three times a week with the added benefit of greeting other teachers doing the same thing.

"I found the tiniest drum!" proclaims Marietta as she holds up a 2.5 inch tall brightly painted ceramic vessel covered with goat skin. "No way, look at this one, challenges Nick as he holds his slightly smaller version next to hers. "OK, I give, you win," laughs

Tiny drum   Marietta along with the rest of us. Last night the school sponsored a "Cairo by Night" scavenger hunt. Two busses carried the new teachers and families down to the Khan-el-Kahlili Bazaar, a market area since the 1400's. We were instructed to find the price of the smallest drum behind the mosque, discover the number of floors of the largest antique shop, find the cheapest source of cinnamon and capture a live cockroach among about ten tasks. We had a fun time asking people strange questions while trying out some new language skills.

We end our tour with a delicious authentic Egyptian meal in the

Naguib Mahfouz restaurant lounging on Persian carpet-covered benches under soft lighting from the hanging brass lamps. "Here, try some of this, it's delicious." Terri passes me a ceramic red plate filled with stuffed grape leaves. "I like the Ful even better," announces Dave as he takes some more of the large fava beans doused in a dark spicy sauce.

Egyptian food is pretty tasty. It seems to include lots of Lebanese, Turkish and Greek influence. The hummus and laadies (yogurt with mint and cucumber) and babaghanush (tahini and eggplant) are dips sprinkled with fresh pressed olive oil served with warm chewy pita bread. I often enjoy these so much that I barely touch the main dishes. We eat good grilled fish that comes from the Mediterranean and tons of fresh fruit and vegetables. The other day I had my first fresh date. It was red and crunchy, slightly sweet but a bit green tasting. They say there are many varieties and they get better as the season rolls on and they begin to turn more brown, soft and sweet. We have eaten lots of fresh figs, grapes and mangos and enjoy trying out little neighborhood cafes.

We like the friendly Egyptian people. Although Muslim, they are more tolerant to Western ways than Pakistan was. The local women move about freely on the streets with some of the young ladies even wearing the latest in modest western fashion. Others wear a more traditional thin veil across their shoulders or over their hair and a cotton dress to their ankles. Some western women even wear knee length shorts around Maadi and only a few Egyptians wear the full burka and are in black from head to toe. Our Arabic language teachers are the only local teachers at the school so we've really only met shopkeepers and taxi drivers and are looking forward to meeting more of the professional Egyptians.

We think we've hired a maid. Someone cleaned the house last week and made dinner on Thursday. We haven't seen her yet. The servant situation is much different here than in Pakistan or Bangladesh. They usually work about three days a week while we're not there. Unlike our help in Lahore and Dhaka who lived right behind our house and came every day. Dinner is ready on the kitchen counter when we arrive home. Very few of the servants here speak English. I guess we'll need to learn some Arabic. We learned the numbers the first week because prices are in Arabic. The maid across the hall, Mona, is Pilipino, speaks but does not read English and has volunteered her translating services. If I need something done, I'm to leave a note that will be taken to the store to get translated. We'll see. Maybe this will work, maybe it won't.

We're keeping our eyes out for a suitable car. Prices are quite high because of a huge import tax - over 100% the cost of the new car, doubling the price. Fiats are cheaper because they are assembled here. But then, who wants a Fiat? A four-wheel drive would be great but most of those we've seen are either junkers or over $30,000. Ken is thinking about a Niva, a small Russian four-wheel drive. Taxis are cheap but I think we could do a whole lot more exploring if we could just jump in behind the wheel and follow our noses. There is word of a special "grey market" procedure in which foreigners with some diplomatic pull can import cars without the tax. Sounds like information we will pursue. Patience, research and persistence will help, and money.

Even though the city is dusty it is fascinating and we like it here. Our everyday life includes friends as co-workers and neighbors and an excellent school with ambitious students. We come home to a clean house and can go just across the hall for good company. On weekends there will be parties and excursions. And of course, everyone's already making plans for the next vacation. Kilimanjaro? Israel? Alexandria? Diving in the Red Sea? We think we'll stay and travel around Egypt at Christmas, but summer? "Where've you been?" and "Where are you going?" We all talk the same language.

Dusty Cairo sky

The mass of city lights are twinkling to the clamor of bus horns, truck brakes and steel stacking in the street below and somewhere behind it all stands the Great Pyramid. I lean on the balcony bannister staring into the distance, lost in wonder about the mysteries we may uncover in this ancient land. The western sky is fully ablaze in a glowing scarlet haze as the red sun sinks slowly over the land of the Pharaohs.

Sacred Bulls and a Maid Named Adam
Letter home. Cairo year 1 – Dec. 1991

Just tonight we received the bill of lading on our brand new four-wheel drive Mitsubishi Pajero that we purchased out of a catalog brought to the house by a car dealer. If that's not risky enough, the payments are killers. $8,200.00 down and $8,200.00 when we get it. The school has pulled some strings and helped us buy it through some diplomatic loophole that allows us to avoid the 100% import tax. Of course it should be here last week. Made in Japan and shipped through Saudi Arabia, it is in Port Suez now and the last of the paperwork SHOULD take less than five days. Since we have planned our entire Christmas vacation to include wheels, we are a bit anxious. "Insha'Allah, bokra" (God willing, tomorrow).

School keeps us busy. Besides the preparation of advanced science courses there are lots of meetings with administrators and parents excited about the importance of preparing our students for good colleges. They say 95% of our students will enter higher education somewhere in the world and many will vie for top universities. Cool. We like teaching smart, motivated students. We might enjoy fewer meetings and more planning time.

"Do you think those are ripe enough to eat? I know you can eat them when they are still red." I whisper to Ken as I stare up at the dates hanging in bunches from the palm tree swaying above our table in the hotel courtyard. Just a few weeks after classes started the entire high school staff came to spend the day at an in-service at the Palm Club, a resort near the Saqqara Pharaonic ruins about an hour south of Cairo. We are learning more about school policy but our attention is waning. "They say date season is beginning so I imagine we could try" Ken responds as he quietly reaches up and picks a few red dates for me to taste while we listen to an administrative pep talk. "They are crunchy and sweet but have a bit of a green after-taste. Maybe not quite ripe yet." I report. I love new experiences in food, especially fruit, and cannot resist picking one right off a tree. Ken wrinkles up his face after a small nibble. "I think I'll wait till they turn squishy brown and sweeter."

Shaded with date palms and eucalyptus trees, the road on the way to Saqqara lies near the east bank of the Nile River. It is a step backward in time and deeper into nature. Women in long black traditional dress carry large baskets of freshly gathered dates on their heads as they heard their goats, donkeys and children slowly along the way. The trip from Cairo is less than 20 miles but takes us over an hour as we leave the slow vehicle traffic of the city to come upon the even slower foot-traffic of the countryside.

Country road near Saqqara

We anxiously wait for our conference to end as just outside the hotel grounds lay the ruins of the city of Memphis, the ancient capital of Lower Egypt. It dates back to the first dynasty of the pharaohs and boasts some of the oldest pyramids. The necropolis of Saqqara is the vast burial ground outside of Memphis that has been partially restored and preserved as a World Heritage site by UNESCO. We have booked a room beside Curtis and Denise at the Palm Club so we can spend the night and have more time to explore. It is hard to concentrate on school stuff when so many discoveries beckon just over the wall.

"The guide book says this Step Pyramid was the first of the monumental edifices for the dead and was built about 46 centuries ago by King Imhotep." Denise reads to us as we finally stand in awe before it within minutes of leaving our conference. "The steps were to carry him and his family to the afterlife and their tombs were filled with objects they might need." The Pharaonic civilizations worshiped many different gods but all of them seemed to agree on the importance of preparing for life after death. Their lives came and went but for thousands of years we have learned most about their deaths. The more I study these ancient places the less impressive our modern civilization seems. We may have fancier technology but our lives still come and go in the short skit of life. Eat, pray, fight, love, die. Use up resources until there are no more. Are we any happier? How much have we really learned? Does it even matter?

Step pyramid of Saqarra

Bull worship has been pictured in stone almost as far back as Neanderthals. The life force of these robust tenacious animals was believed to reincarnate in the gods and have magical powers. According to the Old Testament of the Bible, Moses and the Hebrews rejected Golden Calf idolatry when they fled Egypt. The Serapeum Temple of Saqqara was built in the thirteenth century B.C. as an underground tunnel over 350 meters long to bury the remains of these perfect bulls that embodied their gods.

Bull coffin

"A long series of bulls were ritually identified by the priests, housed on temple grounds and then each entombed in a giant granite coffin called a sarcophagus." Denise reads. We admire one weighing over 70 tons carved with hieroglyphics that stands partly open and askew in an underground tunnel having never quite reached its destination. Supposedly it was the last one ever constructed when the worship of bulls declined. I wonder if the gods we worship and our religious practices of today will ever seem as strange as this worship of the mighty bull.

Thousands of years of drifting sands have covered and uncovered past civilizations here along the great Nile River. We walk over a mound in the desert not far from the pyramids and the hollow thump suggests there could be more ruins below. A group of Egyptians are erecting a tent and preparing for an archaeological dig.

If you like old stuff, Egypt is a good place to look. There are ruins all over the place and many are fairly well preserved or refurbished. Stone tools still lie under the sand from some of the first humans hundreds of thousands of years ago. The Pharaonic civilizations built over 82 known pyramids along the Nile River. The Romans conquered the entire region around the Mediterranean and remnants of their forts are found everywhere. We plan on finding our own lost civilization as soon as we get the 4-wheeler. You can see four pyramids from the top of our apartment complex on a very clear day and beyond them is the vastly unexplored Sahara desert, likely hiding even more secrets of the ancient past.

Last weekend was the school's big Christmas party downtown in a fancy hotel overlooking the pyramids. A slow, delicious, four course dinner and drinks were brought to our tables in waves of synchronized red coated, white hatted waiters. There were about 175 teachers with additional spouses and clerical staff invited. Even the band, "The Staff Infection" consisted of teachers who are great musicians (well, at least very good and we love them). We talked and danced till we collapsed.

Jane at the orphanage

I wasn't quite sure why I had volunteered to get up early the next morning and hug babies. Maybe I'm a sucker, maybe I had too much to drink and Kay and John Kruk got to me with sad stories. Anyway, there is an orphanage nearby that is one of Mother Teresa's. Three nuns care for about 20 babies and a few older handicapped children. It is all they can do to keep them fed, clean and clothed and there is no time to hold or love or play with them. So some of the faculty from school go over on weekends and hold babies. "This one is so cute! Look at her beautiful face and amazing smile. I can't believe she hasn't been adopted." I remark as I bounce her in my lap. They are all adorable with their dark skin and huge brown eyes staring right into your heart, hoping for some attention. Some are recovering from starvation and are even more heart breaking than pictures can show. A tiny girl, wrinkled and gaunt with thin hair, looks no bigger than a child of three months but is 18 months old. She smiles. Something that only just this week, she has the energy for.

It is very hard to deal with. People should not be having so many unwanted babies. Yet here they are, helpless, smiling and needing love. Some may be retarded for the rest of their lives due to malnutrition before and after birth. But they keep on smiling and we keep on loving. And the world is overpopulated. Who knows? I think I'll go again.

We're getting excited about our Christmas trip. Mom is coming to visit and our best friends Curtis and Denise will go with us to climb all the pyramids and crawl through all the tombs and temples we can find. We will be driving south along the Nile to Aswan and then take a small felucca down river back to Luxor. The small felucca will have cushions around the deck and a bucket under the front floor for a toilet. We will be on the boat for four days and three nights, stopping at ruins along the way, travelling as the ancient Egyptians did. Then we'll head over to the Red Sea to do some reef snorkeling and back to Cairo. At least, that's the plan.

Cairo is a fascinating city. But it is pretty dirty and very noisy. Tall, plain brown concrete buildings, crumbling streets and the few trees have so much dust on them that they blend right into the plain brown background. Vehicle horns are used prodigiously. Cars often park below the apartment building next door and continue to honk until they get the attention of their desired inhabitant – no matter what time of day or night. Trash is sometimes tossed out apartment windows into the streets even here in the new section of the city. But there are pyramids, sphinxes and mummies, Coptic Christian churches, picturesque mosques and wonderful bazaars. Egyptians are friendly and helpful, commonly dressing in the traditional long cotton, wide-sleeved galabeya which a British friend calls a nightshirt but I think looks nicely traditional.

We've made lots of wonderful friends. The apartment complex we are in has 14 apartments, all occupied by teachers. So we pop in and out of each other's flats as if we are family. There are five party invitations sitting by the phone for the next two-week period. This is the first night in several weeks that I've had a few hours' time to write and I don't have to do housework or even make dinner.

Our maid, named Adam, comes in to clean and cook 3 days a week. She may not be perfect, but if it's cooked and the house is clean, I'm pretty happy. Since she doesn't read English, I have made picture cards to show her what kind of dinner to make. Chicken, lasagna, salad, soup and several other main dishes are each drawn with my bad art on a note card and after a little coaching she was able to figure it out. I place a picture card on the kitchen counter in the morning with a little money for groceries and when we come home the meal is ready and the house clean. Her maid friend, Mona, who works upstairs, helps. That was the deal. Mona, a really good Philippine maid, says her Egyptian friend Adam "is dumb" but if we are good enough to give her this job then she will make sure everything is done properly. So far so good.

Ezayak? Kwaisa, Humdulallah! (How are you? I'm fine, praise God!) We are slowly learning a little Arabic. We have a private tutor that comes to our flat once a week to teach five of us. There are not as many English speakers in Egypt as in Pakistan or Bangladesh. It was the French who colonized here. We will need at least some Arabic to travel around but it is difficult to learn. European languages have similarities in both the Latin base and in the Roman letters. Arabic and most Asian languages are totally different in both sounds and scripts. Curtis, Denise and Sheila aren't learning it any faster then we are. But language barriers never stop us. We know that if we use a few correct words and a lot of emotion and hand waving and are willing to be humble and flexible, it may not be easy but we can get around.

Well, things are looking pretty good here in Egypt and we are adjusting. Sometimes wonderful, sometimes lousy, always an adventure. I think we'll stay awhile.

Hash House Harriers

According to Wikipedia: The objectives of the Hash House Harriers as recorded on the club registration card dated 1950 are:
- To promote physical fitness among our members
- To get rid of weekend hangovers
- To acquire a good thirst and to satisfy it in beer
- To persuade the older members that they are not as old as they feel

"On-on!" shout Matthew and Mohsin with the traditional Hash call to move. With about fifty runners and walkers of all ages we take off into the desert to find and follow a sporadic trail of flour. On Friday we joined the Hash House Harriers for a 'run' out near the pyramids. Quite a rowdy bunch, this international, non-competitive running club is well known for it's fun runs and it's British pub-style beer drinking. They gleefully call it a "drinking club with a running problem." We call ourselves Hashers. About 40-80 folks of all sizes, shapes and endurances gather for an hour or more run or walk in search of a mysterious trail of clumps of flour. At certain "checkpoints", marked with a huge toilet paper X, the group draws together to allow the slow ones to catch up while fast running "hares" are sent out in search of the real trail amidst several fake ones.

"Over here, behind the dune!" Ken discovers the lost checkpoint and the others gather around and began to sing "Why are we waiting, why are we waiting" until the slowpokes catch up. Each week different people set the course in new and challenging surroundings. This time we are running over and around sand dunes with the Great Pyramid of Giza as one of the checkpoints. With the Cairo skyline in the distance, the pyramid stands tall and majestic in the evening sun as we trudge through the sand to reach it. As the full moon rises over the dusty monoliths the raucous group finishes the run with cold beers and sodas. The club members welcome newcomers with a "down-down" which is a chanting song ending with the celebrities quickly downing a mug of beer and then putting the upside down mug on top of their head. Those of us who aren't too good at this end up with a beer hair rinse.

We top off the evening with a grilled fish dinner on the outdoor deck of a local restaurant where we can see the pyramids lit up for an evening "sound and light show". It's great fun. A bit rowdy perhaps, but surely more interesting than running alone in the streets. It is a good opportunity to meet other energetic international and local people outside of school. The HHH runs at different locations near Cairo every Friday and also organize some interesting group trips outside the area.

"Danny's here! Come on Hashers, let's go!" I shout up at the open windows of our apartment complex. "We'll be down in a few minutes, Terry lost her shoes!" Dave yells from the fifth story window. "We're ready!" Ron declares as he helps Vicky climb into the back of the roomy SUV. "Leave space to pick up Rick and Annie and the girls" reminds Danny.

Almost every Friday (our day off) we run with the Hash House Harriers. Luckily we have a friend, Danny, with a very large 4x4 Chevy Suburban we call "The Beast" who doesn't mind picking up some teachers who don't own vehicles. We can pack eight or ten adults and a few kids into the back if we lay down all the seats. Most of the runs are out in the desert and we enjoy getting away from the city and taking ourselves less seriously. Occasionally there can be as many as 80 people of all nationalities and ages who run, walk or just watch. Sometimes we go to dinner afterwards. We get good exercise and have fun with friends.

"On-on!" we shout and laugh, squeezing together as The Beast revs up for the short journey.

Hashers gather to run in the desert.

About three weeks ago the HHH organizers set up a weekend in Luxor for us. We flew down, stayed two nights, ran around some great ruins and had a wonderful time with about 80 other crazies. Luxor is even more amazing than Cairo for the Pharaonic remains. Although Cairo has the largest pyramids, Luxor tells a much bigger story. The area has been called the "world's largest open air museum" with the extensive tombs in the Valley of the Kings and Valley of the Queens. The Karnak temple complex, dated about 1400 BC, is over 850 feet long. Luxor, the ancient city of Thebes, was the capital of the Pharaonic Empire and probably the grandest city in the world for close to one thousand years. It is awesome to stand amidst the 32 giant pillars of the hypostyle, to walk in ancient footsteps along the avenue of sphinxes and to study the mysterious hieroglyphic pictorials on the walls of tombs and monoliths.

Karnak Temple in Luxor

The sky is black, and darkness surrounds the ancient spot-lit monuments before us. It is time for the sound and light show at Karnak, the ancient temple complex of Luxor. "Imagine yourself walking down the avenue of the Sphinxes, four thousand years ago," booms a deep voice from the loudspeakers as we follow our guide. The God Amun-Ra and his Goddess spouse Amaunet were champions of the poor, the troubled and of personal piety. We immerse ourselves in a tale that stirs the imagination. What was the world really like four or five thousand years ago? Were people then so very different from us now? And what about twenty or even forty thousand years ago? Surely there is so very much we do not know. They say that Homo sapiens has been around for over 250,000 years, plenty of time for the rise and fall of hundreds of cultures. These ruins still stand because they were built in hard stone in a very dry area. What of the rest of the earth? Perhaps stories of Atlantis are true. The Middle East was not the only spot on earth where ancient cities flourished. These engravings show ships and if there were ships there must have been places to go. Wetter climates rapidly cover up broken buildings with plant life that eventually turns them into soil. Recently they have been re-evaluating the dating of some structures around the world. Even in the Americas there are some that may be over fifty thousand years old.

There has been speculation that some sites like Luxor, Stonehenge and Machu Pichu were abandoned due to destruction of local resources by growing populations. Once lush areas were stripped barren, changing to deserts. When people left these places there were still plenty of greener pastures to move to. How will our still growing global population fare in our future?

We didn't think they could possibly cancel a flight with all 80 of us. I guess we weren't thinking clearly. We had to spend the night on the floor of the airport waiting lounge using our suitcases and backpacks for pillows, piling clothes on top of us for warmth. Now we know why the school asks teachers to tell them whenever they are leaving town. After a long night on the cold, hard airport floor we got home at 4 a.m. and started class at 8 a.m. We made it - this time.

The International Hash House Harriers will be in Cyprus this spring and we have already signed on for the adventure. On-on!

Hash House Harrier friends on a felucca after a run.

Red Sea Rainbows (see map p. 245)
October, 1991 Dive Trip

"Did you see that beautiful speckled puffer fish under the rocks?" "No, but did you see those turquoise and purple parrot fish on the red coral?" "Yes, and did you spot that school of bright yellow tangs with the angelfish darting around the brain coral?"

The numbers and diversity of colorful fish on the lush reefs surpass anything we had ever seen in Florida. We are in the Gulf of Aqaba at the northern tip of the Red Sea between the Sinai and Arabian Peninsulas where the rift between land masses is less than 15 miles across and more than 6,000 feet deep. Biological diversity is so high because of the warm waters, drastic changes of depth and the low populations of people in the desert areas that surround it.

Taking an afternoon break on the deck of a dive boat we share fish stories after a strenuous morning of snorkeling in pristine waters filled with colorful life. October 6 is Egyptian Armed Forces Day and to us, a school break with a three-day holiday. Just time enough to cram in a diving trip to the Red Sea. Leaving Cairo we passed through the Ahmed Hamdi tunnel under the Suez Canal and traversed the length of the Sinai Peninsula to get to Sharm El-Sheikh at the southern tip.

Although we left Cairo early in the day, with eight friends traveling in a van that has two flat tires along the way, it is close to midnight before we arrive at the dock. The choppy sea in the black of night is not inviting and I quickly take some Dramamine before boarding. Holding tightly to the ropes with the ramp twisting and turning we tenuously climb aboard the charted dive boat that sleeps 10.

The crew gets us settled into our tiny berths and then feeds us dinner on the main deck, since in Egyptian culture, it is just late evening. Kusheri, a tasty local food made of tiny noodles and chickpeas in a tomato sauce topped with fried onions, is served along with fresh fish. After filling our starving bellies and exhausted from a long day, we hit the bunks quickly in hopes of a good sleep.

"Ken, are you awake?" I whisper.

"Yup, can't sleep. It's too hot and stuffy in here," he sighs. "Let's go up on deck and see if we can sleep on the benches." Stuffing our pillows under our arms, we climb the ladder to find we aren't the first ones with the idea. Eventually most of us end up on the top deck, stretched out on the floors and benches, sleeping under the stars, rocked to sleep by the Red Sea.

Our dive boat on the left

"Here, let me help you with your tank," Curtis offers as Vicky struggles to get it on her back. Curtis, Ken and Denise are the only experienced, certified divers on the trip, along with the boat's dive master. Ron and Vicky are beginners who have just completed a course in the school swimming pool. Curtis is their NAUI certified instructor and will keep an eye on them. "Let me check the valve on your regulator," Vicky asks her diving buddy, Ron, as she is supposed to. "And don't forget to breathe!" Reminds Ken as he makes a final check of his gear and rolls forward into the water.

A couple of us just came to snorkel. With the topography dropping from three-foot depths so quickly to thousands of feet, we can choose any level to experience. I am not a diver. Having had asthma as a child I don't like the dependence of breathing from a big pressurized can deep under water. I prefer snorkeling. The most beautiful part of the reef is near the surface anyway, since most color is lost in the dim light below thirty feet of water.

I gasp as my body hits the cool water. Not only from temperature shock but from the sight of a gorgeous masked unicorn fish. Black-bodied with bright yellow fins, orange-red spots and a sweeping forked tail, it comes right to my face to meet me. A yellow butterfly fish and a stingray with a meter long tail skirt out of my way. A hefty red grouper hides between the corals about twenty feet below me. She better keep hiding if she wants to avoid joining us for dinner. Each little cranny under the water is a world of its own, based in different coral structures, populated with so many beautiful fish, each more exotic than the last. One surprise after the other. Red sea urchins, blue tailed sunfish, yellow, purple, brown and golden fish and corals. A fish so fluorescent purple that I cannot quite see its body well – just a flash of vivid light shining in the water. Rainbows of life on display.

"Hey, Jane! Denise! Look over here!" Loud calls come from Curtis and Ken who have risen from the dark depths to report a huge whale shark moving slowly along below us. I am too close to shore to see it.

The boat is hooked to an anchor, one of many that are permanently fixed in the edges of the reef in order to preserve it. An excellent idea that is being implemented in endangered reefs of tourist spots everywhere. Between the excess carbon dioxide making the oceans more acidic, the warming temperatures and the pollution from cities, most corals and their systems are dying around the world. We soak in all the beauty we can.

Curtis and Denise ready for the Red Sea

Face painted with turquoise warrior stripes, a large Queen triggerfish bears down, directly attacking us. She courageously chases us from her nesting place and even flapping our big swimming fins in her face does not curtail her determination. Ken tries to capture a picture with his disposable underwater camera but just gets a blurry open fish-mouth in his face.

The first-mate spearfished two large red snappers for our deliciously fresh evening meal that we share on deck, under the stars.

"Anybody interested in a night dive?" Asks Ashok, the dive master as we finish our meal. "The sea shows a different nocturnal face. Come on over here, I want to show you something," he continues. He stirs the sea with a long-handled net and the black water glistens with tiny lights, like the stars of the heavens. "Wow! Bioluminescence! I've heard of that but have never seen it," I lean over the boat rail to get a better look as the tiny glowing organisms invite us into the sea for a nighttime excursion. The divers don their tanks as the snorkelers slip on fins. Armed with flashlights and trepidation we jump into the darkness.

The earth teams with life no matter the hour. As day creatures dependent on color vision and seeing long distance, we are often not just reluctant but fearful of the dark. Armed with bright underwater lights we are able to see another world of creatures rarely visited. Scorpion fish, Lionfish and a variety of beautiful Puffer fish display their awesome, poisonous bodies before us. They dance in a theatrical pageant in the beam of our flashlights. We keep a respectful distance from these toxic beauties and do not overstay our welcome.

Jane snorkeling on the reef

After breakfast and another morning dive, the boat moors close to Tiran, a small desert island in the middle of the Red Sea. We feel like Star Trek visitors from another planet as we swim to the beach and clamor over the barren rocks and explore in our slick, black wetsuits. At the top of the hill on the edge of the island we can see the coastal mountains of Saudi Arabia on the distant shore, only about seven miles away.

Little did we know we would someday work on that far shore; in Saudi Arabia, which is something like another planet. We would eventually look back both in time and distance to this very spot, from Ash Shaykh Hamayd on the northwest tip of Saudi. This little island of Tiran is part of a strip of land that connects the tip of the Sinai, across the Red Sea at the mouth of the Gulf of Aqaba. Although it is now mostly submerged, it could have been above water in the time of Moses. Maybe this is where the sea was parted. Who knows? I don't.

We visited the Red Sea several times over the four years we were in Egypt. Other times we stayed in camping "resorts" where we could pitch our tents on the beach. We only had to walk about six meters across the shallow water before diving right off the edge of the reef and didn't really need a dive boat.

There were usually Israeli tourists at these camps. During one of the Egyptian / Israel conflicts the Israelis gave up most of the captured Sinai under the condition they be able to use the beaches on the eastern shore.

Once we brought our friends Joe and Marilyn Halusky who had come to visit from Florida. Joe was the director of Marine Biology for Marineland and Marine Extension Agent for most of the northeast coastal counties, from Jacksonville south. He even has a reef named after him that he built right off St. Augustine Beach. We have known them since college where Joe taught scientific diving to Ken at Florida State University. As marine and diving experts the two of them pointed out little secrets of the reef we had not yet uncovered. We had a hard time getting them out of the water.

Break between dives on the beach of the Red Sea

Christmas Down the Nile (see map p. 245)
A Not So Easy Adventure in 1991

"A good traveler has no fixed plans and is not intent on arriving."
  - Lao Tzu

We were supposed to have our nice new four-wheel drive Mitsubishi Pajero weeks ago but it took way longer than promised and was still "on the way" when vacation started. What did we expect when answers were "Bokhra, inshallah" or "Tomorrow, God willing". Mom was coming from Florida and we had planned to ride with Curtis and Denise all around Egypt, spending much of our time camping off-road at ancient ruins in the desert. Time to re-structure.

So we totally re-designed our itinerary to share a rented car and arranged last minute hotel reservations through a friend of a friend that ran a small travel agency. Having paid about $2000 in advance for 12 nights in five cities for five people we expected everything to be ready as planned.

December 22

"Do you have room enough to breathe back there?" Asks Ken. All five of us squeeze into the small blue rented Renault, packed to the hilt with stuff tucked between and around us. Ken and Curtis with their long legs claim front seat driver positions.

Our Egyptian rented "dune buggy"

Mom, Denise and I snuggle in behind them with backpacks at our feet, snacks and pillows stuffed between us. We are ready to make our tour around the Nile valley of southern Egypt as best we can, determined to see and experience to the max.

"I can't believe so much trouble went into worshiping bulls," Mom remarks as we show her around the finely engraved black granite tombs of the Serapeum. "It was believed that bulls became immortal after death and here in the ancient city of Memphis there would have been plenty of devotees. Not much different than spending time to build churches or temples to our Gods of today," I reply. "And bull worship is still common today in some high schools and athletic teams," Ken adds with a grin.

"Who are you again?" Asks the clerk at the desk. After a long day of touring Memphis and some pyramids south of Cairo we arrive late in the evening ready for a relaxing night's rest at the Badr Hotel in Asyut. "We have no reservations for you and no rooms open." She continues while closing the black scheduling book before her.

So much for expectations and proper prior planning. After much heated discussion and a few phone calls and muzzled cuss words the manager is able to "find" a room for us and accept that it was indeed prepaid.

It turns out that using a small tour agency during the height of the travel season in Egypt is not a good idea. You may be "bumped" by larger tours, losing your room and your money. Either use a larger, well-known agency or book it yourself if your dare.

We try to make the best of it by spending our days delving into our full itinerary of Pharaonic ruins along the Nile River, hoping to find decent lodging at night.

December 24, Christmas Eve

I think my favorite Pharaonic temple is in Abydos, the ancient capital of northern Egypt and one of the oldest cities. The finely carved reliefs of the Seti Temple tell unique stories embedded in stone and well preserved. It is an immortal tale of death, resurrection and good conquering over evil. And is it coincidence that we are here on Christmas Eve?

From earliest times Abydos was a cult center of the gods Osiris and Isis, believed by some to be buried on the site in the 24th century BC. For over fifteen hundred years an annual procession was held in Abydos to honor Osiris and Isis and their son Horus. The most elaborate and influential stories of ancient Egypt honors these great rulers who brought law and order, agriculture, music and civilization to warring tribes. Murdered by King Set, Osiris was resurrected by his loving wife Isis long enough to conceive a son, Horus who eventually grew up to re-unite the kingdoms of Egypt. It is a timeless moral tale and powerful feelings of light and wisdom seem to emanate from this ancient center of worship. I stand in the doorway looking out across the bright empty desert, feeling grateful for and connecting to those who have spent their lives trying to improve their worlds against tough odds.

December 25

On the frontier of southern Egypt about 150 miles from the Sudan border lays the massive earthen Aswan Dam. Since the 1970s the dam has prevented flooding of the lower Nile valley and supplied hydroelectric power to Egypt. Aswan is the driest city in the world with barely a sprinkle of rain every five to seven years. Many homes do not even have solid roofs, as it is more important to let out heat than to keep out rain. The Aswan Dam holds back the fresh water of the Nile in one of the largest reservoirs in the world, Lake Nasser that is over 340 miles long and 22 miles across.

All Egypt has depended on the fresh water of the Nile for thousands of years as even the heaviest rainfall in Alexandria near the Mediterranean Sea is only eight inches a year. There are many areas in the country where a white crust stretches out across the land due to salt build up from too many years of irrigation from this mineral rich river. Any desert land that is continuously irrigated will eventually be poisoned by salt accumulation as it takes heavy rain to move and distribute these minerals more deeply into the soil. We plan to sail down the Nile on a felucca from the Aswan dam to Luxor, taking about three days.

It was Christmas day when we arrived at the Cleopatra Hotel that was booked for us in Aswan. Although it had been rated as four-star by our travel agency our small room was a dump. The window faced a crumbling brick wall, the toilet had flushing problems and an old dingy brown chenille spread covered the sagging double bed. After several days of poor lodging and dusty, crowded, bumpy roads I sat on the bed and cried. Mom, Curtis and Denise had taken the car and gone to visit Abu Simbel for the afternoon and had left their luggage with us to move in so we were on our own.

"You lay down and take a nap, sweetheart," Ken says as he hugs me tight and covers me with a blanket before walking to the door. "I'll go see what I can do."

While I curl up exhausted, Ken heads out to hit the pavement. Tired himself from driving he decides to change our fate and charges out to scour the area on foot and taxi. In less than an hour he comes back to surprise me. "I have cancelled our rooms here and reserved two gorgeous suites at the grand, five star Oberoi Hotel sitting on a private island in the middle of the Nile River." He proudly announces with a wide smile. It is indeed Christmas and Santa Ken has truly brought presents.

We left a detailed letter for Curtis and Denise at the front desk. The five of us spent Christmas night in total luxury lounging on high balconies overlooking the city lights on one side, the expansive empty desert on the other and small wispy sailboats on the wide dark river below. As an extra coup, the cost was only five dollars more a night than the Cleopatra, as Ken had negotiated. We enjoy roughing it but sometimes we really need a break. And a Santa.

December 28

It is our second day on this small felucca sailboat, floating with the gentle slow current northward on the Nile. We planned this adventure to be a major focal point of our trip. Anyone can book an easy cruise on a ship. We wanted to be close to the water, to nature and to Egyptians with more options for self-discovery and surprises.

Wearing typical long brown and grey galabeyas with lightly wrapped beige turbans warming their heads, two village men work around a small felucca pulled up on shore near our hotel. Our captain, Samir and "the crew" are supposed to have everything ready for us to board at 8:00 A.M., but our passports are not yet registered and the drinks have not been purchased. By 11:00 they finally have most of it together but the cook & captain (the only 'crew' on the small boat) were heatedly arguing in Arabic and Gamal the cook left in a huff. Samir said we would not be able to make it all the way to Luxor without him but we decide to set sail anyway and enjoy what we can.

Felucca at full sail

Ahhh! Simple and free at last. Floating, thinking, watching and enjoying life on the river. The wind is just enough to ripple the water in this cool December air. The dry, bright sun keeps us warm as we bask on deck lying on cushions and covered with blankets. Wings spread wide in the breeze, an osprey dips down to glide just above the dark lapping water near shore. The white cotton main sail is kept just a little slack so we do not move too quickly as we want to stay on this felucca journey for three to four days. Our adventure is more important than the destination.

"Oooh what a beauty! Take a look! See that red and yellow bird atop that bush hanging over the water?" exclaims Curtis as he shares the binoculars all around. Denise quickly flips through the pages of our Birds of East Africa guidebook. "I think it is a Four-colored Bush Shrike, a species of great beauty with bright green above, a yellow forehead and belly divided by a scarlet throat," she reads. Denise is our self-appointed and much appreciated tour guide. She dives into our small collection of guidebooks to identify everything we can. As educators we can't help but want to know all about it, whether a bird, a village or a Pharaonic ruin. "Owing to its shy and skulking habits it is often overlooked. It inhabits thick coastal shrubs and dense riverine thickets." She continues as we watch the beautiful specimen flitting in and out of the bushes on shore.

"Can we make a little stop over near those shrubs, please?" I ask after a few hours. Although there is a covered gallon-size metal pot aboard to use as a toilet we prefer to have the captain pull over on the side of the river every now and then. It is surprising how little greenery there is for cover. A thin line of salt-tolerant bushes and reeds are backed by endless stark, serene desert, golden dunes cresting in the distance.

With no rain everything that grows wild has to have roots enough to get water from the river. Much of the land within miles from the shore has been salted by the irrigation of ancient agriculture using the mineral rich water of the river. Here and there we see chunks of stone and other remnants of buildings.

Boarding the felucca on the Nile

The mystery of lost civilizations is becoming clearer. Egypt, Machu Picchu, Sparta, Carthage and other ancient cities used up their resources, poisoned the soil and then moved to greener pastures. Sometimes, with good rain, the earth recuperates. Sometimes it does not, and only poor salty soil and crumbles remain. The whole world could look like this if we don't take more care. Greener pastures are getting scarce.

Night is coming so we pull over to the edge to tie up near another small boat. Samir the cook has finally caught up to us with some of the food and drinks he was supposed to bring.

"Where is the beer that you promised?" Curtis asks Samir as the last of the supplies are loaded onto our boat. "I was robbed at the market and was not able to buy it," explains the cook. Usually quite intuitive about people Ken's suspicious nature takes over. Amazingly Samir finds the beer money in his pocket just as Ken grabs his shoulder to throw him overboard. After Samir apologizes we settle into a better understanding of each other.

"Come on, get up! Come on over and join us" calls Mom as we wait for our evening meal while warming our hands by the fire. While the cook, humbled from our earlier confrontation prepares our dinner, a few of his friends decide to entertain us with song and dance. Two donkeys rest not far from our warm glowing campfire as the troubadours accompany some simple tunes with a drum and a tambourine.

After dinner fun on the shore of the Nile

Mom is having the most fun and before long she gets us all to join in, clapping and moving to the music, getting over our earlier hassles. The musicians are taken aback and smile broadly when I begin to chant a Sufi song in Arabic. Maybe they are surprised, or maybe I'm not pronouncing the words properly. We relax and communicate with the globally shared ancient language of smiles, rhythm and music around the warm fire in harmony with the great Nile River swirling north to the sea. Finally curling up in our sleeping bags under the bright stars of the dark desert night, we doze off to the lapping of small waves against the shore. A timeless sound in a timeless place.

While enjoying a few quiet days immersed in thoughts of lives once lived we travel on this simple boat with accommodations little different than those used thousands of years ago. Farther down along the edge of the Nile we stop at the Temple of Edfu and a few other remnants of civilizations long gone.

Mom, Ken and I leave the boat at Edfu to take a taxi back to Aswan to pick up the car. Denise and Curtis remain on the boat to finish the last leg of the trip to Luxor where we will meet them.

We could have taken a tourist cruise on a big, hotel-like riverboat and been much more comfortable but we can be comfortable at home. It is far more exciting to do something different, testing our wits, stamina, patience and endurance and getting close to some local people. It was a trip of many trials. We really needed the patience of Mom and Denise, and the aggressiveness and wits of Ken and Curtis. It was an amazing, unusual adventure. Glad we experienced it. Especially glad for the peacefulness of the river, the birds and the desert. But maybe next time we will take a reputable cruise ship.

December 31, New Year's Eve

"I have a special surprise for you" exclaims Razaz, the rotund, balding owner of our one-man, half-baked travel agency. He finally connects with us in Luxor, listening to our tirades and apologetic for the troubles we had encountered. "Meet me back here at 2:00 and I will arrange a very special evening for you"

At 5:30 Razaz finally re-appears ignoring his tardiness and leads us to one of the large tourist cruise ships with tickets for a buffet dinner and a special New Year's Eve "Extravaganza".

A belly dancer shakes her golden bangles in rhythm with her swaying hips. Her jewel pierced bellybutton shimmers with her movements. A Whirling Dervish turns circles in tune with a flute and a drum, emulating planets turning round the sun. A group of rowdy Italians tosses festive party hats over to us. Even though Islam has its own calendar, the New Year is celebrated around the world regardless of religion or nationality. Here in Luxor, we cheer with people from all over the world as fireworks light up the sky irrespective of calendars.

The entertainment was fun but accommodations for the night were not. All five of us squeezed into a hole below deck with two double beds and no space around them, probably servants quarters. It was a chummy night.

January 3

Before heading home we wade into the water at Hurghada, to show Mom the astonishing biodiversity of Red Sea life with rented snorkeling gear. We have never seen such an array of flashing colored schools of fish so close to shore. Red Squirrelfish, Blue Tangs, Yellow Damselfish and rainbow Parrotfish compete in displays of grandeur flowing over reefs of pink Staghorn and yellow brain corals in a system with hundreds of other species of coral, fish and invertebrates. We must come back soon, as pollution, warming water and excessive carbon dioxide is killing coral and the fish that depend on them around the world.

Once again we have hotel reservation trouble before we can rest for the night. Finally heading back on our last leg to Cairo we stop to renew our spirits and converse with the monks at St. Paul's Coptic Monastery just inland from the Red Sea. Drinking deeply from the sweet water of a spring in the center of the courtyard we relax and wait for other tourists to complete a tour of tomb paintings dating back to the fifth century. It would be nice to return here for a quiet retreat in the off-season of spring.

A pile of bubbles mounds up around me as I sink into my first hot steamy bath since last year, washing away the weariness of a not-so-easy adventure. So glad to be home. The wonder of it all is just beginning to seep in, crinkling fond memory folds into my brain as the water is crinkling my skin. No matter what the troubles, in fact often because of the troubles we learn and grow from travel.

"Life is either a great adventure or nothing." - Helen Keller

Into the Fayoum Desert (see map p. 245)

"I have always loved the desert. One sits down on a desert sand dune, sees nothing, hears nothing. Yet through the silence something throbs, and gleams." - Antoine de Saint-Exupéry, *The Little Prince*

Independence comes with wheels. Our brand new 4x4 Pajero finally arrived ten weeks after promised and it feels so good to be self-reliantly mobile. We purchased the shorter, sturdier and cheaper two-door version with red-flame decals on the side. We will miss our local friendly taxi driver arrangement and promise to recommend Ahmed to others. Each morning other teachers from our complex who are ready climb in for a ride. Curtis and Denise are also raring to go adventuring and we are setting plans to explore new places almost every weekend. They have ordered their very own Pajero, exactly the same make as ours, except beige to tell the difference from our white one. It may be more than a few weeks before it arrives. Ron and Vicky are also talking about buying a small used car. Many folks just employ cheap taxis and avoid never-ending parking problems and logistics of local maintenance. We are too independent and love to discover life on our own, especially where taxis cannot go.

It doesn't take us long to get our new vehicle off-road. The very next weekend we fill up the car with seven friends in our five passenger SUV and head out to the desert to run with the Hash House Harriers.

"What about that hill over there? Do you think she can do it?" Ken asks our passengers. Shifting into low range 4x4 gear he revs the engine for the climb. "Hold on tight everybody! He's going for it!" I warn them as we make our first rocky attempts. "You're nuts!" Vicky laughs from behind the back seat as we bounce down the other side.

We are likely to get stuck when we go off-road. So a lot of proper prior planning and practice helps to make it routine. When we first got our new 4x4 we also bought shovels, tow ropes and sand ladders and then headed out with other more experienced drivers to learn the moves. Sand ladders are strong metal "ladders" about four feet long and just wider than the tires, providing a surface with traction. We have to dig out the sand in front of the tires and stuff the ladders underneath them. After weeks of trying to purchase some without success Ken had them special-made by picking out some metal trash from a junkyard and finding a welder.

For our fist big desert foray we head out for a weekend on the edge of the Sahara, just a couple hours from Cairo. Quiet light breezes, clear bright blue sky, expansive views across rolling golden dunes and no people. The stark simplicity of the Sahara desert has a serene beauty that calms the spirit. We visit whenever we can now that we have our own, cool, capable, brand new 4x4 with red-flame decals.

"Maybe just a little push will do it?" suggests Ron.

"I don't think so. Try flooring it?" is my two cents. Wheels spin deeper into the sand as shouts from backseat drivers try to help. We are stuck again.

"No sense digging it deeper. We need the shovels for this one. Maybe even the sand ladders." Ken decides as he turns off the ignition.

"OK, lets get to work!" Vicky cheers as she jumps out of the back seat and sets out to collect some rocks for traction.

Curtis and Ken use sand ladders to rescue the Pajero

With Ken's attention to detail and mechanics and my organizational skills it wasn't long before we were better at desert travel than most. Still, we never went far off-road in Egypt by ourselves. One can die in the Sahara in less than 48 hours if it is hot enough and there is no water. Someone who is injured doesn't stand a chance. (No such thing as cell phones at the time.) We carry extra water and notify others where we will be going and when we should be home. The school actually requires us to do this as they will need us to teach come Sunday morning.

Curtis, Denise and Lynn Putzke are in the other Pajero and Ron and Vicky Nelson are riding with us. We enjoy taking friends to Fayoum because it isn't too far from home or from a road so we don't need to be quite so careful or carry so many provisions.

The expansive Fayoum Depression is our favorite week-end camping destination from Cairo. It is well off-road in the quiet desert, with remnants of ancient towns lying in a once lush valley peeking out from under centuries of sand. It takes less than two hours to get there if we leave before sunrise on Friday but sometimes almost three hours to return home in heavy traffic on Saturday evening. The area is in a large depression that still holds the saltwater remnant of a once large lake supplying fresh water for over eight thousand years to thirsty people and crops. There is more hard ground than sand so navigation is manageable and there are many cool campsites.

The Fayoum depression on the shore of a lake mostly gone

"Hey! I found one! Look over here!" I call to the others to gather round to admire an unusual find, a chert arrowhead I had discovered barely sticking out of the sand. "It is chipped on one tang but has a beautiful golden brown sheen. Definitely the real thing" remarks Ken as he buffs it on his sleeve and dons his reading glasses for closer inspection. The others rush over to see the prize and to scour the site where there may be more. "I found the biggest arrowhead! Look its worked!" teases Ron as he holds up a large triangular chunk of rock. We all join the laughter and continue to search and play.

We like to argue and tease about whether the stones we find are actually real tools that have been "worked" or just naturally chipped rocks. Spending hours slowly gazing at the sands on the desert floor, meandering in the peaceful barren landscape, chatting occasionally with friends is a relaxing hobby and a get-away from the city. Finding artifacts uncovered by millennia of shifting dunes is an alluring bonus.

Showing off prizes found in the sand

Over years of visiting this site we found Roman iron fish hooks, stone scraping tools and some chert Neolithic arrowheads, probably 4,000-8,000 years old. A piece of human skeleton was sticking out of the sand next to the decayed city of Dimeah that has not been occupied for 2,000 years. What will be left of us thousands of years from now? Are we learning anything or are we just repeating cycles of rise and fall.

The Dimeah ruin is our pet camping spot within the Fayoum. It has stones from an ancient Pharaonic temple and remains of a Roman fort built on the edge of a depression that is now forty meters below sea level. It is well enough off-road to be nicely isolated, fairly easy to find, and a great location for camping and exploring surrounding desert hills and dunes. Archaeologists have already collected the valuable antiquities for the Cairo museum. But among the remaining rubble we have already found lots of broken pottery bits and a few stone carving tools just lying on top of the ground.

"Look at this nice blue one. It even has a tiny stripe around it." Lynn uncurls her fingers to show us her small prize. Ken, Denise and Lynn are focusing on finding tiny beads and have gathered almost enough for an ancient bracelet. They are probably Roman but some may be much older.

Lynn, Denise and Ken search for tiny artifacts

There are a couple of good books in our school library that have definitive information about historical ruins in Egypt. *"The Desert Fayum"* is the best. Done by two British archaeologists for the Royal Anthropological Institute of Great Britain, it is incredibly detailed with contour maps and pages of photos of stone tools, pottery and building remains. Two tough ladies, Gertrude Caton-Thompson and Elinor W. Gardner, did all this work in the 1920's. We can only imagine what kind of adventure that was. They scoured a fairly large part of the country west of Cairo where the land had been inhabited since Neolithic times before it turned to desert. Some settlements date back more than eight thousand years. We will use their information and coordinates and hope to follow in some of their footsteps.

Local museums are good places to find physical information on geology and historical anthropology. I was never that interested before coming to Egypt. The Sahara desert is pretty uninteresting and inaccessible to most people but is a wide-open fantasyland for the adventurous. The Geological Museum of Cairo tickled our excitement about re-discovering ancient civilizations just sticking out of the sand.

Humans, after all, evolved in Africa and our ancestors have been making stone tools for over two million years. The dryness of the desert preserves the ruins and prevents greenery and people from moving in on top of them.

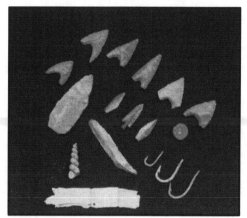

Neolithic flints and Roman fish hooks

The dark red sun settles down in the dusty haze across the sands. It is time to pitch the tents, blow up the air mattresses and make dinner. "Is everyone ready for some of Mona's vegetable soup?" asks Denise as she dumps the half-thawed bowl prepared by her maid into the large aluminum pot sitting on the camp stove.

"You bet, bring it on!" answers Curtis, dragging a few Egyptian Stella beers from the cooler and pulling up some canvas chairs.

"Have some Pringles vinegar and salt chips we found down on Road Nine," offers Vicky as she takes them from Ron and passes around the unusual treat.

There are always people at school wanting to ride with us because it is such a unique opportunity. Next time we're taking the new superintendent, Dave Chojnacki and his wife, Clair. Hopefully we can eventually share the adventure with all our friends.

After a while we travel only with Curtis and Denise to the really tough places. Our Pajeros are identical. We brought extra parts that are interchangeable. We know that if both break, between Ken and Curtis we can scavenge any part and still have one good running vehicle. Ken was a mechanic in the Army and can fix anything. Curtis also has repair experience. Both are physics teachers and great at analyzing technical problems. Ken once replaced a lost oil filter cap from the Pajero with an empty Heineken can and a coat hanger we found in the trash. We call it the "Heineken fix."

Ken fixing oil cap

Sand ladders, shovels, extra gas, lots of tools, plenty water, several maps, a few compasses, extra tires, cork screw, more water, wine, food...... We had a camping list a mile long. After travelling with a few folks who came unprepared we often opted out of group expeditions.

The Fayoum was just the beginning of many exciting years of sandy excursions throughout the Middle East. When we took new jobs in a desert country our first question was often "Can we get a four-wheel-drive and go off-road?" It was our passionate weekend pursuit in Egypt, Tunisia, Saudi Arabia and Dubai. Each trip was a journey into a different world with a story all its own.

Spring Serendipity
Egypt, 1992

It started while we were at school, like a temper tantrum it thundered and thrashed growing darker by the minute. Visibility clouded to less than 25 meters on campus in late morning and we could not see the elementary building across the playground. Our first real dust storm. Fine brown powdered sand blowing in from the Sahara thickened the air all day long. It obscured the view out the window and sifted through cracks causing us to cough and gag. Finally in late afternoon the storm abated and was followed by a brief, unusual rain shower, covering the entire city in a thin layer of mud. With only one inch of rain a year Cairo does not have a drainage system and streets are never washed clean. As cars, trucks and people slid across the muddy oily roads hundreds of little accidents piled up. Luckily, with the slow traffic, most of them were just fender-benders.

We arrived safely home to find the back bedroom window had blasted open and the whole room was coated in a thick layer of dust that would have to be removed with brooms and shovels. The bed, stuffed chairs and carpets would need vacuuming and washing. The maid will have a few days' work cut out for her.

Scientists have analyzed soil chemistry to discover that dust from the Sahara can be found all around the earth and even on top of ice in Antarctica and mountain glaciers in Alaska. Small, dusty, connected world.

"We can't sleep at night. The owner of our building yells down to the unloading, clanking, steel re-bar trucks all night long, while the busses are blowing their horns at the station next door and loaded trucks lumber down the busy four-lane street below our window." I've been complaining since we moved in and have gathered research that describes the deleterious effects of noise and sleeplessness on health and job performance. Ken has measured the decibel readings using a meter from the physics lab. I have a petition signed by everyone in our apartment building to move us. Even though the head of housing is adamant about staying in this apartment for at least two years, our headmaster, Guy Lott is much nicer and gives in after visiting and reading our research. They will move all 14 families. We can see our new apartment complex just a couple blocks away, closer to school and more residential and quiet. The flats are larger and newer and I think we will like it there, especially since we will still be close to our friends. The noise of hundreds of people packed in high-rise living will still be trying but at least it won't be industrial all night long.

It is so dark in the mornings now since winter that we have almost given up running. There is too much debris and too many cracks and bumps in the road to run in the dark and the afternoons are far too busy with traffic. Weekend mornings are better as we can wait for dawn but that is not enough exercise for us. So I have been going with Denise and Vicky to Annie Camp's aerobic class and using the gym at school a few times a week after running the track. Annie is so full of energy she keeps us all bouncing and the class is an enjoyable diversion from solitary exercise.

School is a bit more hectic than expected. With a student body of about 1700 and about 175 faculty there is not quite the closeness with students that we experienced before. More teachers and administrators means more meetings. Many of the families are posted in Egypt with big business or oil companies who have their own social groups and are not as chummy as the AID agency folks in Dhaka or the diplomats in Lahore. But there are plenty of great folks at the school. With two chemistry, two physics and four biology professors Ken and I have fewer subjects to prepare and more professional interaction.

Every country, every school, apartment and social circle has a whole different essence. The challenge lies in uncovering the joys on which to focus and put central in our life, to change what we can to make it better and to learn from all of it.

St. Paul's Monastery, February 15

After our brief visit during our winter Nile trip, without any reservations Ken and I arrive at the front gate and ask to spend the night. None of our friends are interested so we have come alone. "Please, join us. We are very happy to have you. We will serve a simple meal of soup after our evening services," the kind monk invites us into the courtyard. Since it is a cold and slow time of year the generous monks are able to accommodate our needs and even allow us to sleep in the same room, which is not usually acceptable.

Monk at St. Paul's

The Coptic religion is an early sect of Christianity derived in Egypt. The Monastery of St. Paul the Anchorite is a Coptic Orthodox monastery dating back to the fifth century. Although it was repeatedly attacked and destroyed over the many centuries by Bedouins, it is still going strong and is celebrated as a precious inheritance of the Coptic faithful. The adobe structures rise up out of the edge of the barren desert mountains near the Red Sea, just south of the Suez Canal. A small group of monks manage a year-round retreat center for visitors.

"Just let me know if you need anything." A helpful, heavily-bearded monk named Macaree takes over our care, shows us around, makes sure we have the food and privacy we need and informs us of the schedules.

"I'm thirsty and my water bottle is empty. Have you noticed any place to fill it?" I ask Ken as we sit on the wall of a well in the courtyard. "I saw some monks drink from this well we are sitting on. Want to try it?" As we draw water to fill our bottles from the ancient well in the center of the monastery, Macaree appears again. "Would you like to have one of our blessed breads?" He offers. Still warm from the stone oven, imprinted with a Coptic cross and offered from generous hands it seems to fill more than just our belly.

Following a short afternoon service we climb the hills behind the monastery. Sitting down against the stone mountain in the warm sun we overlook the Gulf of Suez at the north-western tip of the Red Sea. The focus of so many stories of the Bible. Some say there is a reef not far below the surface nearby that could have been exposed during strong winds in the time of Moses parting the sea for the Israelites. A light breeze brushing the rocks and the crinkling of the paper on which I write are the only sounds at this site of a possible miracle.

I believe in miracles. The definition is "surprising, welcome, unexplained events." These happen every day and the more science I know, the more I appreciate the miracle of it all. Nothing can ever be completely explained. There is always a core of unknown in the timing, the physics, the chemistry or the biology. "If you ever think you really know something, count yourself a fool," I tell my students, "for there is always a fact behind a fact and a cause behind the cause."

The pink glow of the setting sun illuminates the monastery below, tucked into the walls of the golden desert mountains. As the stars begin to appear in the clear sky above we hike back down to our simple quarters for a quiet, peaceful night.

Rising at 4:00 A.M. we join the monks for early morning services in the underground tomb of an early Christian saint. The soft chanting rhythms of the Kyrie-Eleison resonate in my body as it echoes off the damp, candlelit walls deep within the cave. The Coptic hymns and chants are familiar but not identical to the Catholic masses I had known as a child so I can chant softly right along with them. Spicy odors of frankincense wafts from the smoking brass burners swaying from the wrinkled hands of the elderly priest. The soft golden light of dozens of candles flicker gently as we pray shoulder to shoulder with the monks. Standing on the worn Persian carpets of the small cave, we face the altar built next to the tomb of St. Paul. The red and gold decorated robes of the priest contrasts with the simple black garments of the monks as we joined them all to chant before the sun brings the day.

No matter what religion, monasteries throughout the world are havens for those who wish to dedicate their lives to God. Although I could never live this kind of life, the simplicity, honesty, and devotion of those who do is a wonderful retreat from the materialistic, busy life of the city. Each of us makes lifestyle choices and I am learning to appreciate the amazing diversity of ways in which we serve each other.

Coincidence in the Holy City

"Paul!" "I can't believe that you are here, now, of all places, in St. Peter's Square, in Rome at the exact time we are!" I shout with joy, throwing my arms around my brother as he lifts me, twirling around in a big bear hug. "It's a miracle!"

We had won a free trip to Italy at a big Christmas charity ball in Cairo. Air Italia included three nights stay in Rome in the four star Hotel Forum right across from the Forum and Coliseum. Biggest prize we ever won and we had never travelled to Italy so we were wired for the adventure.

We had ten days for spring break and the tickets had to be used before summer so we started making arrangements right away. As we were getting the details sorted out a letter arrived in the mail from my youngest brother, Paul who was living in New York. He was excited to tell us about his plan to travel through Europe in spring and he included his Eurail itinerary. "Oh, my god!" "Paul will be in Rome the same time as us!" I shout to Ken as I read the letter. "I can't believe it! We must call him right away before he leaves."

So, as magical coincidence or blessed karma would have it and a phone call confirmed, we ran across the plaza of St. Peter's Cathedral to jump into each other's arms with the squealing abandon of long lost siblings in a different part of the world.

Having been brought up Catholic the spiritual significance of the Vatican as the center of our religion is still meaningful to me even years after leaving the weekly services. Studying many different religions I have learned to appreciate their good purposes regardless of their flaws. Michelangelo's Pieta and the magnificent murals of the Sistine Chapel epitomize the creativity of man meeting God in art and devotion. I stroll through St. Peter's Cathedral, head thrown back straining to examine the vaulted displays. The Stations of the Cross and the intricate stories unfold in the stained glass windows, all bringing up memories of my childhood reverence.

Ken and I had already spent three days exploring ruins and small, delightful Italian restaurants and are ready to discover more of Italy. So the four of us – Paul, his friend Joe, Ken and I rent a very small white Fiat. "Do you really think we can all fit in this thing?" Paul asks as Ken tightly stuffs four big backpacks into the vestigial trunk. "Come on, Paul, don't

you remember getting all eight of us into dad's car when we were little? There should be plenty of room for you on the roof." I tease. "As long as you don't leave me behind like you did once when you were being a brat." He smiles as he grabs my arm.

With tour guides in hand and no reservations we head north out of Rome. It is a cool, sunny spring day as we motor up highway A1

Paul, Ken & Joe piling into the Fiat

toward Florence. After a few hours of driving through the scenic land of olive trees, vineyards, spring wildflowers and ancient castles we spot a dramatic looking hill-town perched on top of a craggy cliff surrounded by thick old fortress walls.

"The highway sign says Orvieto," Joe declares from the front seat.

"I'll pull over so you can check the books," Ken offers as he drives to the edge of the highway.

"Orvieto has stood far above the valley of Umbria with its impregnable walls for thousands of years. Julius Caesar was the last one to conquer it." I read from the *Lonely Planet Guide to Italy*. "Seems like it should be a safe place to stay the night." I remark and continue reading, "The town has a festival every spring to celebrate their family heritage."

"Sounds fun," Paul remarks, "What are the chances it'll be today?"... Laughing, we turn towards Orvieto. Without too many set plans we have time to investigate off the beaten path, so we chug up the winding hill and into the village on the mountain.

A quaint hotel of chipped cream-colored stucco framed in dark brown trim faces the central town square. For a reasonable price, they have two cozy rooms available with an adjoining terrace so we bring in our bags. After a quick rest we hustle out to see the magnificent Gothic cathedral just across the street for which, according to our book, this town is known.

"Hey, did you see that group of people on the street just outside the cathedral? Paul asks as he catches up to us wandering around inside. "It looks like a group of actors or something. You might want to come see what's happening." Figuring we can come back to the church later we turn to follow his lead.

Robed in beautiful medieval costumes more and more local people are gathering in the streets. A woman in her tightly bodiced lace-topped burgundy dress holds the tiny hand of her little boy dressed in blue knickers, tall white stockings and a red cape thrown over his shoulders. Several men in green or purple velvet pantaloons proudly carry their family coat of arms strikingly displayed on large cloth banners swaying from long poles. Like a scene from the movie of Romeo and Juliet, there are many families represented. Men, women, children and even dogs are decked out in their sixteenth century best. And we just happened to be here, in this main street of Orvieto, waiting for them.

Orvieto celebration

"This looks like it could be the spring festival that was described in our guidebook." Paul remarks. "What are the chances?"

"It is Corpus Domini, a yearly event to celebrate the Body of Christ and the ancient noble families who have been here for more generations than they know," answers a young Italian man watching from the sidelines when we ask. "The crown on the top of the banners is the Royal Coat of Arms given to Orvieto in the Middle Ages and the red cross on the white background symbolizes heroes of the crusades." He knows the story well and is happy to share it with us. Sitting on a mossy old stone wall in the afternoon sun we chat with the young man and his girlfriend who speaks just a little English. We learn more about these families marching by to the beat of their drums and long brass horns, proudly waving their family coat-of-arms.

Unplanned itineraries are sometimes difficult but we like to travel more for the purpose of discovery than convenience. This amazing medieval parade in this ancient hill town of Orvieto with its grand cathedral is an unanticipated pleasure.

Searching out the beauty, art, history, food and personalities of Florence and Assisi fills the rest of our week before we have to separate from Paul and Joe and head back to Egypt. Different from the dusty noisy streets of Cairo, Italy was a refreshingly different spring break. Especially when sharing it with family in unexpected serendipity.

Eco Update 1992

The school is especially keen on professional development so Ken and I offer to do a seminar on the latest facts and figures of the ecological status of the world. Since ecology has always been a subject close to my heart I keep up with the latest and enjoy sharing recent scientific research.

With about 25 teachers in attendance we use video clips and slides of photos, facts and figures along with a ten-page booklet we had printed for them. It is fun to organize and especially nice to get all the raving appreciation. It's hard for busy teachers to keep up in a field that is not their own and quite nice to be able to summarize it for them. With our highly educated faculty presentations are frequent and diverse.

Unfortunately the environmental news is not good. Even though our hearts and hopes want to make things better, a rising population focused on using resources excessively makes it very difficult to see a healthy sustainable future. I try to be hopeful because the alternative is not acceptable. Surely we can make changes when faced with adversity, we always have.

Easter in Cyprus and Dreams on the Mountain

The Hash House Harries are having an international run in Cyprus over a long Easter holiday weekend so we join them to buy group rate plane tickets. Running with a couple hundred Hashers through masses of yellow wildflowers in stony fields of spring on a Mediterranean island is a boisterous break from the Egyptian deserts.

Dave and Terry have brought their twelve-year-old daughter Elizabeth along to Cyprus. Many of the international faculty have children. In some countries it is cheap to hire a full time nanny and other servants to make child-rearing easier. It is an amazing experience for children to grow up in different cultures with friends from all over the world. They learn to feel like a citizen of the planet instead of identifying with only one country. Many of them pursue international careers as adults.

After the HHH running event along the rocky beaches of a Cyprus bursting with the fresh flowers of spring we rent a car with Curtis and Denise and head out to look around the Greek side of the big island for a couple of days. This island has been in political conflict for centuries. Officially an independent country, the Republic of Cyprus has more than a third of its land claimed by Turkey and calling it the Turkish Republic of Northern Cyprus. We stick to the Greek side and avoid the disputed border.

Last night, restlessly sleeping in a chilly hotel room, I dreamt of asking my grandparents countless questions. Having passed away many years ago they have occasionally guided me in my dreams. Grandpa drives me to a temple at the top of a hill and tells me to follow the teachings there.

It is Easter Sunday morning and we get an early start. As we tour through the Cyprus countryside in our blue Corolla sedan we spot a monastery at the top of a steep hill. "Looks like a beautiful spot," Denise admires. "Turn left here," exclaims Ken. Curtis reacts quickly to turn into the steeply winding driveway. Only men are allowed entry to the monastery so Denise and I stroll over to a small chapel perched on the edge of the mountain overlooking the colorful countryside all the way to the sea.

There are over 2,000 species of wild flowers here and this cool, sunny spring day is aflame in shades of yellow, orange, blue and purple. The wildflower hillside flows down to a patchwork of fenced in farms, which flow in turn to a grid of town streets running their paths to the sea.

Cyprus Flower Girls

A knurled oak tree spreads its wide branches next to the chapel. Beneath its sheltering boughs I sit down quietly on a boulder to contemplate. The vibrant multicolored patchwork spreads across the terrain below. Wildflowers and a few bushes of the steep hillside are the only part that is natural. The rest looks beautiful but is unnaturally cut into segments designed solely for human use.

We are cutting it up too much, replacing nature with agriculture, factories, cities and yards. It occurs to me that in order to continue to thrive on this amazing planet we need to look at it from a bird's eye view. All creatures share the earth, air and water in intricate complexity. With education we may be able to shift our priorities from individual consumption of our land to a shared global stewardship and protect larger areas to let nature reign.

Dreams on the mountain. They can only come true if we believe in them.

Guts and Guppies
Letter home from Egypt, Fall 1992

There's a cool breeze blowing, sparrows are chirping and doves cooing in the swaying branches of the courtyard trees. A donkey brays in the distance and a 1950s rusted wreck of a car rumbles down the empty street as the warm sun peeks up over the horizon. Curled up in a white wicker chair on our small back porch, I'm sipping a hot cup of Barney's cinnamon coffee and all is quiet and pleasant on our Friday morning off in Cairo.

It is year two here in Egypt and things are better. We are enjoying our new apartment located just one block from the last one but away from the busy four-lane street, the rebar factory, the bus terminal and the amusement center. Even with thick blankets stuffed into our bedroom window we were getting pretty grouchy with little sleep in our last apartment. Egyptians can be very late-night people but we need to rise early for school. So school facilities' workers moved eleven households into this newly built seven-story complex we call New Fontana.

Our flat at New Fontana with friends

Surrounded with large windows, the living room is almost as big as my classroom and now includes a forest. We covered one wall with a 9' x 12' mural of a wooded park scene we brought from the States in our luggage. The Hawaiian beach is on the wall in the bedroom, complete with glow–in-the-dark stars on the ceiling. Philodendron vines, crotons and small palms fill the living room with green life. Red geraniums and white gardenias grow from window boxes and surround our tiny back porch. Our friends come over for picnics. We try to bring some nature inside our apartment. There is so very little of it outside in this city of millions tightly packed in high-rise apartments in a long band between the Nile River and the Sahara desert. Pant life must be carefully tended; as the average rainfall is only one inch a year and we have not yet seen it rain here.

School has been keeping us incurably busy since arriving in August. But that is nothing new as good teaching is a never-ending pursuit. The students are ambitious but can be rowdy, as usual. There is a bit more American influence here than we had at other schools. Cairo has the largest American embassy in the world and U.S. oil companies are big businesses. Cairo American College is the place to send these international kids to prepare them well for university.

Not only are we totally redesigning the high school science curriculum but a whole new science wing is under construction and everything must be ordered by the middle of this November to receive it next August. I stuck my foot in my mouth and agreed to be science department head this year. What was I thinking? All these changes and having to get 12 independent, science teachers to agree on them is a serious challenge. After a few rounds in the ring with some old-timer teachers who want to keep things as they were, we're finally clearing the air and beginning to work together. Usually. We will be starting the International Baccalaureate Program here next year. It will be even more intense than the Advanced Placement college classes we have been teaching and more paperwork but it will prepare our students for top universities all over the world, even allowing them to skip some college courses.

I asked our lab assistant to bring me some whole chickens from the market to dissect and he brings five, very much alive and squawking. "Can you kill them for me, please?" I ask with a grimace. "Yes, Ma'am," he answers as he takes them out the back door.

Yuk! Look at that!" The students arrive a little too early, just in time to go shrieking and running to the back window to watch. Despite the whining they eventually get down to work and have fun learning.

"Make a nice straight cut down the middle of the breast and be careful not to slice into the organs," I instruct as the students begin dissection. Amira dives right in but Becky is a bit queasy. Mohammed thinks it's "way cool" and strings the small intestines like a garland over his wide-stretched hands. Unraveling the long squishy intestines to measure the length is always a highlight.

Stephen complains of finding a heart on his lunch table later in the day and blames it on Brian. It isn't easy to monitor all the little parts.

Students dissecting chickens

The City of the Dead is very much alive on Friday mornings when this largest graveyard in the city becomes a big open market. A wide variety of products is sold but mostly pets and all their supplies are displayed between the ancient graves. The tombs are built like small one-room brick houses, complete with walled in courtyards for the wealthy spirits. It's not surprising that more than a few live people inhabit these graveyards, even though relatives of the deceased pay caretakers to run them off. But early on Friday mornings ghosts are neglected and the alleys fill with a dense concentration of vendors. Pigeons, lizards, parakeets, fish, hawks, hedgehogs, puppies, falcons, finches, snakes, parrots and, I'm sorry to say, an occasional Fennec fox or eagle. As the morning progresses, the crowds of buyers get thicker and the cars, trucks and donkey carts continue to lay on their horns as they bulldoze their way down the narrow streets.

It's fun, disgusting, interesting, dangerous, sad and exotic. Some of the animals being sold are endangered species. The falcons are so beautiful with their thickly feathered bodies and big black intelligent eyes. It's sad to see five or six in a small cage instead of flying freely over the desert. There are twelve separate vendors with fish tanks full of swordtails, guppies, goldfish, angels, and occasionally a different tropical. We buy a 25-gallon aquarium plus everything it needs so we can enjoy watching and feeding some easy-care fish. With a couple of bags of swordtails and guppies we head home and hope they'll live. Some will. They're not expensive so it is easy to buy more.

Tropical fish market

It's relaxing and fun to have some kind of pet again. The swordtail had babies the other day and we monitor closely to see how long they will survive. Five are still hanging in there, hiding in the grassy forest of their tiny world.

This Christmas we will be somewhere in the Sahara desert, alive, we hope. The plan involves driving a one thousand mile Sahara Desert loop west of the Nile River. The roads will take us through the Kharga, Dhakla, Farafra and Baharaia Oasis. We will adventure mostly off-road in pursuit of ancient ruins and good camping spots. Curtis and Denise will have their own 4-wheel drive and both our vehicles will be filled

301

with water, food and gas to last ten days. There will be remnants of Pharonic and Roman civilizations all along the way in places inaccessible to most travelers. We may even attempt crossing a corner of the Great Sand Sea where impenetrable golden crescents of sand run west into Libya. Camping will be primitive. It will be cold, windy, sandy and isolated but no real adventures are easy. The desert will be serene and beautiful with some of the cleanest air in the world. There will be historic civilizations to discover and no problems with rain.

Our weekend camping trips to the Fayoum desert a few hours from Cairo have given us enough experience and bravado to tackle this more complex excursion. We still have lots of proper prior planning to accomplish.

Another big plan in the making is to attend the NESA teacher's conference in Nairobi in spring. The NESA organization includes more than 100 international schools from the Near East & South Asia. They facilitate high-quality workshops for educational improvement and professional development. We attended one of their conferences in Bangkok when we were teaching in Pakistan.

Our school will help to pay the fees. The conference will be over spring break. The latest is - we have to fly out at 2AM on March 17th on Ethiopian Airlines and spend about 14 hours in transit with a stop in Addis Ababa. Both the Lahore American School and the American International School in Dhaka will be participating and we are excited about catching up with old friends. NESA conferences present renowned speakers and are great venues to learn more and revive our enthusiasm for teaching.

After four days of conference we plan to go on Safari. Mom will fly in from Florida to make the trip to Kenya with us. It's fairly expensive to fly across Africa. The continent is gigantic and airfare is high with no bargains. But traveling is what we're here for so we are seriously excited. Egypt doesn't feel quite like Africa. Everyone says it will be worth every penny as there is nothing else like a safari on the wild open savannahs of Kenya.

There have been more terrorist attacks focused on tourists here in Egypt. But statistics show that one is more likely to get shot in a big American city than in Cairo where crime is much lower. Besides, the military has just gone out and 'taken care of' anybody they thought was making trouble. Tourism is down and there are police escorts for tourist buses, but there have been no attacks on individuals so we think it should be safe for Christmas. At least safer than Pakistan was. We keep a low profile – sort of. Since we spent most of our first year going to the big tourist attractions like the Giza pyramids and the Cairo museum, we can focus on more out-of-the-way unusual places.

Knife sharpening

"Ya la sikkina!, Ya la sikkina!" The frail brown man in his weathered bare feet calls out as he carries his large wheel on a wooden stand. He calls to sharpen our knives. Wandering through the streets in tattered clothes he comes by our apartment about twice a month. This is likely his only form of income and he is good at it. For about fifty cents he'll turn his strapped wheel with his foot and sing a little tune as he moves the knife rhythmically back and forth until it cuts like a razor. It's worth the money just to watch him.

A younger man with a donkey cart loaded down with potatoes and yellow onions slowly walks by calling out his own selling song as his boisterous young son rides atop the pile. The donkey moves slowly with head down, as if tired but resigned to his path in life.

A run-down car pulls up below the high-rise apartments across the street and honks the horn to get the attention of an invisible friend waiting for their ride.

It is Saturday morning, the air is cool and clear (well, almost) and the daily activities begin outside our window.

We spent Thanksgiving on the Sinai Peninsula camping on the beach of the Red Sea and the Gulf of Aqaba, stopping at Mt. Sinai where Moses received the 10 commandments. I wonder if I inhaled some of the same molecules that he did and what wisdom he would have to offer to us in this busy, technological world of today. Maybe we all could use a bit of solitude, a bit of wondering. The desert is a quiet, contemplative place. No distractions.

Somebody in our neighborhood died the other day. A large white tent was erected on the street and a mullah (Moslem preacher) sang chants over a loudspeaker from late afternoon till late night. Oh well, it wasn't much worse than our neighborhood mosque of Pakistan or the nighttime construction of Bangladesh. The incessant din of big city life has always been a challenge for us. Yearning for the quiet life of our country home in America constantly pulls our heartstrings.

After a busy week teaching, it is finally SHIT day (Sure Happy it's Thursday) so we take out after school with our friends for a quiet ride on a felucca sailboat down the Nile. On a pleasantly warm evening, with a deep orange sunset and a sliver of a moon, we float peacefully down the same river that carried the golden ships of the Pharaohs. Some perspectives on life slip into place as we share the evening. We forget the troubles of living, dip our fresh chewy pita bread into some tangy eggplant babaganoush, toast to each other, relax and breathe in the essence of Egypt.

Earthquake!
Egypt, Oct 1992

It is about 3:10 in the afternoon and classes have just been released for the day. The high school building is not busy, as kids don't dally much after school. I am discussing an assignment with a couple of students when the room begins to shake. At first I think it is just a big truck but the deep rumbling immediately intensifies, sending a primal warning to my very core. EARTHQUAKE?? –BOMB!!??- Then an urge to get out fast. "LEAVE THE BUILDING" I yell as l rush the kids to the door. I am from Florida, the flat sandy remnant of the continental shelf. I have never before experienced a shaking of this kind and don't know the protocol. I don't trust buildings, especially those of questionable construction. The instinct to get outside takes over. Ken emerges from his class down the hall and we spot and grab each other on our way out. We rush the kids before us and try to make sure we have everyone clear and safe. We learned later about the practice of hiding under the desks.

"I'm not going in there." I inform Ken at the entrance to our apartment. "Look at those cracks in the wall near the front door. When there are earthquakes there are aftershocks and just because it looks OK doesn't mean it is." I decide. The school building is just 2 stories high and designed by American architects, but our apartment is six floors and designed locally, where building codes are not necessarily followed.

"Oh, come on. We'll just run in, change our clothes, get a few things and come right back out. We'll be fine," he insists. I finally agree to Ken's coaxing on the promise of just a quick change, a brief look for any damage and then a fast exit down the stairs for a dinner out.

There are some cracks in the plaster of the living room and back bedroom. The fish tank has dripping aquatic plants hanging over the side, has lost several gallons of water, and the fish look a little dazed. Otherwise the place looks OK. We eat at an outdoor cafe on the Nile, along with a lot of other nervous, excited people exchanging experiences.

"Buildings have collapsed downtown, possibly hundreds dead, and lots of destruction. They say it was a magnitude 5.9." Someone from another table gives us the report as he listens to his small portable radio.

Weaving our way home through the busy streets after dinner we see many frightened families curled up to sleep outside to avoid the same fate. Small aftershocks continue to move the earth beneath our feet. Electricity is still out as we climb into bed. A few small tremors shake us in the fitful night.

No one was hurt at the school, but of 15 million people in Cairo there were about 500 deaths. It could have been much worse. Or much better. For a magnitude of just 5.9 it was quite destructive, the worst in a century of Egyptian history. Some of the local structures are unbelievably dilapidated and people are injured by building collapses even without an earthquake. It was a thirteen-story apartment building downtown that caused most of the deaths and injuries. It had no steel reinforcement, was not made to code, and the top stories had been added without permits. The whole thing just pancaked into a pile of concrete. The owner and builders are under verbal and even physical attack as families continue to pull loved ones from beneath the ruins.

The tremors continue for about four weeks, shaking up to 4.1 on the Richter scale. Long cracks in the living room plaster still remind us. Of course we try to call family, as we know it must be international news, but the lines are tied up for days. Ken's sister, Sybil, using her contacts in Washington D.C., was able to find out that no one from our school was hurt and passed her information to our families.

There are a lot of seismic fault lines in and around Cairo that cause occasional problems. For months, I jump to attention when I hear windows rattle. Nature's power is humbling.

"Let's go see what's happened in the Fayoum," suggests Ken two weeks later. "The epicenter was not far from our favorite camping spot."

"Yeah, right. Jumping right into the center of an earthquake sounds like a jolly good time," I smirk.

"We would be sleeping in a tent and even if there was another quake, there would be nothing to fall on us." He answers.

"Well, I guess it could be exciting to see what happened at the epicenter." I concede. Curtis and Denise are also interested so we load up the trucks for a weekend camping trip.

"Would you and Clair like to go camping with us in the Fayoum?" Ken asks David Chojnacki, our superintendent.

"We've been wanting to go but is this a safe time?" David responds.

"No, but it should be interesting and there haven't been that many aftershocks lately." Ken assures. "Besides, it may be safer than your house."

David and Clair ride with us, and Curtis and Denise bring some friends in their 4x4. Newly opened cracks in the sandy desert floor make driving difficult as we can't tell how deep or wide they are. "Stop! There's another crack!" I demand as Ken tries to slam on the brakes without throwing everybody through the window. Jumping out of the truck, I walk ahead to check it out. "It looks like its only about four to six inches wide but I can't tell how deep. Sand is pouring into the cracks and it appears bottomless. I think we should try to go around it to the right," I report. We drove right over the top of a few cracks before we could even see them.

Looking for earthquake cracks in Fayoum Desert

We have longitude and latitude coordinates and we use our new GPS to camp close to the epicenter. But not too close. We are nervous, but actually hoping to feel the ground shake right from nature. It doesn't happen so we enjoy a nice quiet campout with friends, away from the city under the sparkling clear desert sky.

I am sure people in California and Japan would not flinch at such a small earthquake. I find our emotions amazing. How easy it is to be unprepared and afraid of things we are not familiar with. Also, how easy it is to get too familiar with danger.

Ghosts of the Sahara (see map p. 245)
Winter break Dec 92 - Jan 1993

Day one – The Black Hole

"OK, everyone show your passports and wallets," Denise demands and we comply, knowing that it will be disastrous to forget them. At six AM on Dec. 20, the day after finishing our last exams and turning in our grades for the semester, Curtis, Denise, Ken & I meet below our apartments to check each other for the essentials: passports, money, water and extra gas. Our two Pajeros are packed to the hilt with everything we feel we might need to survive ten days in the Sahara desert: maps, compass, 50 liters of bottled water, 20 liters of tap water, 60 extra liters of gas split between the extra 25 liter can on the outside and 2 large red plastic jugs behind the seats, shovels, sand ladders and towropes, extra car parts, tools, camping gear, food, extra sunglasses, sunscreen and of course warm clothes and sleeping bags for the freezing desert nights. Our lists were a mile long and we plan (hope?) to re-fuel and re-stock supplies at the oasis towns.   Good thing we are not backpacking.   We have been planning for more than a year, even collecting detailed maps on a trip to London, which could not be found elsewhere. We have bought a GPS for $600, fairly cheap for this brand new technology, and have practiced with it on shorter desert journeys near home.

The road out of Cairo looks like something out of the Mad Max movies; like a nuclear bomb wasted the place years ago and man has degenerated into little more than survivalists living in trash.   A lifeless, rocky brown landscape is littered with tattered plastic grocery

Highway just outside of Cairo

bags of faded smoky shades that cling to fences and thorny, bare, scrub bushes. Hills of household and industrial waste dumped right on the roadside for miles make the new four-lane highway an unsightly two-lane obstacle course. The air is so dense with dust and pollution it is hard to see the sun rising. Clouds of grey cement particles spew from nearby factories covering the desert, the garbage and the village buildings with the same dingy ashen blanket. High-rise housing units of brown plaster are packed together in a few isolated compounds and surrounded by garbage. In this harsh climate of scouring dust storms instead of cleansing rain it is hard to work at exterior beauty. Paint wears quickly and there is not enough water to spare for decorative gardens. On a hill shrouded in white dust, three men "mine" phosphate with shovels. Children, mostly boys about middle-school age, gather in a soccer field to organize a game. The garbage has been pushed to the side, and the dirt packed down to make a fairly flat spot for their favorite outdoor pastime; a sign that human beings can survive under bleak conditions, make a go of it and even have fun!

"Ken, look! Over on that billboard. It's the Michelin Man waving to us. Better wave back, quick!" I remind him as we drive past on the way out of town. Tongue-in-cheek, we wave heartily to the rotund man made of white tires, taking our luck wherever we can get it. We heard we must wave to keep from getting flat tires. I stick my hand out the window to remind Curtis and Denise, following right behind us. We each have our regular spare tire as well as an extra tied to the bull bars on the front, along with the sand ladders. We had the metal ladders made at a local junkyard. Ken scrounged through a mound of metal trash till he got the types of rough, strong steel to make a four-foot ladder strong enough to support the truck struggling out of a sand trap. Longer would be better but we could not find a good roof rack so we have to carry them on the front or inside.

Our desert itinerary includes driving through Asyut to get to the Kharga Oasis, a depression more than 160 kilometers across that once watered both Pharaonic and Roman outposts. Asyut is near the Nile and linked to the desert loop with only one paved road. It is an area where shots have been fired at tourist busses traveling down the Nile roads to Luxor. Because we have private vehicles we hope that we won't be identified as targets.

We have been through here before on other trips without problems. Checkpoints are everywhere and when they study our driving permits and passports to find out we are Americans, the military usually gathers a contingent to escort us through town. We aren't sure this is the safest thing, as it clearly identifies us as a tourist or someone else worth shooting at. But that is their job and they take it seriously, even stopping with us at the gas station to stand guard. Our Raggedy Ann doll sitting on the front dash makes them smile when Ken waves her hand at them. Smiles and a little silliness relieve tension. Especially helpful when there are guns around. Little Raggedy Ann and Andy dolls have traveled with us around the world to remind us to play and enjoy life no matter what happens.

Egyptian military escorts us through Asyut

Standing guard over the road entering Asyut, an imposing steel-grey Egyptian military tank is manned with vigilant rifles sticking out the small narrow windows. There is a large military presence in general here, with armored trucks posted along the Nile roads. Police and army personnel are everywhere. There have been several terrorist attacks on foreigners just in the last few months so we are especially edgy and anxious to get out of this area pronto! The plan is to fuel up quickly and move out of the city, into the desert and off-road away from trouble. Gas will be more difficult to find in desert towns so we need to tank up. Everything is going fine until we meet the "black hole."

To work our new GPS we must enter the geological coordinates for our intended destination and then just try to head in that direction. It is useful in the desert but not in cities. We do not have cell phones or any way to connect with Curtis and Denise except to stick close together, in visual contact.

We are negotiating our way around a busy choke (round-about) in the middle of Asyut where two major roads cross. In some thick traffic moving slowly in a large circle around a raised garden median, C&D's Pajero totally disappear in the maze. "Where are they? Can you see them?" Ken asks concerned. "They were ahead of us just a minute ago. Maybe they are in front of that truck," I answer. "I'll go around once again. Maybe we'll see them down one of the side roads," Ken suggests as he merges back into the flow of traffic. Panic is hard to hold down. We keep circling round the choke, looking down all the roads to see if we can spot them. No luck. There are four possible directions to turn down and we spend about thirty anxious minutes driving in circles desperately trying to find them, wondering how we could possibly lose them right here in the beginning of our journey. We finally decide to get our gas and head out of the city and off into the desert toward the Kharga Oasis, our prospective destination for the day. We hope they too will make the same choice. Not knowing if they are ahead or behind we keep stopping and waiting, discussing a million different possible scenarios- including the possibility of capture or shooting by terrorists.

It doesn't go very well. As we are leaving the city on the desert road to Kharga we are stopped by police at a checkpoint station and asked to wait for an escort. We really want to keep moving on down the road hoping to catch up with our friends. Most other cars are driving right by, so Ken decides he isn't into hanging around and takes off, with the surprised guards yelling and running after us blowing their whistles. At this point we are sure that C&D must be ahead so we bolt to try to catch up. Then panic rises again. Maybe they are behind? So we circle around off road to come up behind a hill where we can see the checkpoint with binoculars. The guards cannot see us and we watch and wait for a while without any sign of our friends. So they must be ahead? (The Hash House Harriers in Cairo eventually applauded this wild maneuver by awarding Ken the nickname "Checkpoint")

So we drive on all the way, about 200 kilometers to the town of Kharga, stopping, waiting, worrying, wondering how they disappeared into the black hole. Are they ahead or behind? Are they in trouble? Surely they will eventually go to Kharga. Surely? Maybe they decided we stayed in Asyut or even gave up and went home. Desperately wishing we had made better plans for losing each other, we continue down the desert road to the first hotel of the oasis, and park our truck in full view.

It is a very long and depressing evening. Our first night of our big, "well planned" adventure might be our last. Christmas carols echo around the dining room as we join some German travelers in hearty yuletide songs as they try to cheer us up after dinner. We still crawl into bed anxious and disheartened, knowing we should be having fun camping in the desert with our friends.

Day two, December 21

After several phone calls made by our friendly hotel clerk to police stations and driving around in the early morning to checkpoints, we finally found out that C&D were in the Kharga Valley. They had gone through and registered in the Asyut checkpoint as we had not when we bolted. Good news. They are OK – most likely. But where? We finally give up driving around and decide to leave notes of our whereabouts with the two valley police checkpoints. We'll just sit and wait for another day or two at the hotel, with the truck parked on the main road, hoping they will find us.

Only about an hour after giving up I open our hotel door to some rambunctious pounding. "You're OK! I can't believe we finally found you!" screams Denise as we all jump into a group hug. They got our checkpoint note, saw our truck, found our room and amid lots of hugs and kisses the ordeal was finally over.

Their story was even worse than ours. They had been in front of us at the choke in Asyut and turned down a side road where they spotted a gas station, expecting us to follow. After filling up with gas and waiting for us they decided to head on out of town. But when they got to the checkpoint the police were ready for crazy foreigners. The guards took their passports and insisted that they wait for a police escort. They were told that "some crazy Germans just ran the stop but, no, not Americans in a white Pajero". (Maybe they were colorblind and just assumed white people are Germans?) The military then became worried about the missing Americans and escorted C&D all around the streets of Asyut looking for us, with a police car ahead and one behind. If we had not gone through the checkpoint they surmised we must still be in the city somewhere. As evening was closing in, C&D decided we just might have gone to Kharga, despite what the guards were telling them. Getting into the desert near dark they pitched camp just off the road where we could see them, desperate to know where we were and if we were OK. After a rough night sleeping on the side of the busy road they headed into Kharga where they were stopped at the valley checkpoint where we had left our note just hours ago.

We immediately discuss some plans for never getting separated again.

After hot showers and a good brunch we check out of the hotel to continue with our expedition. We finally make it off-road, less than fifteen kilometers away, to El Deir, our first really planned destination to pitch our tents mid-afternoon. This Roman fortress ruin near Kharga still stands with its crumbling mud brick remains of twelve tall towers and ten feet thick walls. It is a beautiful site.

El Deir - Roman fort outside Kharga

Isolated from the nearest villagers by about five Km of graceful sand dunes and not far from the cliff range that separates the oasis valley from the main desert. There was sand to negotiate but we managed it without too many problems. We are enjoying a leisurely inspection, wandering freely through the ruins, enjoying the warmth of the afternoon sun and isolation of the desert. "Hey everybody! Over here!" Yells Denise excitedly from a hilltop not far from the fortress. "There's an open tomb!" she continues as she disappears over the hill. We amble over to check out her discovery.

Mummies. Real ones. Skulls, bones, and wrappings are tossed all around a hole on the side of the hill from a dug out burial chamber. "Looks like this tomb had been opened recently," observes Curtis. "Could it be an archaeological dig?" I ask. "This mess looks more like grave robbers looking for Pharaonic gold," suggests Ken. Body pieces are strewn all over. Some are still partially wrapped in ancient cloth, the skin leathered by the dehydration of the desert, torn but still largely intact. One complete skull with black, withered skin still had traces of red hair. The bones of the face look young and strong and we name him Big Red. Curtis is brave enough to climb down into the deep, dark hole of the tomb to explore. Among the bones and debris of the long-dead and disturbed he finds a tiny fully wrapped mummy, possibly a cat or large bird. Ancient Egyptians used to wrap beloved pets of the dead so they could be together in the next world.

"Big Red" the mummy head

We tell mummy stories by the campfire and don't wander too far in the dark. Late in the middle of the still moonless night we are startled by three distinct taps on our tent, like small stones from nowhere. We are camped not far from the fortress tombs and the ancient ghosts must be bugging us for our indiscretion in disturbing them. Curtis swears he didn't do it. Big Red stares in silence.

Day three, December 22

"Is it dawn yet?" I stick my head out of the tent to ask Ken. He is trying to quietly make coffee on the camp stove in the glow of a small miner's flashlight strapped around his head. Curtis and Denise are still fast asleep. "Not quite but there is some light on the horizon." He answers. It is easy to rise early when we were anxious to climb into our

314

sleeping bags by 8:30 at night in the dark, cold, winter desert and our bodies ache from tossing around on a thin air mattress all night long. But mostly because dawn is my favorite part of day, as black turns to deep scarlet then to the golden pink hope of a new day of adventures. We fill our insulated coffee mugs and climb the nearest dune to witness nature's awesome gift of sunrise over the crumbling ruins, the elegant rolling mountains of golden sand, and the vast desert beyond. This daily treasure of glowing light is worth far more than something we might find in a tomb.

We are in the area of a spectacular series of un-charted Roman forts, many built over Pharaonic ruins that lie within the Kharga Oasis. Archaeologists have only begun their studies here. These ancient towns used up most of their available ground water from their fertile oasis land well over a thousand years ago. The town of Kharga still thrives along with a few other oasis outposts where the deep water below the Sahara has not yet been depleted. This fossil water may have gathered thousands or even millions of years ago when the Sahara was a forest, but today there is no rain to replenish this source of life and every drop of water is precious.

Smooth sand near Ain-um-Dabadib

Day four, December 23

Our next major destination is much farther off-road and far less travelled. According to our maps Ain-um-Dabadib is about 40 kilometers from Kharga as an eagle might fly. We type the estimated coordinates into our GPS and head down the road.

Like slow motion monsters, towering sand dunes move across the landscape and ever so slowly cover roads and entire villages without even noticing. The dunes are phenomenal waves of flowing tawny brown, some over a hundred feet high. They beckon us to stop and climb and play and slide down their soft warm slopes and we succumb rolling, gliding and laughing with abandon. This is our first big excursion into the Sahara desert. We have the compass coordinates of two Roman ruins charted by G. Caton-Thompson and E.W. Gardner. The same two British women who studied the Fayoum in the 1920's. We have read lots of books on how to navigate the desert and how unprepared people have died horrible deaths. The four of us, in our two identical, heavily supplied vehicles, hope we have it right. We will not go so far off road that we cannot walk out in a couple of days. Our new GPS technology should really help us to find "trails known only by a few old Bedouin guides," who we don't have.

Dunes overlapping dunes prevent us from taking the direction indicated by the GPS as we fail to weave between them. We've only been off the pavement for about thirty minutes and have bogged down twice. "Look over there between those dunes. It looks like there might be a passage to drive through. I think I see some tire tracks," I announce to Ken as we drive along trying to go in the right direction. "We'll try this path and if it doesn't work out we can come back to this point," Ken says as he stops to discuss tactics with Curtis and to record the GPS coordinates.

Denise & Ken try pulling out the Pajero

The GPS gives a heading but does not tell us how to get over the dunes, around a mountain or across a deep ravine. The coordinates on an old map show the ruins to be just south of a steep, six to eight-hundred foot high scarp that separates the valley from the plateau above. We try to travel parallel and keep it in sight as it goes on for over a hundred miles.

316

Curtis drives behind us as I hold the GPS forward in the front window, the only place it works, to lead our caravan of two. When we get stuck we hook on the towrope and Curtis pulls us out from behind. We stop and start, making constant decisions.

"Is it too soft here?"

"Which way should we go now?"

"What happened to the tracks we were following?"

"Is it safe to go down this hill or will the truck turn over?"

"How can we ever get around this huge sand dune?"

"Will we come upon terrorists out here all alone?"

"We're STUCK! How do we get out of this pit?"

"Dig! Get out the sand ladders!"

"Pull with the other truck!"

"This is the fourth time we're stuck in the last hour!"

"Does this place really exist?"

"Have we gone too far? Should we go back? Can we go back?"

Our two trucks finding the way in the Sahara

Sand dunes pour down over the scarp and block our way but we spot some tire tracks from past explorers and try to follow. "Some tracks can be covered over in minutes by blowing sand but others might remain impressed in the ground for more than twenty or thirty years, " Ken informs me. "And just because there are tracks does not mean they got anywhere successfully. We have already backtracked on some of our own." "I read up on it. Curtis loaned me this 400 page book called *The Physics of Blown Sand and Desert Dunes* written in 1941. It is a definitive work on the subject and even focuses on sand right here in the Libyan

Desert."

The sand dunes here are the largest we have seen yet. From the hilltops we can get a perspective of how they move. The ground itself is fairly solid, sometimes rocky and often flat for miles. But discrete waves of sand from a few feet to hundreds of feet grow with wind-blown particles. The ground is fairly clear before and behind them as they line up and march away from the prevailing north winds. A few may intersect and form an interference pattern. Totally smooth, changing color in the light, tawny brown to amber to golden pink. Some are hard enough to drive across, some are soft enough to totally burry us. We try driving across a few and get stuck often. Even after reconnoitering on foot it is chancy. The flat dunes seem to be harder and we risk crossing a large expanse directly in our path. I jump out to run ahead and test. If my ninety-five pounds sinks in, so will the truck. Once we get onto the dune Ken keeps the speed up so we don't dig in. So ssssmooooooooth. Like sailing or driving on a cloud. We worry about coming back over it heading uphill.

Stretching after a difficult drive

In the last four hours we have travelled about twenty miles. Our GPS and maps say Ain-um-Dabadib should be right here where we have stopped to discuss the options. "I don't see anything but sand with bits of brush in all directions," observes Denise. "Shouldn't we be closer to those mountains?" The seven-hundred foot high escarpment of the valley edge is quite distant so we decide to go straight to it, squinting in the afternoon sun, tired and getting discouraged. I bound out on foot in front of our vehicle for a few minutes to test drivability. "Head directly north toward the scarp, the ground is not especially soft here," I encourage.

Pulling both trucks together we get out to stare with our binoculars. "Is that a ruin or just a hill?" We argue, hearts racing along with the car engines. We jump back in and carefully move another mile closer over soft ground. "Yes! Those mounds have some straight edges!" Ken cries out the window to Curtis. We slowly move even closer. Emerging from the sand, the mud-brick square outline of a tall crumbling fort takes shape. We stop once more to confirm, to rejoice, to shout our relief and to plan our final approach around the dunes and crusty soft ground.

"I can't believe we have finally made it!! Can you believe it?!!" We each exclaim as we jump around hugging each other. After spending most of the day to travel less than forty kilometers through an unchartered maze of sand dunes and mountains we finally find the coveted prize that others said was impossible without a guide. We are ecstatic with victory!!

Emerging from the sand, the crumbling fortress walls with corner watchtowers still stand sentry, guarding only small foundations, tombs, and mounds and mounds of broken pottery, the garbage dumps of the

The Roman Fort at Ain-um-Dabadib

ancient. This Roman fort once connected desert towns of the Sahara to the Nile River. It is said that Ain-um-Dabadib was inhabited for thousands of years, even before the Romans, in an area of about 60,000 acres. There are bits and pieces of past civilization scattered wide. We find a level spot to set up camp and spend the rest of the late afternoon wandering around with elated feelings of winning a grand prize after lots of hard work.

319

Day five, December 24

We rise early and have all day to explore this expansive ruin. But there is so much here we already know we must return again someday for more thorough explorations.

A gaping hole in the ground is too exciting for us to pass by. For over an hour we hike through the dark passages of an underground Roman aqueduct that brought water from the hills long ago and still has traces of moisture in it, and a few bats. "It's getting pretty tight in here but I think I see some light ahead," Curtis calls over his shoulder as the rest of us follow with our flashlights. The narrow, dark, tunnels carried water from the top of the scarp down to this town thousands of years ago. Although dry and partially filled with sand, it is amazing how well they have withstood the millennia. About every fifty feet the tunnels widen into a chamber with an opening to the air and light above, possibly locations of ancient wells.

Aqueduct entrance

A few old, gnarly acacia trees dig their roots up to 100 feet down into the oasis aquifer and still provide life here in the middle of nowhere where it does not rain. The sweet smell and nectar of their tiny yellow flowers attracts insects and birds to form a small but lively ecosystem. Even a tiny Fennec fox with its perky tall ears comes to visit our campfire looking for food and not afraid to ask. We tent near the trees, careful to sweep away thorny twigs from below our air mattresses. We plan to stay for two nights before continuing on our journey.

With at least 25 miles of sand dunes, rocky hills and desert between the nearest village and us, we are isolated. Impressively alone - we think. The four of us are up on a mound of pottery near the fortress walls quietly looking around with only the sound of a faint breeze blowing across the sand. Suddenly, a wrinkled old Arab man, long flowing grey and brown robes, head turban wrapped, appears out of nowhere. No water, no food, no pack. He moves quietly toward us with nothing but prayer beads rolling through the fingers of his weathered hands. He proffers silent greetings with a bow, walks right across the ruins, and disappears up the mountain and over the horizon along a path we do not see. With wide eyes and open mouths we all just stare and watched him leave. Was he real? A desert apparition? A ghost of the ancients?

Barack dunes near Kharga

We search for hidden stories in little treasures but this must have been a poor frontier town or it has already been scoured for thousands of years. Only pottery shards, no coins, beads or other artifacts. The place has not been fully excavated by archaeologists and we look only on the surface where locals would have cleaned up years ago.

I uncover a small broken oil pot sticking out of the ground, junk for historians but a real treasure for me. Who used this simple little red clay vessel with its tiny cracked spout that once must have kept precious oil pressed from their own crops? What was their daily life like? The hands that made and held it so many generations ago are long dead and gone but still linger in this little spotted vessel caressed in my palm. Perhaps hundreds of years from now another "wonderer" will ask these same questions. Life marches on.

So many civilizations have come and gone in this very spot. Romans, Pharos, and possibly even more we do not know about. A few stone tools here and there could have been shaped over ten or even one hundred thousand years ago, as we know humans have been here even before that. I am but a tiny spec in the story and love to sit here immersed in a panorama of life gone by.

"We wish you a Merry Christmas...... Joy to the World......" Tonight is Christmas Eve and Denise and I tickle Curtis and Ken, teasing them to sing carols around the campfire with us. Close to the glowing embers, cuddled in long underwear, sweat pants, down jackets, woolen scarves and stocking caps we sip hot chocolate and open little presents we brought for each other. The Milky Way shines brightly overhead in the clear black desert sky and we begin to count the shooting stars and make our wishes.

Day six, Christmas Day

We break camp early so that we have time to dig a deep hole out away from the ruins in which to burn and deeply bury our campsite garbage to leave no trace.

It is easier to backtrack and drive back to the blacktop of the oasis road since we had taken some important GPS points along the way. Now we are able to go around most dead-ends and sand traps. We vow to come back soon, with so much yet to explore. Knowing the way will make it a shorter trip from Cairo, perhaps possible on a long weekend.

There is a small hot spring, the Roman spring of Ain-Bishay, near the Farafra Oasis that the locals use for bathing and washing clothes. It is a little distance from the village, flowing into near-by date groves. It is Christmas day and after five days of just baby wipes, we think a real bath in warm water will be a luxurious present. So we manage to go early to slip in and immerse our crusty bodies in warm fresh water coming from deep within the earth. "Ahh! Does this ever feel good!" exclaims Denise as she lowers her body down into the warm water. "I think I have enough sand in my ears to grow a garden," Ken adds as he emerges from under water shaking his wet head. Denise and I bathe in our long underwear, shoving soapy washrags inside to scrub. We don't want to upset the locals by disrobing and anyway, the garments need cleaning too. No one comes so we relax and enjoy soaking in the steamy pool on a fresh winter Christmas morning, cleaning the sand from our eyes, the dust from our caked hair and the grime from parts where baby wipes just can't do the job.

The White Desert north of Farafra is our last camping destination. White crusty mounds stand like armies in the creamy brown sand, some like pinnacles jutting from the desert floor, others like fields of giant cream puffs, sculptured by the wind during fierce dust storms. The unusual soft chalk bedrock carved into whimsical white shapes over eons is a sight to behold, a geological anomaly.

Here, among miles of desolation, two large, sprawling Acacia trees sit atop a white mound visible in the distance. We camp here for two nights, hanging our hammocks, which Ken had packed for such an unlikely chance, between the heavy lower limbs.

Following our guidebook we walk 30 minutes east until we spot another small oasis. An Acacia droops over a watering trough for camels fed by a withering spring. Foundations of ruins, probably Roman, are poking out of the sand. Wherever there is any sign of water in Egypt there is likely to be traces of human history. I find two fragments of Roman coins. Denise finds a few beads and some pottery shards.

People have been sloppy with their garbage since time began. Ruins we've seen around the world seem to be surrounded by pottery shards. Mounds of them. Pottery is easy to make and easy to break. Today some houses are still surrounded by garbage but most is collected at huge dump sites. I guess there is a positive side: future archaeologists will enjoy searching for these treasures.

The White Desert of Farafra

We carry only small amounts of wood that we must conserve for evening fires and play an Egyptian trivia card game by the dim flickering light. "What is the name of the greatest pyramid?" "What was the name of the one God of the pharaohs?" We again try to stay awake till at least 8:30 in the long, cold, dark night of winter in the desert. Denise holds her knitted moccasins near the flames; driving me crazy thinking her feet will burst into flames any moment. At my suggestion, Ken finds some big stones to heat in the fire and bury in the sand below our tent since it will be near freezing tonight. Forget the stones; they didn't work. Snuggling is better anyway.

At the first pink blush of day there is only a fine line between desert and heaven. Ken is already firing up the camp stove to make hot coffee. We fill our thermal mugs and look for a hill to climb. Standing in awe we watch dawn turn the chalk mounds of the White Desert into glowing pink works of art displayed in a vast gallery across the sand.

Returning to camp we share breakfast with C&D. Hot instant oatmeal with lots of nuts and raisins along with the last of the apples hits the spot.

Last day, December 29

From Asyut to Kharga to Dakhla to Farafra to Bahariya and back to Cairo there is a road of sorts that joins these small oasis towns of the Sahara desert. People eke out a living much as they have done since time immemorial, drawing water from ancient wells to grow their crops. Villagers are kind, helpful and worried about all the problems of the cities, hoping to be left in peace to raise their families.

Our last day on the road is a long one, all the way back to Cairo. Although we find some gas in Bahariya, the power is out and we have to pump it out of the tanks ourselves by turning a hand crank; not getting all we need. We empty the extra gas tank from the backs of our trucks and the five gallon containers we each carry behind our back seat. We arrive on the edge of Cairo running on fumes and are thrilled to finally pull into a real gas station.

"Oh, man, is it good to be home or what?" I ask, opening the apartment door for Curtis and Denise after a full hour of soaking in a hot bath. Ken returns with chicken take-out from across the street as we pop a feel-good movie into the VCR. Our warm clean apartment feels wonderfully perfect as we share fine wine with Curtis and Denise to celebrate our accomplishments. "Here's to our amazing, successful expedition and all four of us and our two trucks making it home in one piece!" Curtis toasts. So good to enjoy the simple pleasures of home. At least until we leave for Jerusalem in a few days.

Polish comes from the cities; wisdom from the desert.
- Frank Herbert, *Dune*

Israel or Palestine?
Winter break
Dec 92 - Jan 1993

"Hatred does not cease through hatred at any time. Hatred ceases through love. This is an unalterable law." - Buddha

We returned to Cairo on the eve of 30th of December after a tour of the Egyptian desert west of the Nile. After washing a few clothes, we repacked our bags and went to a New Year's Eve party. At dawn on the first day of the New Year, we jumped into our Pajero to head out of Egypt and into Israel.

We had hoped to take our truck into Jerusalem but after checking on it, decided that it may not be worth all the inspections and the paperwork. The Israeli Embassy had sent us four signs to put in our windows written in Hebrew saying "This vehicle belongs to Americans," so that the car would not be stolen or rocks thrown. We got suspicious that driving our new truck in a Jewish state with Egyptian Arabic license plates could be tempting fate. So we drove our truck across the Sinai to the border at Taba, parked in the Hilton Hotel parking lot, walked across the border to Eilat, Israel, rented a car, and drove to Jerusalem. They put a removable sticker visa into our passport so that future travel to Muslim countries would not be refused entry as Israeli sympathizers.

The Negev desert of southern Israel is an extension of the Sinai but kept much cleaner. Israelis have an agreement with Egypt to travel along the eastern coast of the Sinai Peninsula without visas. So there are a lot of beach resorts and tourism in the area, especially near the border. Expats and some Egyptians often cross into Israel just to buy good wine or other products not available at home. We have to pay top dollar to rent a car for a week in the Jewish beach town of Eilat but we don't need signs to protect us from attack.

"Is that the Dead Sea?" Ken asks as we traverse the depression between Israel and Jordan on the way to Jerusalem.

"Must be. It looks and feels pretty weird, kind of depressing." I remark. "The air is misty cold and dense feeling."

"So, you're saying depressions are depressing? Probably because we are over 400 feet below sea level with a dense, salty humidity in the air."

"The whole area around the water is white. Must be salt. I think those white mounds on the water are actually floating salt bergs."

"The water is nine times saltier than the ocean and this is the lowest land on earth. At 1000 feet deep it lies along a major fault line that cut off the fresh water millions of years ago," I read from our book.

With its milky turquoise water topped with chunks of salt, the Dead Sea is a uniquely strange place. There are salt mining industries in the south and health spas in the north. Although I can't see how healthy bathing in saturated salt water can be for your skin, many swear by the curative powers. It is too cold to swim or I would try it out.

Israel's Dead Sea with salt-bergs

Driving into Jerusalem is a kind of spiritual experience in itself, especially arriving from a trip through the Sinai and past the walls of Jericho. A place of so much history and so many legends, there are few people whom it could not emotionally impress. The hills are high and rolling with sparse grassy vegetation, barely green now in winter. Newly planted young pines dot some of the slopes in an attempt to re-forest.

Bedouin camps lead the way into the city. Tattered gray canvas tents cover sheep, people and belongings. The immediate area is overgrazed and dusty. Women in long black dresses with red trim, men in dirty robes, grimy children playing in the mud. I've read that the Israelis have made several attempts to settle these nomads. Government housing was built. The people kept the sheep in the house, pulled the sinks from the walls to water the animals and slept outside under the stars. Not so easy to change a culture. "Perhaps they should just let Bedouins alone if they like it." I muse. "They are using a lot less resources and are closer to nature than we are."

"Turn right here," I instruct Ken as we enter Jerusalem. "Can't. It's one-way." Ken responds as he slows down to see the sign. "Then turn left and go around the block?" as I try to see on the map what will happen then. Arriving in Jerusalem at dusk on a Friday evening means very little traffic since it is the beginning of the Sabbath. It still is not easy. Poorly marked one-way streets means an hour of driving around in circles before we reach the hotel that was recommended. It was full. Two more hotels and we are finally in a room for the night. Israel is expensive. Not as bad as Paris but expensive. The hotel fee does include a large buffet breakfast that becomes our main meal of the day. The Israelis like fish for breakfast, with sour cream and chives or olives, especially smoked salmon. I love it too, but I like to add some fruit for a little balance. A late afternoon 'dinner' from food stands selling falafel or shawarma includes salad and bread, which is all we need for the day.

Saturday morning we head into the Old City. Surrounded by a high stone wall, this area includes remains of the Temple Mount with the Jewish Wailing Wall, built by King Solomon. There is the tomb where Jesus was buried and the jail cell where the apostles were held during the crucifixion. The gold painted Dome of the Rock is the oldest Islamic monument.

*Muslim Dome of the Rock
& Jewish Wailing Wall*

It is built over a stone where the Prophet ascended into heaven. Muslim mosques, Jewish temples and Christian cathedrals stand wall-to-wall. Significant history here is claimed by all three Abrahamic religions.

"This place is a mess." Ken admits as he kicks aside some garbage. "I can't see where we are on this map. Maybe we can just turn around and re-trace our path," I suggest. This morning we got lost winding our way around the Arab quarters in the Old City. Dark stone alleys, crumbling plaster, painted graffiti on the walls, garbage, and shops of merchants calling to sell trinkets. We got tired of being disoriented, found our way to the nearest gate and left.

It's a good thing we returned to the Old City later. This time we find our way to the Jewish Quarter, a very different world. The difference reflects much of the problems of this land. The streets are immaculate here, the stones kept clean and scrubbed and re-built where needed. The little stores have glass fronts, nice displays, first-rate goods and prices clearly marked. Archeological digs are fenced, glassed over and described in nice plaques in Hebrew and English (but not in Arabic). The Wailing Wall is heavily guarded and police diligently patrol all the Jewish streets.

Hasidic Jews at the Wailing Wall

It takes money to keep a place up and it is clear the money is not so evenly distributed. Not so different than slums within most fancy cities.

There are two separate and very different cultures in Israel; Arab and Jew. Two separate languages; Arabic and Hebrew. The children are taught in two different school systems. Although the Arabs are allowed in the better Israeli schools, they must speak and learn in Hebrew. They must be proficient in Hebrew to go to the national Universities. The Arabs here are mostly poor, with little education, few modern work skills and very strong, extensive family ties. The Jews have come from all over

328

the world. With a strong work ethic and a better education they learn Hebrew and have united to form the country of Israel. The Arabs are treated like second-class immigrants in their own land. Their opportunities are very limited unless they learn Hebrew and abide by Jewish cultural norms.

We are able to converse with several Israelis and Palestinians over a few days. Neither of these terms is even acceptable to the opposite group. It was quite an eye opener. The problems are much deeper and more complex than I had ever imagined. What a place! Truly, if they can ever have a peaceful country, the rest of the world has a chance.

They are mostly pessimistic. The Palestinians want autonomy but depend on Israel for their livelihoods. The Jews don't like the Arabs but need them to do much of the work. Much of the problem is more about socio-economic differences kept strong by competing cultures; not so different than blacks in America. The Jews moved into an Arabic land, declared it theirs, and required everyone to learn Hebrew. This language imposition alone is likely to forever separate the people.

Of course, there are many good, peace-loving people who just love each other regardless of religion. It only takes a few hotheads to cause a whole heap of trouble and a global media to keep fanning the fires.

Then to make it even more complicated, there are different, clashing Jewish sects. "Let's jump into the car and drive out to the suburbs to find a mall or a grocery store." Ken suggests when I say we are out of shampoo. "OK. Sounds good. I'd like to walk around a little just to watch typical, simple, daily life in Jerusalem," I answer.

Easier said than done. Crawling along in traffic, we don't see any malls or large groceries on this major road. We finally find a pharmacy to buy shampoo. It takes us about two hours to do this and we only drive about four miles. On the crawl back home we find out why.

"What the hell is happening here?" Ken asks in frustration as we creep to a stop in bumper-to-bumper traffic.

"I'm not sure but there seems to be a lot of tension," I surmise from watching other drivers.

"I smell something burning. Look over there, just off the road on the right!" Ken points ahead to a large garbage dumpster turned over with trash on fire.

"Great! We've chosen to go for our little afternoon jaunt in an area of Jewish riots! Do you think we can turn around?" I urge.

"No way. Too much traffic," he responds as we inch along, stuck in a real mess. A bit farther down is a large group of Hasidic Jews with long side curls, black robes and tall black top hats gathered around an ambulance yelling at the driver.

"I think I see a road to the left down at the bottom of this hill. Try to get in the left lane and maybe we can get away from this. I'll check the maps" I try to navigate as Ken tries to maneuver. Just as he pulls toward

Burning briefcase in Jewish clash

the left we see a smoldering car turned over in the left lane, window smashed, with a Hasidic man gathering his papers into his burnt out brief case. Two police vans try to come through with screaming sirens and flashing lights. Police are swinging clubs and Jews are shouting all around.

"What are you doing? Put that thing away!" Ken yells at me.

"Just trying to get some pictures! Don't worry! Nobody can see me," I insist stubbornly.

Ken is trying desperately to drive out of this chaos. I am trying desperately to get pictures with a slow camera that keeps flashing when I don't want it to. Ken tells me again to put the camera away. I won't listen and keep shooting, not having much success through the car window and the traffic.

Of course we thought it was an Arab-Jew clash. But when we read the papers the next morning we found out it was the Hasidics against other Jews, mad about some bones being dug up at an archeological site. Lots of stone throwing, fires and angry people but no major injuries.

I guess we found our typical, but not-so- simple day in the life of Jerusalem.

A young American man working at an army surplus store confides that he has been here for five years and has become a citizen. He was required to join the army, as every Jew is, male or female, unless they are doctors or have some other special dispensation. Non-Jews are not required to join. He says that the Israeli boys who come into the army at 18 are usually terribly spoiled by their Mamas who know that they may loose their babies at this tender age. He professes that although from the outside it seems as if Israel is in constant strife that the streets are usually safe. "Most people do not want violence and will come running from all corners if you yell out that you are in trouble." He feels a great sense of brotherhood here.

Leaving the capital city, we drive north to Haifa, a much calmer place than Jerusalem. There we visit a Baha'i shrine and spend the night high on Mount Carmel, overlooking the Mediterranean Sea, near the cave of Elijah.

The Sea of Galilee touches me deeply. Probably because I heard so much about it as a child, growing up as a nature-loving Catholic. I take off my shoes to walk in the cold water along the beautiful shores, where Jesus once walked. Jesus was a Jewish heretic standing up for a new way to live and worship. A strong man with a new message. Instead of "an eye for an eye," he taught, "Blessed are the Peacemakers for they will be called the children of God." The Sermon on the Mount took place right here. It is just a small grassy hill with a church at the top and the Sea below. No one is here but Ken and I. The awe is overpowering. All my childhood teachings seemed like fairy tales. But here it feels real. And my favorite teaching, "Blessed are the pure of heart, for they shall see God." If we can be pure of heart, open to the hearts of others, we can surely become Peacemakers.

Sea of Galilee

Israel (Palestine) is a cross culture of Jews, Christians and Muslims who all claim it as a very holy place, centrally important in their religion. It is too bad they cannot get along well as they believe many of the same truths. Most of them want to live in harmony, but like so many places in the world it is the fanatics who cause the problems for the quiet, peaceful majority.

I have learned to listen to my enemies as they often have valid points that I am ignoring. Aggression often comes from feeling cast out. Perhaps if we listened more closely to our fanatics we might find some common ground.

The next day we spend the afternoon & evening wandering around a classy little Jewish shopping area where every corner musician competes for tips. A couple of recently immigrated Russian men bow their violins in front of a bagel shop. A white-robed bearded man strums guitar while singing that he is the Messiah. A stout darker fellow in a red and black outfit plays his heart out on the saxophone. All kinds of people, sounds and food. Eating falafel at the outdoor cafe we decide that our trip to Israel has been quite an experience. Not a place for a vacation. It's much too intense for that. But surely a place of many lessons.

Israel is not recognized as an official country in most of the Muslim world. "Palestine" is written on their maps. It is a fascinating place of extremes and high tension. From love to revenge the emotions are intense. I have heard it called the 'Heart" of the world. Perhaps, if this heart of ours can stop the war, our world can one day make peace.

Israel or Palestine. May peace be upon them.

Surreal feelings of disconnection overcome me as I sit down at my computer in my apartment after the experiences of the last three weeks. We went from the still timelessness of the Sahara desert to the intense conflicts of life in Israel. This computer in this modern home seems like an alternate universe. I feel like it's been years since we left Cairo. Yet when school begins tomorrow it will seem as if the whole experience was a dream. Travel is otherworldly that way.

Goddess in the Sinai (see map p. 245)
December 1993

Earlier this year Ken was asked by Sandrine, a French student in his physical science class, if her parents could go on an off-road trip with us. Ken hesitated and said he'd be glad to speak with her father. We don't like going with strangers on serious desert trips. In fact, we have some good friends we would not take. It is a dangerous place to have trouble and coming well equipped is paramount. Bringing plenty of water, food, gasoline and a vehicle in top running condition are mandatory. We have been on more than one group trip where those that came prepared were crippled by those who didn't.

The next day Ken found a book stuffed in his school mailbox. It was a beautiful, hard-cover, table-top book filled with amazing photographs of the Egyptian deserts. The author and photographer was Sandrine's mother, Nicole Levallois. We were impressed.

"Hello! Jean-Pierre!" Ken answers the phone. "Sandrine gave me your wife's book and told me about some of your desert travels. Yes! We would be honored to travel with you."

Jean-Pierre is a French banker financing the Egyptian metro and has some local connections. He got permission for us to travel across a military controlled area to explore the area near Siwa in the Libyan Desert in the northwest of Egypt. It was a grand trip and a story all its own.

So when Jean-Pierre and Nicole invite us to go off-road in the Sinai with some of their friends, we are quick to accept. "Parlez vous Francais? Do you speak French?" Jean-Pierre asks. "Not really - only oui–oui and merci, but we can make do," I reply. With five French adults, two French children and one Egyptian who is fluent in Arabic, French and English, we head off into the Sinai desert in search of a Pharaonic temple on top of some obscure mountain about 60 kilometers from the road.

Traveling with the French is an experience on its own. Boy, can they get into the food. When I ask what I should bring, Nicole hems and haws until I finally suggest fresh fruit and vegetables. We Americans are known as bulk eaters. The French have a more elegant idea. Here we are, out in the middle of the desert, and the French put on a spread that I expect to see only at a fancy party. We dip eggrolls wrapped in fresh herbs of mint and endive into a sweet sour dip while we watch marinated beef strips grilling on a portable barbecue pit. The mashed carrot-potato dish complete with sour cream complements slices from a sizable round of Brie cheese. Four choices of personally imported French wine fill our plastic goblets. It was a good thing I brought those epicurean cucumber and carrot sticks. OK, I also contributed my wickedly delicious dark-chocolate brownies that are almost gourmet.

Our French friends camp in style

The Sinai is not quite as barren as the Sahara. It gets some moisture from the Mediterranean Sea and an occasional seep of water comes forth from mountain springs. Small oases of palm trees can be found tucked in narrow valleys. In the land where Moses hid the Jews for 40 years there are now tiny villages and wandering Bedouins who eke out a minimal existence. One of these settlements centered around a large turquoise mine used in Pharaonic times. It was these ruins that we sought.

Hanni, a multi-lingual Egyptian, leads our four-vehicle convoy in his red SUV. He stops in a small village to get directions and to arrange for a guide to lead us to the temple tomorrow. As we unroll out of the trucks to stretch, we are greeted by black-shrouded Bedouin women with jewelry and trinkets to sell. Five of them sit on the ground between the trucks and set out their wares on a blanket. "Come," "Look," "See," they urge.

I have my eye on a couple of face veils; similar to the ones they are wearing. The long rectangular cloths are sewn with beads, coins, shells and sometimes weird pieces of who knows what - bottle tops, buttons etc.

And so - the bargaining begins, "100," she says.

"No, mish mumkin," ("not possible" – one of my favorite phrases) "I'll give you – 40." (all spoken in Arabic, of course)

"No – 70."

"No – 40."

Bedouin women

She finally gives it to me for forty but then says "No! – 10 more". So I hand it back. But I eventually give in and offer her 50 Egyptian pounds (about $15). Then another woman sells me one for 40. So now I have a present for Mom. Meanwhile Ken is getting some great pictures.

"Come on! Want to get up and see the moons of Jupiter? The sky is so clear I can see one of them casting a shadow on the planet." After a peaceful night camping in the clear cool air of the desert Ken tempts me up before dawn to gaze at the brilliant stars and planets through our telescope.

As the morning glow of orange and pink flow across the landscape we climb the nearest hill to see the sunrise, hot coffee in hand. The most wonderful spaces of Egypt are in the stillness and stark beauty of the desert. Vast expanses of golden sands topped with a bright cloudless sky. Perched on the quiet hilltop, it is a perfect place for contemplation. No distractions, just simple raw beauty.

As the sun pops over the horizon and we finish our coffee, we notice a black speck moving in our direction. Then two others come from different areas. The Bedouins know where we are and have walked for kilometers to catch us. Even before the others in our camp are awake we watch the women with their children come into the campsite and spread out their collections. We enjoy dealing with local trinket dealers as long as we're interested in their wares. It's not so fun when we want to be alone, as they are very persistent, knowing that it sometimes pays off well. As we put up our tent the women pull at my sleeves wanting me to buy. Camping in the Sinai is not quite as private as in the Sahara.

Our village guide finally arrives to lead us to the ruins of Serabit el-Khadim. Built about five thousand years ago, it is the only known Pharaonic temple built outside of mainland Egypt. On the top of a flat mountain in the middle of the Sinai desert is a temple dedicated to the Goddess Hathor, one of the most important and popular deities throughout the history of Ancient Egypt. She personified the principles of joy, feminine love, compassion and motherhood. Hathor was also the patron goddess of miners.

Ruins of Serabit el-Khadim, a temple to the goddess Hathor

The goddess figures of different religions have always attracted me. These feminine aspects are lacking in our Abrahamic religions where god has become masculine, authoritative and warrior-like. This masculine dominance has had a profound affect on the global spread of aggressive cultures and the repression of women in our world today. If we really want peace in this world we need to address the male dominance in our religions and cultures and honor the qualities of the goddess.

"Here, grab my hand," Ken offers as I struggle to step over a gap

336

in the crumbling path. It takes us close to two hours to pick our way climbing up the steep cliff, following the guide. We are about a thousand feet or 300 meters above the valley below. I can't imagine how or why the ancients came all the way up here to build this temple. They must have really loved their Goddess Hathor.

The view from the temple site is marvelous. Hathor was often referred to as the "Mistress of Heaven," and from this barren tabletop mountain with its steep sides we can see for miles in every direction. In the ruins there are hundreds of stones and pillars cut with Pharaonic carvings and hieroglyphics. They were excavated and cataloged by the Israelis when they had possession of this territory. Our guide says there is an ancient deserted mine shaft about a kilometer away, in the valley. Turquoise was mined here for centuries. How did they survive here in the desert? Perhaps there was more water then. Perhaps wells supplied a village. There is nothing but the silent stones to tell us of thousands of years gone by.

Stele of Hathor

In the afternoon we travel much farther off-road to find some old lava tubes. They are remnants of volcanic activity, probably formed millions of years ago. We escape the paths of the Bedouins to enjoy a quiet evening of hill climbing and another spectacular French dinner. The goddess Hathor still watches over the valley from her pinnacle in the distance. Perhaps compassion will one day reign again.

Canterbury Tales
December, 1993

> *"Yet do not miss the moral, my good men.*
> *For Saint Paul says that all that's written well*
> *Is written down some useful truth to tell.*
> *Then take the wheat and let the chaff lie still."*
> — Geoffrey Chaucer, *The Canterbury Tales*

Paris and London at Christmas time sound so romantic. Maybe even some chestnuts roasting on an open fire and a white Christmas with sleigh bells ringing. This year we will go to Europe for winter break instead of traveling in Egypt again.

"It's just six o'clock. Want to get up and try to see the sunrise over the Eiffel Tower?" Ken asks as we are both stirring restlessly in bed. On our first morning in Paris we are awake early because of the two-hour time change.

"OK, let's do it. I think the hill up this street will take us high enough to overlook the city." I respond. "Looks like it could rain so we better bring the umbrellas."

It is completely dark as we step outside. It is still completely dark thirty minutes later as we stand at the top of the hill and by now it's drizzling rain. We wait another fifteen minutes and still no sign of light even though there are clear spots in the sky. We give up, return to the hotel, bathe, eat breakfast, and prepare for the day. Not until 9:30 does the sky finally begin to show signs of morning. We of the tropics are not used to these short days. Where's the sun? Us morning people expect to be out hiking and ready for a nap by this time. How do people survive? And what about Finland and Alaska and such? Do people really live there? Maybe that's why cafes and pubs are centers of life at high latitudes rather than parks and sports.

It is drizzling rain most of the time and cold but we have anticipated that. We use our trusty umbrellas and ski jackets and spend a lot of time in museums. The nights are a bit long. If it were summer we would be out sightseeing till 9:00 but when darkness comes at 4:00 we tend to retire early. We are staying in a small hotel SW of Paris in Suresness. Pronounced Soor-en, believe it or not. The French seem to have made an art of spelling things quite differently than pronounced.

We visit the American School of Paris to check on possible future employment options and are very impressed ---- at how nice our Cairo school is. A school in a hardship post is often the main focus of the community. At CAC the hallways and rooms are decorated with artwork, the staff know each other well and the atmosphere feels inviting. The Paris school has bare hallways and feels more like a business. "Most teachers who come from schools like yours do not enjoy it here," offers a teacher I meet in the lounge. "There is not much community spirit at this school. Americans who come to Paris are usually more interested in the city and don't hang out together very much," she adds, giving us information that will color our future choices.

We finish our breakfast of fresh croissants and a strong cup of French-pressed coffee. Our rental car is packed and ready to travel west out of Paris. We are heading to the city of Calais on the coast to catch a ferry across the English Channel to the British Isles. Soft snow is falling lightly on the beautiful French countryside on Christmas morning, powdering the landscape white. A special treat for us Floridians.

"I'd like to stop at the town of Wisques on the way to Calais. *The Lonely Planet Guide to France* says there is an abbey there where monks are known for their chanting."

"Sure, sounds interesting. We have the time and it is on the way," Ken responds.

We follow the scenic roads marked on the map to St. Paul's Abbey. We are lucky to find a cozy *pension* to spend the night just a mile from the monastery so we move in quickly and head over to evening services.

"Adoremus in aeternum...," they chant in a soothing harmony, "Let us adore for all eternity...". It is Christmas night in the abbey sanctuary. There is a chill in the air so we keep our coats on but warmth is coming from the monks in the flickering candlelight. Forty Catholic Benedictine monks have devoted their lives to God and to the Gregorian chants that warm our hearts and raise our spirits. "Ave Maria, gracia plena..." They sing in Latin of Mary and her baby Jesus as we listen to the beautiful harmony of their devotion. In their long, black-hooded robes with worn hymn books in their hands and rosaries attached to their waist it is a medieval scene continued because of its beauty and their love of tradition.

The monks lead a very simple life. With only a small room of their own, they share daily household and garden chores. They also make wines, jellies and cleaning products to support themselves. I can see how the famous scientist, Gregor Mendel, had the time and focus to do all of his genetics experiments in the garden as a monk in the 1800s.

We leave our *pension* at 3:00 in the morning to arrive at the docks before the 5:00 AM ferry departure, having heard that we are more likely to get un-reserved tickets for this early ship. Driving the car onto the ferry at Calais we cross the winter-rough sea of the English Channel to arrive at the white Cliffs of Dover just as the sun peeks over the horizon. The town of Canterbury is our next destination on our way to London.

"Nothing Ventured, Nothing Gained"
— Geoffrey Chaucer

Canterbury's cathedral was the site of pilgrimages beginning in the twelfth century with the murderous beheading of St. Thomas Becket. Geoffrey Chaucer used these pilgrims as a focal point of *The Canterbury Tales* written in the fourteenth century. Many lessons of these stories still live on in familiar sayings of today. Just like a

Jane on ferry to Dover

fairy tale, the cobblestone streets and old buildings are kept beautiful as a UNESCO world heritage site.

The center of town is blocked to cars and filled with fun shops alongside historic places. It is also the beginning of their famous January clothing sales so the place is packed with shoppers. We enjoy a turkey-cranberry pie for lunch at a quaint local pub and find a nice bed and breakfast about a ten-minute walk from downtown. I join the shoppers to buy myself an English outfit: a woolen burgandy skirt that flows to my ankles and a fuzzy turtleneck sweater to match.

I can't believe how much we are enjoying England. After living abroad for so many years using minimum words and maximum sign language it is a treat to be able to communicate freely with the local people. We find it much easier to laugh. Humor is often a play on words and more difficult when we don't understand the language.

From a small bookstore in Canterbury we purchase Staying *Off The Beaten Track*, by Elizabeth and Walter Gundrey. So instead of going to London we head to a historic English estate north of Stonehenge in the small town of Newbury.

Nalderhill House is an impressive Victorian mansion siting on a hill overlooking park-like gardens and the pastoral countryside. Pheasants come to beg breakfast in front of the tall picture windows each morning. Our hot generous English breakfast is served at a cozy table near the fireplace. The English are much better than the French at designing breakfast. Cereal, eggs, sausage, tomatoes, biscuits, fruit, juice and tea or coffee are the norm. The French usually serve only croissants

Country chapel

and coffee, always leaving me hungry. However, I would rather be in Paris for dinner than eat more fried fish and chips in London.

"Let's walk around and explore a bit," suggests Ken. "OK. It's sunny and as warm as it will get today. It might even be above freezing," I respond as I gather my coat and gloves. The grassy landscape here is greener than I imagined. Even though we are close to the same latitude as Quebec the English winter is far warmer. Relaxing for a few days at the mansion we find some inviting paths winding through the forests and farms to hike in the sunny afternoons.

Our four-poster bed was made in the 1600s. The cushioned seat below the large plate-glass window looks out over the hills and into the garden. Our over-stuffed comfy couch faces a color TV that has programs in English. We are the only guests for New Year's Eve and have some friendly conversations with our hosts who show us photos of their auto-racing hobby displayed in the hallway.

We decide to stay at Nalderhill House an extra day. Stonehenge is only about an hour away so we spend an afternoon to check it out. This stack of stones was built about the same time as some of the pyramids and Pharaonic temples of Egypt. The rise and fall of cultures and civilizations seems to be a given. I wonder what ruins will be tourist spots a few thousand years from now. And if there will be tourists to wonder our rise and fall.

"And high above, depicted in a tower,
Sat Conquest, robed in majesty and power,
Under a sword that swung above his head,
Sharp-edged and hanging by a subtle thread."
— Geoffrey Chaucer, *The Canterbury Tales*

Egypt Population Conference 1994

Along with some of our senior students, we arrive in our yellow school bus to rub elbows with leaders from around the world. Security is very tight. Our bags are scrutinized and x-rayed three times. There are guards with automatic rifles on every street-corner in the city and hundreds around the conference itself.

This is an incredible opportunity. The special nametag hanging from my neck says "ICPD, International Conference on Population and Development." Jean Stal, head of our United Nations program at school, had slogged through the paperwork to get special permission for a few teachers and students to attend. She spent hours sitting in the hot sun waiting and shuffling between authorities to acquire our special passes. Next to the hundreds of governmental officials attending from around the world, we are peons lucky to be admitted.

CAC students and teachers at International Population Conference

It is exciting to see so many international leaders getting together to focus on possibly the biggest problem to ever face our species. For over 300,000 years the human population remained under 500 million across the planet. There was plenty of room to live and use simple resources. By 1800 there were still less than one billion but things were radically changing. It is now well over seven billion and about 85 million are added each year. And each of us uses FAR more resources than we did a hundred years ago. From satellite photos the destruction of our ecosystems is becoming obvious. There have been five other major extinctions since the beginning of life on earth. We are in the process of causing the sixth mass extinction. The human species is highly resilient but the balance of ALL life on the planet is important to our own survival.

Touching my nametag with respect while waiting for the first speech to begin, I have no immediate expectations for the conference. My idealistic hopes about the Ecological conference in Brazil five years ago had cured me of that. All of these forums are essential beginnings but real global change is difficult and slow. I am privileged to watch and listen to the process.

There are two parallel groups meeting here. The United Nations includes the diplomats involved in writing the international proposals. Non-governmental organizations from around the world are also here to include women's rights, education, development, health, right to life, AIDS, ecology, religion, you name it. 179 countries are involved, and it is genuinely exciting.

Jane, Rosemary and Clair at the International Population Conference

With my bag slung over my shoulder I head off to a talk by the Physicians for Social Responsibility. They are discussing a new contraceptive vaccine that is just now undergoing trials in India. It causes a Woman's own immune system to kill her eggs. Its effectiveness is only a year or two (I'm not sure on that point). A few people are concerned that some of the women taking it in trials have not understood what it was for and that it was possible to give it to a woman without her knowing it. "We need more research for better contraceptives that are cheap, highly effective, safe and easy to use," the speaker summarizes.

Women and AIDS are topics for a symposium that includes a panel of six women from different countries discussing the increase of the disease and how it affects reproduction. The worst scenarios are in Uganda and Rwanda. Blood samples from every woman who came into the hospitals to give birth last year found that 20% had the HIV virus. Since this group is considered a cross section of the general population of that age - that's an awfully high percentage. About 40% of pregnant women with HIV will have babies born infected. Even with this rate of disease, their population will continue to grow and double in just 30-40 years as women are having so many babies at such young ages.

Another seminar focused on a movie and discussion about female circumcision in Egypt. I am sickened by this practice in this society. You may have heard about it, it was released on CNN. At about the age of ten, some Muslim girls are subjected to having their clitoris cut off. This makes sex painful for the rest of their lives because the tender tissue does not scar over well and often tears open and bleeds. They say it is to keep them from straying from their husbands, while husbands are allowed to take other mistresses and wives when they tire of their own. This is sadism, not religion.

Some of the talks are more encouraging. There are many on the reproductive health of women. Thailand, India and Bangladesh have made great strides in getting women to use birth control. Birth rates have already dropped and families are healthier. The trouble is with so many women entering reproductive age and most people living longer lives, the population continues to expand.

They say we may reach a global population of nine or ten billion by 2050. I hope our ecosystems can survive the onslaught.

Most discussions are challenging but optimistic. The presentations spark intellectual bantering that spills out into hallways and elevators. If talk could solve problems we would have it made. Leaders from all over the world are working to make changes. We know that the instinct to reproduce is one of our strongest. We know that populations under stress of poverty, warfare or poor health have more children, fearing they will loose them. We know that educated women with good career choices tend to have smaller, healthier families.

After the conference was over, Amira reported to her advanced biology class: "179 nations basically agreed to work on good contraception, health care and education for women as solutions for a bright global future." She leads her classmates in a discussion on how we can work towards that goal.

NESA and Safari
Near East South Asia
Council of Overseas Schools

*"You know you are truly alive when
you're living among lions."*
— Karen Blixen, *Out of Africa*

Woman of the Masai Mara

The tinkling sound of the little brass bell chimes from the hallway as Mary Ann Hass calls us for the opening presentation. This is our second time attending a spring NESA conference. Our first was held in Bangkok where we traveled from Pakistan. About a thousand teachers from over one hundred international schools in Asia and the Near East usually attend. This year we meet in Kenya. An opportunity for us to explore an exotic land of deep African culture and wildlife.

Richard Leaky takes to the stage as our keynote speaker. He is the son of the famous archaeologist couple Louis and Mary Leaky who discovered the skeleton of "Lucy," the first missing link found between monkeys and man. (A seventh grade student once asked me: "Mrs, Cundiff, how did they know Lucy was her name?")

"I hope he will talk about his work as head of the Kenyan Wildlife service," I whisper to Ken. "I've heard he's been able to get local villagers to cut down on poaching in favor of tourism."

"He's also had a lot of political problems with big-wigs who get rich from kick-backs." Ken smirks. "I'd like to hear how he deals with it." We both feel privileged to hear from one of the most famous archaeologists and environmentalists of our time.

NESA does a wonderful job of holding conferences for professional development, filled with topics for teachers and administrators of all levels. "After this afternoon's main speaker on teenage psychology would you like to go with me to the workshop on physics electrical experiments?" Ken asks. "Thanks, but I think I'll head to the one on teaching creativity," I respond.

Although we are enjoying the conference we are especially excited about being in Kenya. Mom flew to visit us in Cairo a week ago just so she could travel with us to Nairobi. After the conference is over we will use the rest of our spring break to go on a six-day safari with a crew of six. Curtis and Denise are with us and Lynn Putzke, our friend and the elementary music teacher at CAC. Lynn is partnering with Mom to share a room. We are staying in a hotel in downtown Nairobi and getting taxis out to the conference site.

"Be sure to cover up your money pouch," Ken reminds Mom as we prepare to leave the hotel and travel around Kenya. "Theft is common in this country and we need to take precautions."

"I feel so white in this sea of black faces." Mom relates as she pulls her pink jacket lower. "I'm beginning to understand what it feels like to be singled out for the color of my skin."

Our first destination is a "tree hotel" perched on the side of Mount Kenya in a tropical rainforest. Our rooms have a large plate-glass window from which to view the forest animals as they come to drink at the pond, twenty-four hours a day. A small herd of elephants are right

"It was wildest, untouched Africa, and it was magic!" - Jane Goodall

out back when we arrive. They are only about twenty meters from our window and it feels like we can almost touch them while they coach their babies to drink.

"Which of these animals would you want to wake up to see?" Ken asks as we look over a list provided by the lodge. "They will knock on our door when any of them come to the watering hole just downhill from our rooms." "Definitely the elephants and lions. And of course, the rhino and buffalo," I answer. "Maybe we should just check everything on the list."

Knocks at the door keep us hopping all night long to watch the wild African animals creep carefully up to the dimly lit water.

Our crew of six rises early to head out to the savannah. "They looked at me like I was crazy when I asked the people at the front desk where I could go running this morning. Now I realize why," I relate as we pass a lioness in the grass right outside of the hotel grounds. "Looks like she's missed her hearty breakfast of fresh jogger," replies Ken. "Here, kitty, kitty! Here she is!" he teases. I laugh and try to push Ken over on the seat.

The top of the safari van lifts up so that we can stand on the seats and take pictures without leaving the vehicle. The animals have become conditioned to ignoring the vans. A heard of giraffes grazes gracefully nearby. One of the tall animals bends its long flexible neck all the way to the ground to get a closer look at a baby ostrich in a nest. Ostrich Momma doesn't seem to mind.

On our way to the Masai Mara Game Reserve we stop to watch thousands of pink flamingos flock the shores and water of Lake Nakuru. A pack of hyenas are feasting on a recent kill below the trees nearby. With their large head and wide, toothy grin the hyenas are fiercer looking than I had pictured. They are certainly not dogs. A cheetah chases an animal into the brush.

Our safari van on the savannah

There are very few wild places left in the world sizeable enough to support such a diversity of large animals, especially all the predators.

Our driver has just gotten a walkie-talkie message from another van. A rhino with a baby is not far away so we head in that direction.

We stop in a village to buy some hand-made jewelry to help support the local people. Local village populations are expanding rapidly and there is a constant struggle between the needs of the people and those of the animals.

Jumping tribal dancers of the Masai Mara

Bright red cotton wraps around them and thick layers of red and yellow beads around their necks accent their smooth black skin. Women have clean-shaven heads and men sport long black ponytails. The deep-voiced men chant a tribal song as they pound their feet and jump in unison. All of their feet are off the ground at once. The women sway to the sounds and bounce their necklaces in rhythm. They seem to be proud of who they are and how they fit into this wild tapestry. I hope they can keep their culture alive in such a fast changing world.

Cairo American College friends meet at NESA in Bangkok, 1997
Back –Vicky, Curtis, Debbi
Front – Ron, Denise, Clair, David, Ken

Cairo best friends meet at a NESA conference in Bangkok, 2006
Ron & Vicky coming from India,
Ken & Jane coming from Saudi Arabia
Curtis and Denise coming from Bangladesh

People Matter Most

"In everyone's life, at some time, our inner fire goes out. It is then burst into flame by an encounter with another human being. We should all be thankful for those people who rekindle the inner spirit." -- Albert Schweitzer

"Good morning everyone! I hope you've had a wonderful summer and are raring to begin a new year!" David Chojnacki, our superintendent, begins the assembly of 175 faculty and staff on our first official day back to school. Ken and I are beginning our fourth year of teaching at Cairo American College. Without the anxiety of being new to the school and with the pleasure of seeing friends after a couple months of vacation, it feels more like a family reunion than a job.

Each of the seven countries we taught in was both remarkable and difficult in their own special ways. CAC had an amazing staff. The 175 teachers and dozens of administrators from all over the world included mostly Americans. All were risk-taking, adventure-seeking, fun-loving, and highly qualified. At the time, the salary and benefits package was considered a "golden cage" as sign-up bonuses got larger the longer we stayed. There was no tenure. Most were terrific instructors and top notch in their field as competition was high for these positions. Paying and treating teachers well made a difference in the quality of the faculty hired and therefore a difference in the accomplishments of the students.

"Want to join my darts club?" Debbie finally asks.

Normally, we would have thought – "Darts? Are you kidding? Sounds pretty boring." But we knew better. "Sure! Love to! We have been hoping for an invitation!" is our quick reply.

Debbi Fintak is known to be the best party gal on the faculty. Darts is just a focus to gather once a month with the coolest people on campus to have fun. Debbi has just two strict rules - we come every month and we host for a turn. Darting ability is optional.

I learned about good clubs from Debbi. Find some topic to gather around once a month to get friends together. Do potluck meals and share hosting. Don't be too fancy or picky. Laugh a lot. Social connections we can count on are good for everyone, especially in tough places.

"See you tomorrow night at the party!" Betsy and Mark wave to us as we leave school. Our housing complex New Fontana probably hosts more parties than any other. *The Rocky Horror Picture Show* draws an enthusiastic crowd to Denise's flat. We come adorned in black and white costumes to reflect the characters of the cultish movie. Carl, John and Betsy wear tuxedos. Denise and Martha sport shiny black satin dresses with white aprons and frilly white bonnets pretending to be British maids. We shout phrases from the movie in unison. "You're lucky, he's lucky, I'm lucky, we're all lucky! What kind of a place is this? Oh, it's probably some kind of hunting lodge for rich weirdoes." We sort-of watch the video as we eat popcorn, drink wine and laugh.

Costume party at Denise's apartment

Debbi was generous with her ideas and theater-costume closet if you felt that yours was lacking. Colorful hippie themes were easy as most of us grew up with bellbottoms and cheap jewelry and were still prone to tie-dye. Although diverse in personality, we always have fun.

Just any idea to get together will do. Terry and Dave Lewis on the fifth floor of New Fontana open their doors for happy hour almost every Thursday evening, after school is out for the weekend. Sitting around with friends we share our problems and successes of the week while getting advice and support whether we need it or not.

Hippie party with Betsy, Debbi, Denise, Curtis, Tara

The school hosts three big parties every year. A galabeya party to open the year, a Christmas feast and a Maa-salama goodbye party. With live bands, good food and plenty dancing they are fun to look forward to. The supervisors at CAC take the social welfare of teachers and staff seriously. It is not only important to hire qualified people but to retain them. Happy teaches make for happy students and parents. The counselors and administrators at CAC made extra efforts to have frequent private conversations with everyone to keep a pulse and minimize conflicts. Living in a foreign country is a roller coaster ride. The tough times need strong shoulders to cry on and the amazing times are so much more so when shared with friends.

"Mercury will be transiting the sun on November, 6. This happens only every eight years or so. Are you interested in trying to observe it? Ken asks Karl Stahl, who has just bought a pair of astronomy binoculars.

"You bet! Where do you think would be a good place to spot it? Karl asks.

"We need to get away from city pollution and have a clear view to the east. Jane and I talked it over with Curtis and Denise. We thought we could go camping on the coast of the Gulf of Suez and climb a hill to get a good observation point," Ken explains. "We think the mountains just south of Ain Sokhna might be a good place."

Ron and Jane Dowty have a four-wheel drive Pajero like ours and have traveled off-road with us before. They offer to give Karl a ride, as our truck will be filled with gear and telescopes. They still have room for another and will bring John Guisti. Ron and Vicky will ride with Curtis and Denise.

Camping spots are usually easy to find in this land of un-occupied desert broken by mountains and sand dunes but the Sinai can be problematic. After a couple of wars between Egypt and Israel there are still some dangerous places where mines are buried. Just last year two British men were blown up when they drove over a mine with their jeep. We back carefully away from a rusted sign hanging from broken barbed wire. We did not see the crossbones until we were too close for comfort. Finally we find a narrow canyon close to the coast that looks like a good spot to set up camp.

Friends camping under an acacia tree

"Yikes! Get these off me!" Vicky squeals as she bounds out of her tent with black specs all over her. Ron and Jane run to help her. The nice soft spot below the acacia tree in the narrow wadi between these stark desert hills seemed like a great spot to pitch their tent. Unfortunately a large colony of black ants already owned the territory and they let Vicky know it.

At 5:00 in the morning, well before sunrise we crawl out of our tents with flashlights. "Be careful of your footing," Ken warns. "Curtis and I checked this path before dark yesterday. The trail is narrow, rocky and steep but it will take us to a fairly flat spot where we should have a good vantage point." I walk in front of Ken to illuminate the path as he carries an eight-inch Celestron telescope that belongs to the school. The path is too narrow to share the task so he has to pause frequently because of the weight. His own four-inch Meade is much lighter and the three tripods aren't too heavy. Karl has his large astronomical binoculars. I have a backpack full of water bottles and snacks. Everybody is trudging something up the hill in the dark, cautiously making their way between boulders and sand.

With our solar filters solidly attached to our telescopes we watch the sun rise slowly over the Gulf of Suez. From this mountain view we are able to catch Mercury already leaving its dark shadow on the sun. We observe its movement all the way across the solar disc as it takes its path along the ecliptic. The sky is clear and we can even see a few sunspots. An astronomer's daylight delight.

Astronomy buffs watching Mercury transit the sun

Ken runs an astronomy club at school during the winter months when dark comes early. Almost everyone loves to look into a clear night sky to watch the stars and ponder life's big questions. It is a fun way to get people together.

"Friendship isn't a big thing — it's a million little things."
- Author Unknown

The students made me cry today. It sometimes happens, that overflow of emotion that builds from the chest. They had been practicing for months and this evening they did it. It was the Broadway musical, *Evita*, about the works of charity and labor rights of an Argentinian political leader. With song and drama and orchestra, many of my students worked together in cooperation and harmony to play their hearts out for this international theatrical production of the school year. Tears of pride welled in my eyes.

Debbie Fintak is the school drama teacher and has directed the best non-professional plays I have seen on stage. We have to get tickets early as they are in high demand in the community. The students work hard as they know Ms. Fintak really understands theater, is a great coach and cares about them. She coordinates with Keith Montgomery's choir and band students for amazing performances. Keith told me once that anyone could learn to sing well if they just practice. I think not. A good teacher makes a world of a difference. His classroom is just down the hall and I love to hear the music and student voices float down into my chemistry lab.

I sometimes feel the same kinds of emotions when I see my own students dive into their love of scientific discovery. When Hanny worked for months to produce a fourteen-page report out of his well-designed experiment on bacteria, I knew he was hooked on biology. In fact, he went on to Harvard with it. Emec enjoyed his chemistry so much that he became a chemical engineer and Joe chose a career in environmental biology. Environmentally aware Amira makes a political difference in Beirut, and Chris becomes a nutritionally savvy chef at a hospital. They also swell my heart with admiration.

It has been an emotional delight to communicate with my students who are now all over the world. To hear that they remember my classes and that I positively affected their lives is worth more than any coveted prize. To find out who they have become and to be proud of their accomplishments is such a gift. I am truly honored to have taught them.

Over four years in Cairo we formed some tight bonds, especially with those who came to the country the same time as we did and lived in our apartment complex. We all missed our families back home and found eager new friends in each other. Over the years, as we shared our trials and troubles, those bonds grew stronger. Although we sometimes meet up again at teacher conferences or sharing new adventures, leaving friends is always the hardest part of departing any country.

"Did you hear that Steve got kicked out of Egypt?" Denise exclaims excitedly. We are together again at a NESA conference in Bangkok a year after we both had left Cairo.

"What??!! Whatever for?? He was there over sixteen years, knew the local language and, as far as I know, was a stellar example of fitting into the culture," I respond.

"Apparently he made a high official angry. Asked to help out as a translator, he was showing Al Gore around the Egyptian parliament. He asked some Egyptian lower official to please step out of some photographs that were being taken by the press." Denise had gotten the story directly from Debbi. "Evidently he stepped on the wrong toes. The guy had a fit, claimed Steve was a spy and insisted that he be thrown out of the country in twenty-four hours."

"Steve is such a quiet, diplomatic person, without a rude bone in his body. He LOVES Egypt! I just can't believe they threw him out." I reply incredulously.

It was wrenching to hear that he got pushed onto a plane without even being able to say good-bye to all his friends and students. His apartment was beautifully decorated with Egyptian treasures in every nook and cranny. He spoke fluent Egyptian Arabic. It was obvious Steve loved the Egyptian culture and had made Cairo his home.

It just shows that whatever happens, no matter how well we behave, we are still foreigners subject to local prejudice and whim. Anything can happen and it can happen quickly. I am occasionally asked if I secretly work for the American CIA. "If I tell you 'no', you won't believe me. If I tell you 'yes' you won't believe me either." I smile, and shrug my shoulders in resignation.

Wherever we go in life and in this world, it is the people who end up mattering most. These connections are more important to Ken and I than wealth or excitement or facilities or even the beauty of the place. We carry a feeling of that country or of that school or that little restaurant by the people we meet and get to know.

From Pakistan to Bangladesh to Egypt and all the countries in-between and after, we encountered so many different individuals and places that enriched our spirits. Every human being has an inner flame, stories and goals that are different than our own. Each religion, culture and way of life contributes to the vast tapestry of humanity.

I sometimes think, in brief moments of insanity, that the world would be a better place if everyone thought like me. But as a biologist I know that diversity is the most important characteristic for survival of any species. Just as we need to protect the biodiversity of species on our planet, we also need to respect and protect the variety in our brothers and sisters around the earth.

The lifestyle of a teacher jumping around the world is not for everyone. We also need all those well-grounded folks who stay put and help to glue our tapestry together. There are so many things to learn and teach right in our own backyard.

I remember Alex, one of my advanced biology students at the American International School of Riyadh, Saudi Arabia in 2005. In his departing speech to the school as senior class president he reminded us, "It is not so much what we do in this world that people will remember us by, but how we make them feel."

We are living in a critical time on this earth, nothing like we have ever faced before. Pressures of exponential population growth are causing political turmoil and alterations in the balance of our ecosystems that will have profound effects. But the answers to our problems are within the seven billion different ways of looking at the world. Perhaps if we listen more closely to each other and recognize our connections we can all share a brighter future. We are, after all, "in each other all along."

"The minute I heard my first love story,
I started looking for you, not knowing how blind that was.
Lovers don't finally meet somewhere.
They're in each other all along."
- Rumi

Epilogue

After leaving Cairo in 1995 Jane and Ken returned to Florida to take a year off to move their home to Virginia, where Ken was born. They bought a home on Smith Mountain Lake near Roanoke and close to his father, where summers would be more pleasant than Florida.

With the mountains of Virginia as home base they returned to teach overseas in four more countries until 2008. India, Tunisia, Saudi Arabia and The United Arab Emirates were all totally amazing in their own right with many new people to meet, lessons to learn and stories to tell.

About the Author

Lifelong student and teacher of biology, chemistry and environmental science, Jane Cundiff never tires of learning more about the world's intricate web of connections. Her enthusiasm for learning and fascination with global perspectives have been shared around the planet with students from sixth grade through graduate school.

Ken & Jane
At play in 2015

Jane and Ken met at the University of Florida in 1970. United by an enduring enthusiasm for science and adventure, they worked together in research for eight years before jumping into the life of an international teaching couple. Having kept journals and thousands of photographs, they share their experiences and lessons learned in a life of teaching and traveling around the world.

Jane and Ken are now adjunct professors at Radford University. They live on top of a mountain, grow much of their own food organically and enjoy hiking through the forest with their dog, Durga. Jane is involved in community projects in her small town of Floyd and coordinates the Wild Edibles Organic Gardening Club.

Jane & Ann (Mom) harvesting in 2014